CW01509638

The never-ending *Brief Encounter*

Manchester University Press

The never-ending *Brief Encounter*

Brian McFarlane

Manchester University Press

The right of Brian McFarlane to be identified as the author of this work has been asserted by him in accordance with the Copyright, Designs and Patents Act 1988.

Published by Manchester University Press
Altrincham Street, Manchester M1 7JA
www.manchesteruniversitypress.co.uk

British Library Cataloguing-in-Publication Data
A catalogue record for this book is available from the British Library

ISBN   978 1 5261 2440 1   hardback

First published 2019

Typeset by
Servis Filmsetting Ltd, Stockport, Cheshire
Printed in Great Britain by
TJ International Ltd, Padstow

For my friends George and Elizabeth Wood

Other books by Brian McFarlane include

Four from the Forties: Arliss, Crabtree, Knowles and Huntington, Manchester University Press, 2018

Making a Meal of It: Writing about film, Monash University Publishing, 2018

Class-Act: The Lives and Careers of Googie Withers and John McCallum, Monash University Publishing, 2015

Twenty British Films: A Guided Tour, Manchester University Press, 2015

The Encyclopedia of British Film: Fourth Edition (ed.), Manchester University Press, 2014

Real and Reel: The Education of a Film Obsessive and Critic, Manchester University Press, 2011

Michael Winterbottom (British Film Makers) (with Deane Williams), Manchester University Press, 2009

The British 'B' Film (with Steve Chibnall), British Film Institute, 2009

Screen Adaptations: Charles Dickens' Great Expectations, Methuen Drama, 2008

The Cinema of Britain and Ireland (ed.), Columbia University Press, 2005

Lance Comfort (British Film Makers), Manchester University Press, 2000

The Oxford Companion to Australian Film (with Geoff Mayer and Ina Bertrand), Oxford University Press Australia and New Zealand, 1999

An Autobiography of British Cinema, Methuen Publishing Ltd, 1997

Novel to Film: An Introduction to the Theory of Adaptation, Oxford University Press, 1996

Sixty Voices: Celebrities Recall the Golden Age of British Cinema, British Film Institute, 1993

New Australian Cinema: Sources and Parallels in American and British Film (with Geoff Mayer), Cambridge University Press, 1992

Viewpoints on the Nineteenth-Century Novel (ed.), Longman Cheshire, 1992

Viewpoints on Film (ed.), Longman Cheshire, 1992

Australian Cinema, Columbia University Press, 1988

Cross-Country: A Book of Australian Verse (with John Barnes), Heinemann Educational Australia, 1988

Words and Images: Australian Novels into Film, Heinemann, 1983

Martin Boyd's 'Langton Novels', Edward Arnold, 1980

Contents

Figures

Acknowledgements

A great many people have helped in the research for this book. For many months, a week rarely went by without a friend sending me the reference to another example of the recurring incidence of *Brief Encounter* in a range of wildly eclectic circumstances. There were so many of what I came to regard as my 'spies' that I am afraid of omitting someone from the following list. If I have done so, please forgive the omission and accept my grateful thanks along with the others named here.

First, I thank the two surviving members of the cast and crew – actress Margaret Barton and production secretary Renee Glynne – for being generous with their time and recollections, and Jo Botting, of the British Film Institute (BFI), who put me in touch with them. I am very grateful to the staff associated with Wymondham Station, Norfolk – including David Turner (who had been responsible for establishing the 'Brief Encounter Refreshment Room' there) and current staff member Lisa Groom, who both gave me very useful information – as did staff at Carnforth Station, especially Kyle Burford who worked the tea room there with sister Rhian. And mentioning Carnforth, I must thank my grandson Dougall McFarlane for accompanying me on the journey to this historic site without expressing any boredom. He felt his name should be on the cover of the book as a token of his support in this venture, but this seemed a little excessive.

Two Melbourne companies deserve special thanks: the Malvern Theatre Company for its staging of *Still Life*, renamed *Brief Encounter*, and the Warrandyte Theatre Company for its performance of Emma Rice's stage version of the film; the people in charge of each were helpful in their comments. In relation to these two events, I also thank Ross and Liz King who brought the former to my attention, and Ian Britain who not only informed me about the Warrandyte production but also arranged transport for us to reach the northern suburb, with Iamm Liew at the wheel. Ian was also indefatigable in providing more leads for research.

Among the other friends and colleagues who were so assiduous in keeping me posted about allusions of one kind or other to the classic film or in giving other kinds of help, I offer many thanks to: Charles Barr, Hannah Boulton, Peter Browne (editor of the online journal *Inside Story*, who allowed me to reprint some of the article I had written for him), Keith Brymer Jones, Steven Carroll, Jan Collins, Jonathan Croall, Charles Drazin, Lucy Fleming, Penny Hawe, Ian Kelly, Rose Lucas, Roger Phillip Mellor, Loretta Mercuri, Hayley Mills, Brenda Niall, Jackie Piper, Jeffrey Richards, John Rickard, Tom Ryan, Alan Sheill, Neil Sinyard, Dan Smith, Andrew Spicer, Billy Steele, Sally Wainwright, Melanie Williams, Hugh Wooldridge and George Wood.

As always, I am much indebted to my daughter Sophie for tidying up my manuscript into an appropriate format to send to the publisher. And I am grateful to Matthew Frost at Manchester University Press for taking on this somewhat unusual project.

The book is dedicated with affection and thanks to my old and valued friends, George and Elizabeth Wood, in recognition of their many kindnesses over the years.

I Title card for *Brief Encounter*

Introduction

When I was writing an article some years ago about the extraordinary afterlife of *Brief Encounter*, I found it was impossible, within a reasonably generous word-count, to include all the evidence I'd come across for suggesting that it has become not just a classic film but something of a phenomenon.[1] It was this that led me to consider writing a book about it – and friends to keep supplying me with new references to it in all manner of contexts. What tipped the scale finally for me was reading, while in the UK, in the 'Letters' to *The Times*, one in which a man, now nearly bald, was complaining that he still paid as much for his regular haircut as he had done when hirsute decades ago – though now his barber dealt with him in a couple of minutes. This letter was simply headed: 'Brief encounter'.[2] This reference and others like it all seem to assume that readers will pick up the allusion, and this of course was simply one of the most trivial echoes of the 1945 film. Most recently, my attention was drawn to the *Hollywood Reporter* (on YouTube) in which a number of directors were discussing the films they might want to have with them on a suitably-equipped lifeboat. Rising filmmaker Greta Gerwig talked of the moment in *Brief Encounter* when Celia Johnson and Trevor Howard acknowledge their mutual love.[3] Just the latest in what seems a never-ending line of mentions of the 1945 black-and-white classic.

Plenty of other films have entered into the collective memory – think of, say, *Casablanca* – but it is hard to think of another which has made its presence felt across such a range of media and other cultural artefacts. Regarding *Casablanca*, phrases such as 'the usual suspects' or 'we'll always have Paris' have often been quoted, but they don't begin to stack up against the reincarnations and resonances of *Brief Encounter*. One doesn't find the word 'Casablanca' popping up in the numerous and often totally unexpected contexts in which the phrase 'Brief encounter' (or puns and other mutations) appears. Nor do other titles that have entered the pages of popular (and sometimes scholarly) film history,

films like *Gone with the Wind* or *The Third Man* or *The Searchers*.
There have been television series derived from *Gone with the Wind*,
including parodic treatments in *The Simpsons* and *The Carol Burnett
Show* and a miniseries sequel, *Scarlett*, in 1994. In Philip Oakes's 1976
novel, *A Cast of Thousands*, a character is watching on television the
final moments from a Vienna-set film in which Valli walks out of a
graveyard and past the waiting Joseph Cotton. The author clearly felt
that there was no need to name the film, *The Third Man* by then having
acquired its recognised place in the culture. And recently, writing a piece
about Australian westerns, I was struck by how often they seemed to
echo *The Searchers*, both in plot manoeuvres and in emotional tone.
So, yes, some films do linger on in various ways, but I rather doubt if
any have kept cropping up in such an eclectic range of circumstances as
Brief Encounter, and exploring this range is the prime motivation for
this book.

What follows in this present study is not a reappraisal of David Lean's
famous film, much as I admire it. There are plenty of perceptive critical
accounts already, perhaps most notably Richard Dyer's 1993 entry in
the BFI's Film Classics series,[4] and my own response to it that was given
a chapter in my 2015 book, *Twenty British Films: A Guided Tour*.[5]
Obviously there will be some account of how the screenplay works,
how Lean's direction gave the original plot, first aired in *Still Life*, Noël
Coward's one-act play, a new lease of life – of, indeed, a very long life
– but my overriding concern here is to trace the amazing diversity of
its influence and manifestations over the seventy-odd years since it first
appeared. Some films and television series 'quote' from it visually: that
is, excerpts from it are on view in the course of their narratives. Plays
and an opera have been made from it; references are made to it in other
films and novels; and there are any number of what may sometimes
seem trivial echoes. Such sense of their triviality, though, diminishes as
one comes to see these in the wider context of a film that has so endur-
ingly entered not just the collective memory, but the culture at large
too. It may well be an instance of what Richard Dawkins characterises
as 'cultural transmission', which he describes as 'analogous to genetic
transmission'.[6]

I want to investigate *why* this film has so persisted and, teaching it
to university students forty or fifty years after its release, I am always
struck by their readiness to engage with it. When teaching it, I used to
imply subtly but firmly that anyone who laughed during the screening
at the wrong place – as, say, a response to changing social mores –
could forget about a Distinction in this subject. Actually, they only ever
laughed when the anguished heroine, after near-adultery (i.e., post-scarf

removal), is running around in the rain and we hear her voice-over on the soundtrack saying to her nice, kind, dull husband: 'Oh Fred, I know you don't approve of women smoking in the street ...'. That seemed fair enough, especially in light of their overall sympathetic absorption in the life of the film. If young people, born more than a quarter of a century after the film first appeared, could show this kind of absorption, this seemed like further evidence of its durability. It was fascinating to observe how they came to terms with the central moral issue raised by the film without seeming to be in the least alienated by the vast social changes of the intervening decades.

There were, of course, other aspects of the film to which they responded, such as the noir element in the cinematography or the effect of the comic couple of railway employees involved in their own relationship – mirroring that of their social betters – or the class issues that resonate in the film, or the atmospheric use of the railway station in which much of the action is set. Above all, though, it was their willingness to engage with the brief encounter that almost changes the lives of Alec and Laura that struck me most in their responses, as they came to terms with such thematic oppositions as adulterous adventure vs the safety of domestic life, or family vs the allure of passion.

Notes

1 'The *Brief Encounter* that Goes On and On...', *Inside Story*, 3 May 2016.
2 *The Times*, Friday 7 October, 2016.
3 The *Hollywood Reporter*, 'Full Directors Round Table', on YouTube, 23 January 2018.
4 Richard Dyer, *Brief Encounter*, London: BFI Publishing, 1993.
5 Brian McFarlane, *Twenty British Films: A Guided Tour*, Manchester: Manchester University Press, 2015.
6 Richard Dawkins, *The Selfish Gene*, Oxford: Oxford University Press (1976), 30th Anniversary Edition, 2006, p. 189.

1

Predecessors

If the chief interest of the present study is in the film's successors, this is not to suggest that its narrative or thematic concerns lacked predecessors. In a novel such as George Eliot's *The Mill on the Floss*, the heroine, Maggie Tulliver, comes to accept that she cannot make her happiness out of the *un*happiness of others when she falls in love with her cousin's fiancé. 'O God is there any happiness in love that could make me forget *their* pain?' she anguishes.[1] Or in Edith Wharton's *The Age of Innocence*, superbly filmed by Martin Scorsese in 1995, Newland Archer, in love with the revenant Ellen, Countess Olenska, cannot destroy his marriage to gratify his own desires. Ellen herself, planning to return to her European husband, asks: 'What else is there? I can't stay here and lie to people who have been good to me.'[2] This is echoed in Scorsese's film when Ellen (Michelle Pfeiffer) asks: 'Is there anywhere we can be happy behind the backs of people who trust us?' In fact, in the film, 'there is a sense of its turning *Brief Encounter* inside out to centre on the man [Newland (Daniel Day-Lewis)] who has a glimpse of passion when it is too late to do more than turn down a glove and kiss a white wrist.'[3] And of course Tolstoy's *Anna Karenina*, caught in a not wholly dissimilar conflict, takes the final step that *Brief Encounter*'s Laura seems about to take and from which she just pulls back.

In the Introduction, I referred to *Casablanca*, and when Humphrey Bogart surrenders Ingrid Bergman so that she can return to her brave Resistance-worker husband, Victor (Paul Henried), something similar is at stake – but, of course, they'll 'always have Paris'; whereas 'Paris', in metaphorical form, is resisted in the other two mentioned predecessors and, indeed, in *Brief Encounter*. Also, the sheer star power of the Bogart–Bergman combination means that the iconic ordinariness of the *Brief Encounter* scene and its protagonists is not part of the emotional charge of *Casablanca*. We expect major stars to be caught up in life-changing passion; it comes as more of a shock to find 'ordinary' lives reacting to unsought emotional complexity. At the time of *Brief*

Encounter, neither Celia Johnson nor Trevor Howard was such a film star: she had had a stage career and had appeared in but three films, with a leading role in *This Happy Breed* (1944), but was by no means a household name of the Bogart or Bergman kind; while Howard had had only a small role in *The Way to the Stars* (1945) and an uncredited bit in *The Way Ahead* (1944). It was, then, likely that as they were not trailing clouds of starry glory, they might more readily convey the 'ordinary' aspect of the lives of Laura and Alec in *Brief Encounter*. Johnson combined film and theatre for the next several decades as a highly respected actress rather than a traditional 'star', and Howard became a key figure of British cinema, in such notable films as *The Third Man* (1949), both always seeming to display recognisable personae – albeit at the service of individually different roles.

As for other films that may be thought to foreshadow *Brief Encounter*, two that in part focus on the emergence of desire in situations where its indulgence is seriously complicated by marriage are Edmond Gréville's *Brief Ecstasy* and Jean Renoir's *La Bête Humaine* (both 1938). The former involves a man returning from India after four years and hoping to resume the affair with the woman he left behind and who is now married; the second complicates matters further with a murder but makes brilliant use of trains – as does its 1945 successor.

The film's immediate antecedent – immediate in the sense that the film is derived from it – is Noël Coward's one-act play, *Still Life*, one of nine such in the compendium, *Tonight at 8.30*, first performed at the Phoenix Theatre, London, in 1936. Re-reading the original play, I am struck by how much more imaginative David Lean's treatment of its plot is in the film. The play, confined to the single setting of the railway buffet, is entirely linear in its approach, beginning with some rather patronisingly presented class-based comedy in the lower-orders exchanges between members of the railway staff: the 'refained' Myrtle Bagot in charge of the buffet, keeping the ticket inspector Albert Godby and her assistant Beryl in their places. Their badinage is interrupted when middle-class Laura, who has been quietly sitting over her cup of tea and has then gone out to the platform to check the train times, comes back into the buffet with a piece of grit agonisingly in her eye. After unhelpful suggestions from Bagot and Godby, a doctor comes to her rescue and removes the grit. His name is Alec Harvey, and from this brief encounter the rest of the play unfolds.

'*Still Life*' seems in fact a more appropriate title for the play because it feels utterly devoid of the quotidian facts of the lives of either Laura or Alec and how these facts interact with the emotional upheaval they are supposedly undergoing. It now seems merely stiff with restraint, and its confinement to the railway buffet gives off a kind of airlessness at odds with the emotional resonance of the film. Unpredictable US critic, Pauline Kael, wrote of *Brief Encounter*, which she mostly admired, that 'There's not a breath of air in it'.[4] If this is not true of the film, it could well be argued to be so of the play.

Two of the crucial ways in which the film reconstructs the play to its immense emotional advantage, and the credit is of course due to Coward for reconceiving it as a film, are as follows. First, the film begins near the end of Laura and Alec's relationship and invites the audience to ponder what has brought them to this unhappy seeming situation; and second, it allows us to see something of Laura's home life and, especially, of her kind, decent husband Fred. Fred may not be exciting but in the characterising of this role, and in Cyril Raymond's quietly sympathetic playing, he makes no small contribution to the film's emotional texture and its power to move us.

In his Introduction to Volume IV of his collected plays, Coward wrote of *Still Life*, which he regarded as 'the most mature play of the whole series [i.e., of *Tonight at 8.30*]': 'Later it was made into an excellent film and retitled *Brief Encounter*. I am fond of both the play and the film with, as usual, a slight bias in favour of the former', and 'reading with detachment after so many years, I am proud to have written it'.[5] By November 1945, two of his other plays, also directed by David Lean, had won a measure of praise: they were *This Happy Breed* (1944) and *Blithe Spirit* (released in May 1945), and it is at least arguable that both, like *Still Life*, benefited from the screen's greater fluidity in matters of time and place. Coward wrote the screenplay for all three, but it is perhaps understandable that a playwright might tend to 'favour' the original work over the more broadly collaborative filmmaking processes. It might have been interesting to know in more detail why he retained 'a slight bias in favour of' *Still Life*: to the viewer, the film offers more insight into the lives of Laura and Alec and the movement out of the railway buffet provides different testing grounds for what is happening between them. By this I mean such settings as Laura's home or the restaurant where they are seen by friends of Laura, who is then forced into minor subterfuge – or, most important of all, Stephen Lynn's flat, scene of the about-to-be consummation of their 'affair'.

By strange coincidence, as I began writing this book, the Malvern Theatre Company, Melbourne, staged a double bill of two of Coward's one-act plays from *Tonight at 8.30*. The more lightweight of the two, *We Were Dancing*, though stylishly enough performed, seemed irredeemably dated. The other play was entitled *Brief Encounter*, and was in fact Coward's original *Still Life*. There was clearly a recognition factor involved here: whereas *Still Life* as a title might not have meant much to audiences in 2017, the changed title did and there were large audiences throughout the duration of the plays' season. The programme contained this sentence: 'The original title of our first play was *Still Life*. It was filmed in 1945 as *Brief Encounter*. The film has been regarded as a classic ever since and we thought it appropriate to use this title for our production.'[6] Another example of this title change occurred when Coward himself and Margaret Leighton, in 1957, made a recording entitled *Brief Encounter*. This was the name on the recording, which consisted of short extracts from *Blithe Spirit* and *Present Laughter* – and 'a complete adaptation' of *Brief Encounter*.[7] In other words, by this time, Coward himself had obviously acknowledged the greater pulling power of the film's title as compared to that of the original play. The Malvern Theatre Company was thus following in the steps of the master, as would later play versions.

The play, extremely well acted, still succeeded in holding audience attention, but it does throw into relief some of the ways in which the film is a more accomplished piece of work than its antecedent. For instance, those intimate conversations between Laura and Alec gain from the camera's way of homing in on them, separating them from the buffet staff and other customers. Speaking of other customers, though, the production struck a note of authenticity not suggested in the original play by having several 'extra' performers simply taking their place at various tables. And the use of two of Coward's most famous songs – 'I'll See You Again' and 'Someday I'll Find You' – as bridges between scenes proved a discreetly satisfying device, giving a fluidity to the proceedings as cast members came and went and changes to setting and lighting were effected.

In other matters, though, the play, however well performed, still misses the chance to take the lovers into the other settings which here they can merely refer to; the absence of Laura's husband, Fred, from the cast is a major loss from the emotional texture the film has taught audiences to appreciate; and the linear approach to the narrative seems a good deal less potent than the film's use of flashback. To sum up, the film's techniques unarguably make for a richer experience on so many levels, however accomplished the play's performance may be.

Notes

1 George Eliot, *The Mill on the Floss* (1860), Harmondsworth: Penguin, 1981, p. 635.

2 Edith Wharton, *The Age of Innocence* (1920), New York: Charles Scribner's Sons, 1968, p. 312.

3 Brian McFarlane, '*The Age of Innocence*: Scorsese Meets Edith Wharton', *Metro*, No. 105, 1995, p. 41.

4 Pauline Kael, *5001 Nights at the Movies*, London: A Zenith Book, 1984, p. 78.

5 Noël Coward, 'Introduction', *Play Parade: Volume Four*, London: William Heinemann, 1954, p. xiii,

6 'About the Plays', programme notes, Malvern Theatre Company, Melbourne, August–September 2017.

7 '*Brief Encounter*', Caedman, New York, audio recordings, 1956.

2

Brief Encounter in 1945

Made during the last days of the Second World War, and (in the biography of Celia Johnson by her daughter Kate Fleming) it is clear that this was much on Johnson's mind at the time – especially in her letters to husband Peter Fleming, then on war service in India – *Brief Encounter* has no hint of wartime.[1] At least, not in any overt way. The preceding play was of course pre-war, first performed in 1936, and it is interesting to reflect on what the film – made after six years of Britain at war – gains (or loses?) as a result of its lack of specificity about the particular period. People better versed than I in matters, say, of costume or of British eating habits may well be able to locate the film temporally with more precision, but there is a timeless quality about it that maintains a grip long after certain modes and manners have changed irrevocably.

Perhaps there is nothing remarkable about this. After all, people still happily read Jane Austen and Dickens long after the lifestyles in which their novels are set have vanished. If we value *Pride and Prejudice* or *Great Expectations* in the twenty-first century, it is probably because they touch on – explore – aspects of human behaviour that remain central to our lives. If Lean's film lacks some sort of 'documentary' realism in the kind of detail that would have anchored it to the mid 1940s, it still, nevertheless, suggests what may have been of wider relevance to the period. The war must have disrupted many relationships, some of which never recovered, many of which may have been re-worked to produce stable marriages. The idea of a sense of obligation in what is owed to others has never become irrelevant, and even though *Brief Encounter* is never tied to a specific time it is not hard to imagine it striking some resonant chords at the time of its first viewing – as well as moving into a popular consciousness in an almost unequalled way.

A recent book, Ken Puckett's *War Pictures*, rather surprisingly includes *Brief Encounter* among the three films he has chosen to explore his theme of 'Cinema, Violence and Style in Britain, 1939–1945'. The other two films examined, *The Life and Death of Colonel Blimp* and

Henry V, are clearly much more obvious choices, but Puckett makes an interesting and largely persuasive case for his view that '*Brief Encounter* is not only a war film but also Lean's best war film'.[2] He claims that the film works as a 'result of the complex, unstable, and pervasive tension between past and present' and that much of this is rendered through close-ups of Celia Johnson's face, when she, for instance, muses: 'I didn't think … such violent things could happen to ordinary people',[3] but also in such moments as 'the appearance of the two drunk and disorderly soldiers in Myrtle Bagot's café, Laura's conversation with Fred about a naval career for their young son, and her largely unmotivated nighttime visit to a World War 1 memorial'.[4] Such references help to place the film in the time of its production, if not in any explicit way in the time of its setting. Those lines quoted from Puckett seem to resonate with Laura's sense of emotional chaos as she stands, distraught, in the shadow of the symbol of major world chaos.

Though the film is introduced as 'Noël Coward's *Brief Encounter*' (reflecting an approach to the film's authorship some would dispute), the screenplay is in fact credited as the work of director David Lean and producers Anthony Havelock-Allan and Ronald Neame, the three key figures in the Cineguild production company responsible for the film. (Cineguild, operating independently under the Rank Organisation's umbrella, was responsible for some of the most prestigious films of the period, including Lean's adaptations of Dickens.) However, though Coward is uncredited in relation to the screenplay, and he was abroad providing entertainment for fighting men at the time of the film's making, his input is nevertheless crucial. Indeed, as Trevor Howard's biographer wrote, it was 'Noël Coward, who carried the whip that spun the top: he had written the script and was to be consulted every foot of the way.'[5] Producer Havelock-Allen recalled the screenwriting processes as follows. He, Neame and Lean had decided that the only play of the *Tonight at 8.30* anthology that 'we could see expanding into a film was *Still Life*':

> We decided to have a go at it, so we did a rough script and Noël supplied the new dialogue we needed: it had been a half-hour play and the film was to be an hour and a half, so we needed more visuals and more words. At one stage during *Brief Encounter* he was actually in India with an entertainment troupe; we managed to get cables through to him saying we needed thirty seconds of dialogue for the scene in the boat and we got a cable back giving us two lines of dialogue and saying, 'This runs forty-eight seconds: if you want to shorten it take out the following words …'.[6]

Neame, in his autobiography, also recalled the screenwriting collaboration: 'When I was in America, David and Tony had started scripting

2 The original movie poster

Brief Encounter and I'd joined them on my return', adding with a frankness that might have been ill-advised at the time, 'we transformed Noël's somewhat static, one-act play into an effective shooting script'.[7] My chief interest at this point is in establishing the film's relation to its immediate predecessor and how its structure was arrived at.

The best – and certainly the most comprehensive – account of the making of the film is in Kevin Brownlow's masterly biography of David Lean, in which he explores matters of its casting, art direction and music, as well as such key structural matters as starting the film with the last meeting of the protagonists, Laura Jesson and Alec Harvey. He quotes Lean as persuading Coward that this would be more 'intriguing' than the straight linear movement of the play: 'supposing we started with a fairly busy waiting-room. There are two people sitting at a table, talking, a man and a woman. Through the door comes another woman who sits down at the table. As she sits talking and talking, you realise there's something not quite right going on and a train comes into the station. "That's your train," says the woman. "Yes," says the man, "I must go".'[8] Thus, and with Coward's approval, the film's narrative is launched – and in a way that immediately grips audience attention.

As to that 'narrative', the film preserves the main outline of the original play, though with the important structural change referred to above and with several additional characters of varied significance. For those unfamiliar with the 1945 film – the loss is theirs and should be quickly repaired – here is a very brief account of its narrative substance. Middle-class housewife Laura (Celia Johnson), after a day's shopping in her nearby provincial town, Milford Town, is waiting for the train to take her home when a speck of grit from a passing train lodges in her eye. In the station's buffet, Dr Alec Harvey (Trevor Howard) removes the fragment, and on subsequent meetings they fall in love. Before this love can be consummated in Alec's friend's apartment, they are interrupted by the unexpected arrival of this friend. She runs to the station, Alec goes after her a little later, and the following exchange, crucial to the film's timeless moral core, takes place:

> ALEC: 'We know we love each other. That's all that really matters.'
> LAURA: 'It's not all that really matters. Other things matter too, self-respect matters, and decency. I can't go on any longer.'

She then returns to her kind, rather conventional husband, Fred (Cyril Raymond). To think of this in Freudian terms, if one must, the instinctual forces of the id have been brought into line by the demands of the super-ego as repository of the critical mores of the outer world, the ego having to negotiate a path between the two. Laura's concern is with how

'Other things matter too', and, if the ego is to be a balanced entity, these will, for her at least, have to be taken into account.

In line with Lean's recommendation, the film is told in an extended flashback, and it has been suggested that it is no more than a dream on Laura's part. A student of mine once gave an interesting paper drawing attention to this possibility, quoting Laura's early comment: 'I completely forgot about the whole incident. It didn't mean anything to me at all – at least I didn't think it did', suggesting that it has built up in her mind so as to *mean* something, and that Fred's line at the end 'It wasn't a very happy dream was it?' may reinforce the notion of fantasising on Laura's part.[9] Even if that were so, it would not lessen its holding power: it would still testify to the repressed emotional life of this decent woman who has been caught unexpectedly by an unsought whiff of passion. As Charles Drazin has written in a brief but perceptive account of the film: 'We are inside her head; we share her thoughts.'[10] And on the matter of starting with the last interrupted meeting of Alec and Laura and returning to this almost at the film's end, Drazin describes this as 'an effect that could *only* be achieved in the cinema'.[11]

Brief Encounter was conceived as a small film (its running time is only 86 minutes), revolving around a simple story, such that its subsequent afterlife was no doubt somewhat of a surprise to its production team. Coward had originally sold the film rights for *Tonight at 8.30* to MGM in Hollywood; producer Sydney Box persuaded MGM to sell them to him; and he in turn sold them on to the Rank Organisation. According to Howard's biographer, its final cost 'lay between £260,000 and £270,000',[12] and its stars were by no means sure-fire draws. As noted earlier, Celia Johnson had made three films prior to this but was no guarantee of box-office success. She had had a long theatrical career but 'still loathed making films', Brownlow records, 'yet she knew she would have to play the part when Noël Coward read it to her in October 1944'.[13]

As for the role of Alec, the first choice was Roger Livesey, but Anthony Havelock-Allan had been impressed by an actor he'd seen on stage in Terence Rattigan's *French Without Tears* and brought him to Lean's attention. 'Then I saw him in a film, then I asked David to see him. David saw him, David thought he was right.'[14] When Lean and Havelock-Allan watched 'a rough-cut of Anthony Asquith's *The Way to the Stars*, they were struck by the actor in the secondary part of Squadron Leader Carter, the commanding officer who gets killed early in the film. The actor was Trevor Howard.'[15] Howard, who had a theatre background, went on to a long and varied career in films, but it is arguable that *Brief Encounter* remains the title with which he is most

3 Celia Johnson and Trevor Howard as Laura and Alec

tenaciously associated. Given how he emerges in Vivienne Knight's biography, it is a little surprising to find how sensitively he renders the role. In this and other accounts, he was totally unable to believe that Alec and Laura didn't simply go to bed as soon as possible. Celia Johnson's view of her co-star, whom she believed to be about eight years her junior (he had actually knocked several years of his age), was that he was 'Rather pleasant but pretty stupid (shhh)', though allowing that she believed he was 'going to be good I think and has the mentality of a born film star'.[16]

Given that their approaches to filming were so different it is remarkable how movingly they play together. Celia Johnson, though she may have 'loathed' filming, was quick and intuitive in getting to the essence of a scene, a gift Harold French, director of her second film, *Dear Octopus*, recalled.[17] Howard, on the other hand, was reportedly slower and required many takes, by the end of which Johnson was beginning to lose the freshness of her performance.[18] Whatever the differences Lean experienced in getting his stars to register the necessary responses, the outcome can only have testified to the wisdom of the casting, even if what subsequently became known of Howard's roistering ways and heavy drinking – as well as the lie about his age – might have seemed at odds with the sensitivity the role required of him. He actually played the role of Alec Harvey again in 1954 in an American TV adaptation of the Coward play, this time co-starring with Ginger Rogers as Laura.

Among the other key members of the cast, Joyce Carey had appeared in several of the other plays in *Tonight at 8.30*, including *Still Life*, and she would repeat her role as Myrtle Bagot in the film. Everley Gregg, who had played the role of gossipy Dolly Messiter in *Still Life*, was not originally cast in the film but eventually replaced Joyce Barbour, who had been unwell and had difficulty remembering her lines; and Stanley Holloway, as ticket inspector Albert Godby, was one of the most popular comedians of the day. As well as these three and Cyril Raymond – whose note-perfect playing of Fred perhaps warrants more attention than it has usually had – there were several other small roles that contribute chiefly to the comedy of the film. Margaret Barton, who played Myrtle's assistant Beryl, was the last surviving member of the cast (apart, presumably, from the two then-youngsters who played Laura's children)[19] and was frequently referred to and interviewed in relation to her role as the chirpy Beryl. At the age of 90, she was still being canvassed for her views on the film, claiming 'how marvellous it was to work with David Lean', but resolutely asserting 'I was never a film star'.[20] Also, in quite tiny roles, Marjorie Mars – as the friend Laura is embarrassed to meet when she's been lunching with Alec – provides a quietly sceptical touch when Laura later phones her to ask for support in a 'domestic lie'; and Irene Handl as the cinema organist who reappears in the restaurant with a different musical instrument and setting, but is just as amusing to the film's protagonists.

While referring to the film's comedy, it must be said that there is no doubt an element of patronage, of class snobbery, in the way Myrtle and Albert and their relationship are depicted. There is arguably a long history of class discrimination in English drama, certainly as far back as Shakespeare's 'mechanicals' in *A Midsummer Night's Dream* or Dogberry and his colleagues in *Much Ado About Nothing*. In these and many other English dramas since, at least one function of the lower orders was to offer comic contrast to the more refined behaviour of their superiors. And Coward was no stranger to snobbish allusion in his plays, though this is not to say that it is the matter of overwhelming importance in *Brief Encounter*. The protagonists *are* middle class but that isn't all that defines them.

Joyce Carey, faithfully following Coward's dialogue, gets laughs for the fake refinement (or 'refainment' as she would pronounce it) she brings to Myrtle. Stanley Holloway's Albert engages in what would have passed in 1945 for suggestive innuendo, as he hints at a later after-hours encounter with Myrtle. Using the word 'encounter' there does, however,

point to another function of these two. In his introduction to the published screenplay, Sheridan Morley wrote that, 'later, several critics, and
David [Lean] himself, admitted they were embarrassed by the "comic
relief" scenes' with Carey and Holloway[21] – a point of view reinforced
by Havelock-Allan.[22] But is 'comic relief' their only contribution to the
film's texture? Yes, with their badinage about Myrtle's late husband and
her response to Albert's sly suggestions, they may seem to offer a comic
version of the serious emotional life of their social betters. However,
it could also be argued that there is an openness about their verbal
parrying that makes a kind of critical commentary on what might be
viewed as the stiff-upper-lipped restraint Alec and Laura's middle-class
background imposes on them. The sense of clear-cut class distinction
may also have been a way of locating the film in a time at remove from
1945, when the effect of wartime life was expected to have made such
distinction less obvious. So, 'comic relief' may not wholly account for
their function in the film.

The interior scenes of the film were shot in Denham Studios, where
the railway buffet scenes were reconstructed, but the station scenes –
platforms, corridors, rails – were filmed in Carnforth in north Lancashire.
Dilys Powell, reviewing the film in the *Sunday Times*, claimed indeed
that: 'the whole film is dominated by trains and the adjuncts, necessities,
and consequences of trains'.[23] There are various accounts of why this
out-of-London location was chosen. Celia Johnson's biographer wrote
that 'it was sufficiently removed from London to be safe from attack,
even with all the film lighting, and also had very little traffic passing
through at night – only the Royal Scot – so that filming could continue
throughout the night without interruptions'.[24] David Lean added that
'there was plenty of time to douse the lights in the event of an air-raid',[25]
not all that likely by 1945, though there was still a remote possibility of
rocket-launched bombs. Johnson had not looked forward to this location filming but, in the event, enjoyed the experience – as indeed did the
unit at large – comfortably housed as she was in Windermere. Decades
later, Carnforth Station has become a tourist venue, as will be seen later
in the book. The other outdoor sequences were shot nearer to London:
for example, the 'Milford' street scenes were filmed in Beaconsfield; and
the boating sequence took place in Regent's Park, London.

Reception

Brief Encounter may now enjoy classic status, and always appears high
in lists of favourite British films; however, in 1945, it didn't receive

4 The railway station scenes were filmed in Carnforth, Lancashire

universal kudos. The film was previewed in Rochester, where Lean received the first print and where he was by this time working on *Great Expectations*, having wanted a break from the Coward connection of his last three films. Rochester, described by Lean as 'a pretty tough town in those days', proved immune to the film's depiction of emotions restrained by obligations to others. Lean recalled how 'at the first love scene one woman down the front started to laugh ... And in the second scene it got even worse. And then the audience caught on and waited for her to laugh and they all joined in and it ended in an absolute shambles.'[26] One member of the audience in the dockland cinema was alleged to have groaned 'Isn't 'e ever goin' to 'ave it orf with 'er?', suggesting that this audience was unlikely to respond to such a tender scenario.[27]

Two decades later, film historian Jeffrey Richards recalled, at a showing of the film in Cambridge, that 'the student audience were convulsed with laughter throughout, incredulous that the lovers did not just leap into bed together and to hell with the consequences, responsibilities or beliefs'.[28] But, as Richards goes on to point out: 'Irrespective of the whims of fashion, *Brief Encounter* remains both documentarily and emotionally true.'[29] What he is arguing for here is the film's authentic evocation of the period of its making *and* the lasting truth of a value

system in which decency and concern for others prevail over sexual sur-
render and self-indulgence.

However, after its rough reception in Rochester, once the film was
presented to the 'respectable' critics in London and elsewhere, Lean was,
for the most part, able to put behind him the response to this first public
showing, as the film garnered positive reviews from the likes of C.A.
Lejeune. She described it in the *Listener* as a film that 'seems to catch, in
words and pictures, so many things that are penetratingly true'.[30] Dilys
Powell, in her *Sunday Times* review, perceptively drew attention to the
film's conflict between falling in love and the values of 'faithfulness and
obligations and the happiness of others' and praised the way 'The whole
story is told with the technical adroitness we expect from Mr. Coward
... [and] with a breadth of sympathy less expected in Mr. Coward.'[31]
Reflecting that some people had felt it was 'more like a French film',
Richard Winnington, writing in the *News Chronicle*, felt they really
meant that it was 'emotionally grown-up' and especially singled out
the acting of Celia Johnson who 'magnificently portrays the wife and
mother meeting passion for the first time'.[32]

But excellent notices such as these were not the whole story. James
Agate, the waspish critic of the *Tatler* magazine, who now seems often
more concerned with being 'smart' than astute or accurate, complained
about the 'very nearly full-length performance of the Rachmaninoff C
Minor Piano Concerto which pounds and drones and rattles in the background whenever the tedium becomes unbearable'. He goes on to claim:
'I know half a dozen Fleet Street hacks who could turn out a chance
meeting which would be every bit as good as *Brief Encounter*.'[33] He ends
his review by referring to Coward as 'a man of near-genius [who] should
have done better'. As to Agate's dismissal of the Rachmaninoff piece
(played by Eileen Joyce), he seems to have been in a minority – possibly
of one – the emotional power of the music contributing significantly to
audience involvement. Is it perhaps an example of what Dawkins calls
a 'meme' in its having been passed on, albeit in altered form, into the
culture as an inevitable reminder of the film that brought it to a vast and
continuing audience?[34]

I don't mean to give a representative sample of the film's critical reception at the time, but, rather, to suggest that the almost reverent status
now accorded it was by no means universally anticipated in 1945. And
in the following year, when released in the US, Bosley Crowther, in the
New York Times found it 'An uncommonly good little picture – and
one that is frankly designed to appeal to that group of film-goers who
are provoked by "the usual movie tripe".'[35] I can't be sure what exactly
that last phrase means, but there is a sense of responding to the film's

particular qualities. Another contemporary US reviewer, James Agee, couldn't resist an element of patronage in his summing up of the film: 'relatively dinky and sentimental as it is – a sort of vanity-sized *Anna Karenina* – *Brief Encounter* is to be thoroughly respected'.[36] Despite Agee's qualified appraisal, the film did pick up several Oscar nominations: for Lean's direction, for the screenplay by Lean, Havelock-Allan and Neame, and for Celia Johnson as best actress. It did not win any, but these nominations testify to its at least being noticed in the US, and it shared the Grand Prix at the Cannes Film Festival in 1946.

Released in early post-war days, the film may have seemed to continue the tradition of realism which had characterised so much wartime filmmaking in Britain; and there are certainly elements of this mode in its use of recognisable settings, for instance. But in Robert Krasker's cinematography there are also frequent reminders, at least in hindsight, of the *film noir* vogue of the period, and the use of Celia Johnson's voice-over narration as the story is revealed in flashback suggests more complex generic affiliations. A recent biographer of David Lean may have been over-simplifying when he wrote: '*Brief Encounter* succeeded because of the "new realism"... that flourished in post-war British cinema.'[37] It is tempting to think that pure realism might not have ensured the long life of the film that the rest of this book will explore.

Notes

1 Kate Fleming, *Celia Johnson: A Biography*, London: Orion, 1991, p. 176–77.
2 Ken Puckett, *War Pictures: Cinema, Violence, and Style in Britain, 1939–1945*, New York: Fordham University Press, 2017, p. 137.
3 Ibid, p. 166.
4 Ibid, p. 168.
5 Vivienne Knight, *Trevor Howard: A Gentleman and a Player, The Authorised Biography*, London: Sphere Books Ltd, 1986, p. 45.
6 'Anthony Havelock-Allan', in Brian McFarlane (ed.), *An Autobiography of British Cinema*, London: Methuen/BFI publishing, 1997, p. 292.
7 Ronald Neame (with Barbara Roisman Cooper), *Straight from the Horse's Mouth*, Lanham, Maryland: Scarecrow Press, 2003, p. 94.
8 Kevin Brownlow, *David Lean*, London: Richard Cohen Books, 1996, p. 194.
9 Loretta Mercuri, class paper, Monash University, Melbourne, 15 August 1994.
10 Charles Drazin, *The Finest Years: British Cinema of the 1940s*, London: André Deutsch Ltd, 1998, p. 56.
11 Ibid, p. 57.
12 Knight, *Trevor Howard*, p. 46.
13 Brownlow, *David Lean*, p. 196.

14 Interview with Anthony Havelock-Allan by Linda Wood. BECTU History Project – Interview No. 139, 23 May 1990.

15 Brownlow, *David Lean*, p. 195.

16 Knight, *Trevor Howard*, p. 174.

17 In interview with the author, July 1990.

18 Knight, *Trevor Howard*, p. 175.

19 Henrietta Vincent (as Margaret) was Celia Johnson's niece and never filmed again. Richard Thomas played two more small roles, the last in the 1957 TV version of *A Man for All Seasons*.

20 www.bbc.com/news/entertainment-arts-36387445. Accessed 23 August 2018.

21 Sheridan Morley, 'Introduction', in Noël Coward, *Brief Encounter* (1974), London: Faber and Faber, 1999, p. xii.

22 McFarlane, *An Autobiography of British Cinema*, p. 292.

23 Dilys Powell, *Sunday Times*, November 29, 1945.

24 Fleming, *Celia Johnson*, p. 171.

25 Quoted in Brownlow, *David Lean*, p. 196.

26 Ibid, p. 203.

27 Quoted in Knight, *Trevor Howard*, p. 48.

28 Jeffrey Richards, *Films and British National Identity: From Dickens to Dad's Army*, Manchester: Manchester University Press, 1997, p. 123.

29 Ibid.

30 C.A. Lejeune, *Listener*, 29 November 1945.

31 Dilys Powell, *Sunday Times*, 29 November 1945.

32 Richard Winnington, *News Chronicle*, 24 November 1945.

33 James Agate, *Around Cinemas* (Second Series), London: Home & Van Thal Ltd, 1948, p. 261.

34 Cf. Dawkins's reference to Beethoven's Ninth Symphony in *The Selfish Gene*, p. 195.

35 Bosley Crowther, *New York Times*, 6 August 1946.

36 James Agee, *Nation*, 31 August 1946.

37 Gene D. Phillips, *Beyond the Epic: the Life & Films of David Lean*, Lexington: University of Kentucky Press, 2006, p. 87.

3

In the wake

It was surely, by the mid-1970s, a rather daring enterprise to undertake a remake of *Brief Encounter*, but the mere fact of its happening is some kind of evidence for the film's stature. On viewing it again some decades later, one can only be struck by the sheer folly of the venture – and the almost total incompetence of the resulting film.

Not leaving well enough alone – another *Brief Encounter* (1974)

The film's most obvious – and most ludicrous – successor is the 1974 remake as a telemovie, improbably starring Sophia Loren and Richard Burton. There may be other films more disastrously conceived and executed than this, but they don't come readily to mind. Nevertheless, one has to consider what attracted the film's makers to the enterprise, almost thirty years after the original's first screening.

Essentially, it is a remake of the *film*, not an adaptation of Coward's play. In narrative outline, it follows the main steps of the original: the grit in her eye; the doctor to the rescue; the series of meetings; falling in love; the near-adultery; then the return to their several domestic settings. I cite this merely as a matter of interest in the sense that a remake would scarcely have dared any major plot manoeuvre, such as the protagonists' going off together for a life of bliss in foreign parts. Filmmaking history offers plenty of examples of remakes, more often than not attracting criticism along the lines of 'not as good as the original', though there seems no particular reason why this should inevitably be the case. In fact, for every lacklustre retelling of, say, Vincente Minnelli's *Father of the Bride* (1951, then 1990) there is probably a reinvigorated success, such as Hitchcock's 1956 version of his own 1934 film *The Man Who Knew Too Much*.

In the case of the *Brief Encounter*, my chief interest is not in an evaluative account of the remake, but in the sheer *fact* of its having been made at all and of what can have inspired its makers to attempt it. It was a UK/Italian co-production, involving Transcontinental Film Productions (London), Carlo Ponti Cinematografica (as A Carlo Ponti-Cecil Clarke Film) and Incorporated Television Company (ITC). Perhaps the most significant name among these is that of Carlo Ponti, who was married to Sophia Loren.

If you want to make a touching drama about love and renunciation in a quiet English setting, you'd perhaps think twice about casting as the leads an international sex symbol and a noted lothario: 'gloriously miscast' as they were described in the obituary of Rosemary Leach who had a supporting role in the telefilm.[1] Intertextuality matters when watching a film: we can't put aside all the information we bring to bear on it, and sometimes this can intensify our viewing experience. But not here. John Bowen's screenplay retains some of the dialogue of the original but in the new circumstances, with such 1970s updating as giving Alec an interest in 'environmental pollution' and setting up Laura (now Anna), as a Citizens' Advice Bureau volunteer, it tends to sound merely old-fashioned. Burton and Loren simply exude a starry glamour that makes their restraint seem improbable. Their private lives, especially Burton's, had received widespread coverage, and their film careers had included such epic-scale productions as *The Robe* (1953) and *Cleopatra* (1963) for Burton, *The Pride and the Passion* (1957) and *El Cid* (1961) for Loren.

This is not to suggest that actors can't and shouldn't display versatility, but the kinds of baggage filmgoers might bring to bear on any new film starring such hugely *known* figures might well make it hard to accept them as an 'ordinary' couple. And this certainly proved to be the case. The point most relevant to this study is that major stars *wanted* to take on what Burton's first biographer, Paul Ferris, described as 'a reckless venture given the quality of Trevor Howard and Celia Johnson thirty years before'.[2] There must have been enough sense of the prestige attaching to the title to attract them; that is, by this time the very title was evocative enough to attract their attention, and it would go on being evocative in the ensuing decades.

And this is essentially what has fascinated me over the years about the original film: that in one medium or another, whether film, television, stage play or opera, there seems to be an unending line of successors. If the producers were serious about recreating the quiet emotional power of the 1945 film, they could well have chosen in director Alan Bridges just the man for this. In 1973, he had shown in *The Hireling* a subtle skill in dealing with an unsought relationship, and would go on to hone such skills in later films like *Out of Season* (1975) and *Return of the*

5 Sofia Loren and Richard Burton, who starred in the 1974 remake

Soldier (1982). He was a director of some sensitivity in dealing with troubled lives, so that one tends to look elsewhere for the film's failure. The adaptation and the screenplay were the work of John Bowen, whose career had been wholly in television – much of it in series such as *Armchair Thriller* (1971) – and there was not much to suggest him as an obvious choice for a reworking of *Brief Encounter*.

However, it is over the unsuitability of the starring pair that the film primarily stumbles. Sophia Loren's autobiography merely mentions the title twice, describing it as 'the remake of a famous movie directed by David Lean'.[3] She includes a letter from Burton who wrote: 'Have read script. What on earth ever persuaded anyone to do it without me? Incredible impertinence … I love you, of course, but it's also a fine piece of work for much as I love I wouldn't do it otherwise. …'[4] There is no comment from Loren to account for her accepting the role. Burton's biographers have a little more to say. The role of Alec had been ear-marked for Robert Shaw, but he was still working in the US on *Jaws*, which was over-running its schedule. According to Melvyn Bragg, Burton's second biographer: 'Sophia Loren suggested Burton and for £200,000 plus expenses, and for Sophia Loren, Burton walked into that disastrous remake.'[5]

It is no doubt unfair to lay all the blame for the film's failure on the unsuitability of the star pair, crucial though this is. Normally when writing on matters of adaptation, whether of literature to film or of one film from another, my interest is in how the adaptation works on its own terms rather than how 'faithful' it is to its antecedent text. With regard to the television version of *Brief Encounter*, though, this approach is difficult to sustain. Because this version keeps so much of the narrative outline of the original, it is almost impossible not to make evaluative comparisons that do the 1974 piece no credit.

In terms of structure, for instance. Bowen's screenplay dispenses with the flashback technique so poignantly employed in Lean's film and with the narrating voice of Laura/Anna – and offers no corresponding method to the latter, so that we never get the sense of her inner turmoil. A few close-ups of Loren's beautiful face, immaculately made-up and with its lush aureole of auburn hair, don't come near to expressing the emotional tensions that Celia Johnson's Laura registers so tellingly in both visual and aural terms. The straight linear presentation reduces the impact of the would-be lovers' final meeting when gossiping Dolly Messiter (Gwen Cherrell) intervenes. In 1945, she is clearly interrupting something in the station's tea room, something of consequence to the lives of Laura and Alec; when we return to this situation at the end, we understand all the emotional upheaval that has preceded it, and Dolly's ruin of their last meeting is so much the more moving. In the 1974 version, the moment passes for nothing.

As regards structural matters, in what other way does this film seek to create a richer texture? For one, making Anna a counsellor brings her into contact with a woman, Mrs Gaines (Rosemary Leach), whose husband has been unfaithful to her. Presumably we are meant to read this as offering further argument for why Anna should break with Alec. If so, the device works crudely, with Anna breaking her workday appointments in order to spend time with Alec as they wander through sunny Technicolor landscapes (not cinematographer Arthur Ibbetson's finest hour). The two actresses seem to belong to different worlds and Loren's cosmetically immaculate image never suggests the careful, considered approach that might be expected of a counsellor at work in such matters. In fact, Rosemary Leach might have been much more appropriate casting for the Laura audiences were expecting. As for the scenes depicting Anna's home life with husband Graham (Jack Hedley), who may have been guilty of a minor sexual lapse, these are both longer and less revealing than the glimpses of the Jesson household in the earlier film; and the brief episode of Alec at home, with wife Melanie (Ann Firbank) asking him to turn down the radio so that she can concentrate on the book she is reviewing, is too fleeting to mean much at all.

Flames of Passion (1989)

Among the many later manifestations of the film's longevity, there was a second remake – to use the term 'remake' loosely. It was clearly derived from Noël Coward's sexuality as an underlying motif of *Brief Encounter*, a matter that will be referred to later in this book. The 18-minute film, written and directed by Richard Kwietniowksi, is plainly intended as a gay take on *Brief Encounter*. In the latter, when Laura and Alec go to the cinema, they see the trailer for a wildly over-the-top romantic epic called '*Flames of Passion*', from which Kwietniowski's short film takes its title. An early title announces a 'seven day pass', and the film is divided into the daily segments in which a suited professional (Richard Seymour) fantasises a passion set in motion by finding a strip of photos of a smiling guy (Donald Grieg). There is no dialogue in the film. What drama there is in it is to be found in the man's face, which registers the growth of his infatuation with the other guy. At one point, he has – or pretends to have – or imagines he has – some dust in his eye and the smiling guy is a doctor. Embraces and fervent kisses ensue; there are close-ups of hands clasped; and the film contrasts the two faces, the one

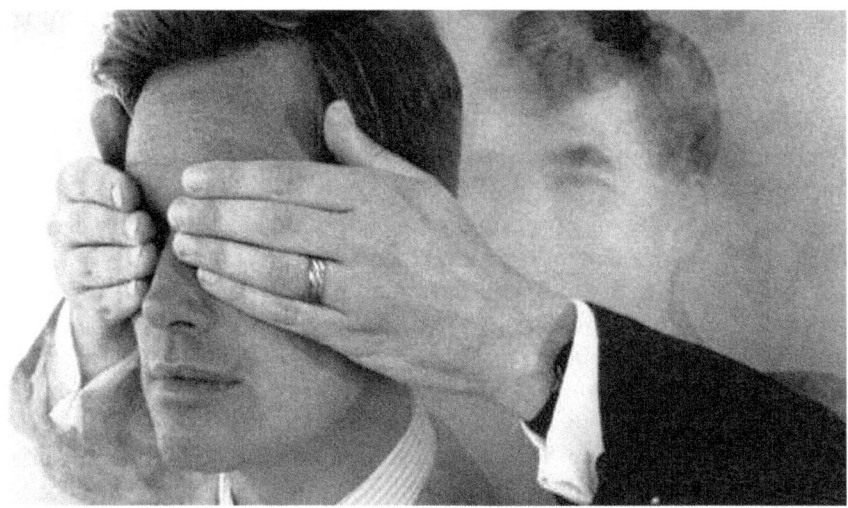

6 Richard Kwietniowski's *Flames of Passion*

sombre, obsessed, and the other much more sure of himself and end-lessly smiling. There's a pounding musical score by Bob Locke and Tim Norfolk, credited as 'The Insects', which grows grimmer as the obses-sion takes over. Also, Oliver Curtis's evocative camerawork and Peter Webber's editing do their best to maintain our interest in this slender tribute (?) to its famous predecessor of forty-four years earlier. Images of men running in the station's passageways and the insistence of the music reinforce Kwietniowski's obvious intentions, but it is hard to imagine the film ever attracting large audiences and it seems never to have been widely released. Its subject and its running-time would have ensured only specialist release attention, but it did win for best short at the San Francisco International Lesbian & Gay Film Festival in 1990.

In considering these two 'remakes', I am less concerned with their intrinsic qualities than with the fact of the original film having given rise to them. Since 1989, no producer has dared to take on the daunting prospect of remaking a film that has so secure a place in British – and other – cinema history. It may indeed be a case of leaving well enough alone.

Notes

1 Michael Coveney, 'Rosemary Leach Obituary', *Guardian*, 23 October 2017.
2 Paul Ferris, *Richard Burton*, London: Weidenfeld and Nicolson, 1981, p. 165.

3 Sophia Loren, *Yesterday, Today, Tomorrow: My Life*, London: Simon & Schuster, 2014, p. 21
4 Ibid.
5 Melvyn Bragg, *Rich: The Life of Richard Burton*, London: Coronet Books (Hodder and Stoughton), 1988, p. 580.

4

Descendants – on radio, stage and screen

On radio

Long before the stage adaptations, discussed next, there had been US radio dramatisations of the film featuring such high-profile screen players as Greer Garson twice – in 1946 and 1948 – as Laura. The first of these was for the Academy Award Theater, aired on 20 November 1946, while the Lux Radio Theater production, starring Garson with Van Heflin, was broadcast on 29 November 1948. Both can now be listened to online.[1] The former is a rather skimpy 25 minutes, divided into two parts and with a tedious, prosy narrator who introduces the play with such profundities as 'Can you judge a man and a woman? Apply a moral yardstick?' and so on. It begins with Garson's rather breathy, over-stated Laura saying 'This can't last', and, accomplished actress though she was, she never cuts through to Laura's underlying pain, whatever she is given to say; while Carl Harbord's Alec lacks the urgency needed to bring Laura to the radio play's near turning point.

Garson's 1948 rendering of Laura for the Lux Radio Theater gives more to work on, but it inevitably evokes recollections of her other famous 1940s film roles. She sounds somewhat more in control and less 'ordinary-under-pressure' than Celia Johnson, but some of the painful truth of the film – and the radio version adapts the *film*, not the preceding play – still emerges. In both these radio versions, the adaptors choose not to use Rachmaninoff for music, and each makes much use of Laura's voice-over, a technique of course readily attuned to the potential of radio. What matters to the present study is the mere fact of there being two radio adaptations within three years of the film's release.

Olivia De Havilland recreated the role in the Lux Radio Theater on 14 May 1951, with Richard Basehart as Alec, but this version appears to be unavailable. The almost bewildering number of big names appearing in other radio versions (Stewart Granger, Deborah Kerr, David Niven, etc.) seem to have been drawn to the prestige of the screen title. None of them were playing *Still Life*, but the enlarged version for the film, the screenplay of which was of course largely Coward's work – despite his not being thus credited. So, even as soon as the late 1940s and early 1950s, the film had taken on a life of its own. It had already displaced the original play both in the public consciousness and as a vehicle for notable actors.

On stage

There were several theatrical versions of the 1945 film, each bearing the title of *Brief Encounter* and owing more to it than to Coward's original, though retaining some of the latter. The first stage version, directed by Simon Redfarn, occurred in the 1996, when it appeared at the Yvonne Arnaud Theatre, Guildford. It starred Hayley Mills as Laura and Simon Dutton as Alec, with Elizabeth Power as Myrtle. Unlike *Still Life*, this production was not confined to a single set, but had several sets on a revolving stage, including one for the Kardomah Coffee House which Hayley remembered as nearly falling on her and Dutton. She also recently shared her responses to playing Laura:

> I fell in love with the film the first time I saw it many years ago. I desper-
> ately wanted to do the play and play the part of Laura. Initially, of course,
> I was influenced by Celia Johnson's beautiful, luminous performance. I was
> inspired by her but I didn't want to copy her, and as time went by working
> on the play I felt more and more that Laura and I were becoming one …
> At base, Laura's terrible conflict is eternal and one that women everywhere
> will always be able to relate to and empathise with; her husband is a good
> man and she does still love him in a way, but her feelings for Alec are so
> powerful, unlike anything she has ever experienced; but she 'does the right
> thing' which in the end is right for everybody.[2]

The fact of the title change offers further evidence for the longevity of the *film's* reputation. I saw the 1996 touring version, slightly modified from the original script, when, produced again by Simon Redfarn, it was performed at London's Lyric Theatre (2000) starring Jenny Seagrove and Christopher Cazenove, popular TV players from the 1980s. Without seriously challenging the reputation of their famous prede-cessors, they made an attractive and convincing pair of the conflicted would-be lovers. Despite there being no attempt at updating, the shift in moral climate since 1945 was not an issue, the film's crucial awareness of the rift between self-gratification and obligation to others still emerg-ing potently. And in its use of a revolving stage it was able to go beyond the confinement of the original play, notably in setting some scenes in

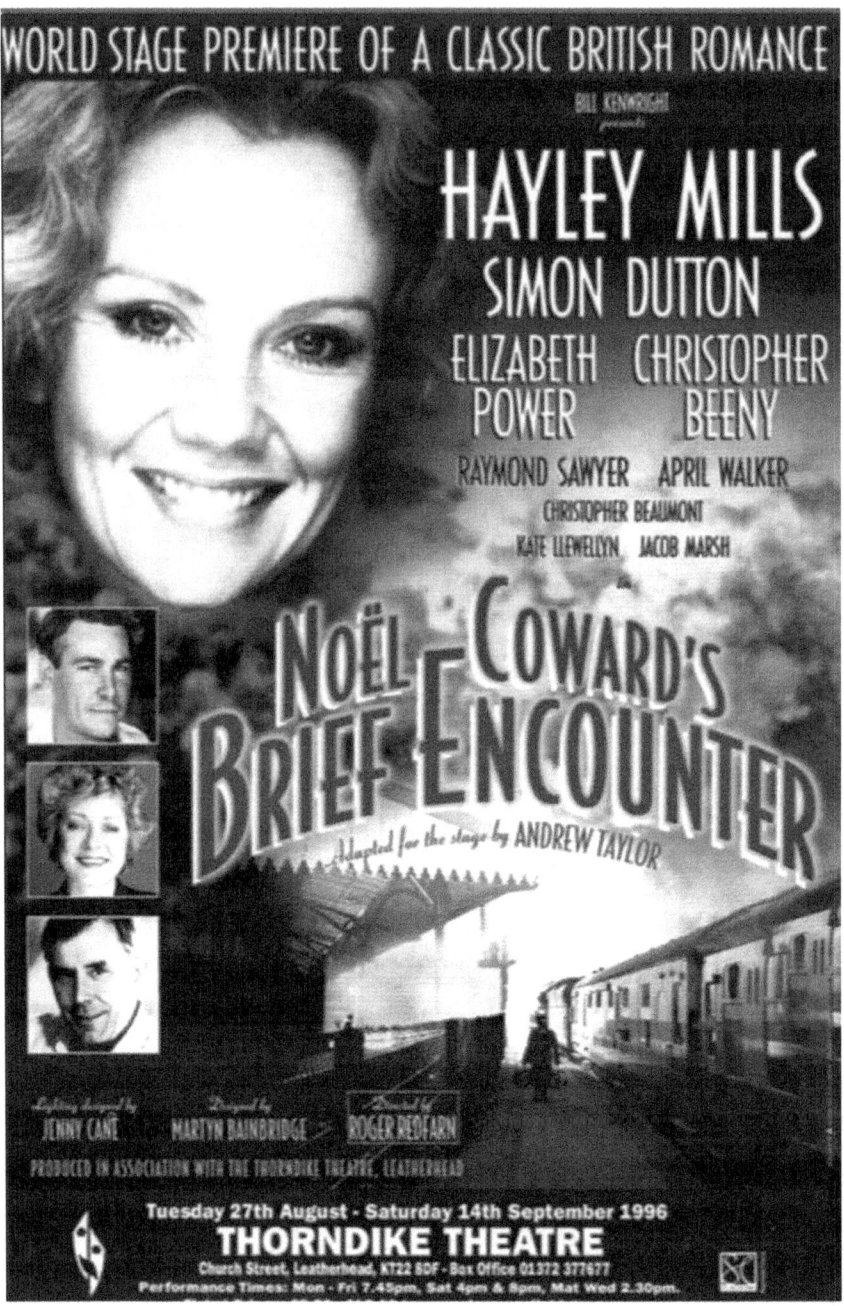

7 The poster for the 1996 production, starring Hayley Mills and Simon Dutton

Laura's home, thus reinforcing the sense of her conflict and of how she eventually resolves this.

My recollection of this production is more benign than those of some of the contemporary reviews, such as that which was headed 'An Encounter with British Drizzle'. This smart-alec piece claims that: 'In an age when people are as likely to change their spouses as they are to change their underwear, Roger Redfarn's stage production of the 1945 David Lean film written by Noël Coward, is difficult to take seriously.'[3] The latter phrase might easily be applied to this review. Another reviewer was more attuned to the central moral/emotional issue of the film and, now, the play when he wrote: 'Their [Laura and Alec's] frustrated love reflects the society of forties Britain, but still touches a major chord for the audience of today.'[4] Some human values don't change with the passage of time.

Jenny Seagrove would go on to play Laura again (this time with Nigel Havers as Alec) on 30 October 2009, in a Radio 2 production of *Brief Encounter*, performed live at Maida Vale Studios, London. The script used was a 1947 adaptation for radio by Maurice Horspool, which had been in the BBC's ownership but never used or performed since then. The script for this radio version kept close to the original screenplay for David Lean's 1945 film, and in 2015 it was performed again for Radio 2 at the Theatre Royal, Windsor, for ten days, with Seagrove once again playing Laura, this time co-starring with Martin Shaw as Alec. According to one account, it was presented in the style of a 1940s radio play. Though this account did not specify what that 'style' involved, the comment was interesting from the point of view of the production apparently being intended to recall not just the film itself but also its cultural context.

The most recent theatrical dramatisation of the film, the Kneehigh Company's version adapted and directed by Emma Rice, in London in February 2008, New York in September 2010 and Melbourne in October 2013, was generally much more favourably received by critics. Unfortunately I was always in the wrong country at the wrong time and missed the performance, so until recently (see below) have had to rely for my impressions on reading the published script[5] and some of the reviews it attracted. It moves fluidly from time and place and is also interspersed with songs, including Coward's 'Mad about the Boy' and 'A Room with a View'.

According to the print version, the band is playing as audiences are shown to their seats, and ushers bid an argumentative couple in the front row to be quiet, and this is all part of the way Rice has chosen to re-present the film classic. The opening dialogue of the Prologue is that between Laura and Alec in which they confirm their love for each other. While this is being spoken, Fred enters calling 'Laura? Laura? Where are you?' and for a brief moment Laura stands between the two men. This Prologue ends with Fred's saying 'Thank you for coming back to me.' In the following 'Scene One', the staff of the Milford Station tea room are going through their paces, Alec and Laura go through the grit-removal ritual, Alec leaves, and Stanley and Beryl sing 'Any Little Fish' before he chases her off, as Fred, Laura and son Bobbie enter.

These details about the way the play begins are worth noting insofar as they suggest that this play is not setting out doggedly to reproduce the film in another medium. It has a zest of its own as it makes its way through the by-now familiar crises until the Epilogue. This ends with Fred's famous last words repeated and with Laura playing the opening chords of Rachmaninoff's Piano Concerto 2 on her own piano, while apparently film is invoked as 'we see her swimming in the ocean. We see her face as she loses herself in the music. She floats freely.'[6] Rice's Foreword refers to how 'Laura talks of swimming wild and free and of playing the piano. Both of these are forms of personal expression – not pleasing anyone but exploring the deep waters of the soul.' In other words, she has picked up a reference from the film and made something new of it, which is surely a key criterion an adaptation must measure up to.

One London reviewer who had gone to the play 'with a heavy heart' finally allowed that: 'Far from being the crude hatchet job I'd feared, the show largely proves a witty and sympathetic homage to Coward's unforgettable portrayal of English reserve and romance.'[7] And in Melbourne, it received critical commendation as 'an inventive leap from the 1945 film to the modern stage, telling the story of hapless lovers … through cinematic projections, live performance, comedy and music.' This almost entirely laudatory review ends by insisting that the play 'cannot be judged against the movie because they are different animals for different times, venues and audiences. Enjoy it for what it is.'[8] The play was performed on Broadway from late September 2010 to mid January 2011, and the *New York Times* reviewer praised Emma Rice for having 'made it possible to embrace *Brief Encounter* once more with feeling, and without irony or embarrassment. Using the tools of music hall, classic British pantomime and story-theater – plus a bit of *trompe l'oeil* technology, via film projections – this production lets its audiences see a familiar movie with virgin eyes and, yes, fall in love with it all over again.'[9] In late 2017, the following headline appeared: 'Emma Rice's Brief Encounter comes to Empire Cinema, Haymarket, from March 2018.'[10] When the play actually opened, the *Evening Standard* ran the headline 'Emma Rice Says Her Own Love Life Inspired Stage Version of *Brief Encounter*'.[11] Of this recent production, one reviewer wrote: 'Rice's production succeeds in taking you to the crux of the agonising dilemma – can two decent people follow their hearts without wrecking their lives?', and ended his wholly positive review with: 'Much more could be said about how finessed Rice's affectionate homage is but in brief it's simply toot-toot terrific.'[12] It could be added that the 'two decent people', at least from Laura's point of view, reach a decision so as not to 'wreck' other people's lives.

By most fortuitous chance, as far as this book is concerned, the Warrandyte Theatre Company, based in a Northern outer suburb of Melbourne, presented an admirable performance of Emma Rice's play in November/December 2017. The company, which enjoys helpful sponsorship from several businesses, made the most of the modest facilities of the local Mechanics Institute Hall. The production maintained a pleasing fluidity between scenes, with rapid rearrangement of minimal props – piano, armchair, tea room counter and tables – to indicate different settings. It also made effective use of black-and-white images depicting, say, the station platform, or the street, or the Jesson home, and of trains arriving and leaving, especially of the express steaming through. Further, three musicians, billed as the 'Trio de Gare', accompanied the musical numbers, which are important for sometimes comic, sometimes emotional, effect. Crucially, though, the actors playing Laura (Gabby Llewellyn) and Alec (Sean Paisley Collins) were both perfectly attuned tonally to the kinds of feeling that have disrupted the pattern of their lives. The fact that the production proved so popular with capacity audiences says something for both the quality of the performance and for the enduring appeal associated with the title. The advertising billboard and the programme's cover both depict that familiar image of Laura leaning out of the train window to say goodbye to Alec, an image that announces the play's heritage.

A further theatrical adaptation that, unfortunately, has never come my way is André Previn's opera, which apparently draws on both Coward's play and the screenplay for *Brief Encounter*. The opera had its premiere on 1 May 2009, at the Houston Grand Opera, which had commissioned it, and its premiere was apparently sold out. Previn had been involved since 1947 as composer, conductor and music director on many famous Hollywood films, including *Gigi* (1958), *Long Day's Journey into Night* (1962) and *My Fair Lady* (1964), until 1967, when he became conductor of the Houston Symphony Orchestra and thereafter worked only intermittently on film. He had previously adapted *A Streetcar Named Desire* to the operatic stage, and the *Guardian* critic felt that his *Brief Encounter* was 'the better piece of the two', even though accusing Previn of 'diluting [the] impact' of each.[13] Previn's score for *Brief Encounter* was conducted by Patrick Summers and had what this reviewer described as 'a carefully crafted libretto by John Caird',[14] while the singing of Nathan Gunn and Elizabeth Futral as Alec and Laura came in for its share of praise. The critic, Tim Ashley, ended by claiming that: 'it all feels very safe and notably lacks passion – unlike the film, which still has the power to tear you in two'.

By comparison, the *Los Angeles Times* had virtually nothing but praise for the original Houston production. This critic discussed the adaptation matter: 'If play-to-film was one level of amplification, film-to-opera is a second level … The opera's job is to spell everything out in easily singable lines … The opera is in 23 brief scenes (divided into two acts) and quick transformations from station to a river's bridge and other locales appear as effortless and commonplace as quick cutting would on the screen,' concluding the review with 'The opera will last.'[15] Writing in *Opera Today* two years later, Chris Mullins astutely noted that whereas a story of suppressed emotions might be 'perfectly suited to the intimacy of close-ups and the relevant restraint of film acting',[16] this is distinct from singers having to announce to the audience what they are feeling. Perhaps only a composer with so sturdy a film back-ground would have ventured to transpose the tender subtleties of *Brief Encounter* into the inevitable grandeurs of the operatic stage. However, given the crucial differences in the requirements of the two media, he seems to have been accorded enough critical bouquets to have made the transposition worth the risks involved – though the opera seems not to have been much performed since.

On television

The telemovie, *Staying On*, directed by Silvio Narizzano, is not really in a direct line of descent from the original film in the way that the radio and stage versions above were. It's more like a second cousin once removed. The 1980 telemovie was adapted by Julian Mitchell from Paul Scott's Booker-winning novel[17] and would not have been thought connected to *Brief Encounter* but for the fact that its stars were Celia Johnson and Trevor Howard. They play an elderly couple, Lucy and Tusker Smalley, who have 'stayed on' in India after the declaration of its independence and whose lives reflect a somewhat precarious balance between the old days of the Raj and the regime of the new India.

As Celia Johnson's biographer writes of these two roles: 'Both she

8 Trevor Howard and Celia Johnson in *Staying On*

and Trevor Howard were tempted: Tusker and Lucy were marvellous parts, and the bringing together of the two of them thirty-five years after *Brief Encounter* was an attractive idea.'[18] Howard's biographer records that he 'revelled in playing with Celia Johnson again … his first screen triumph was with [her] even if he does wince when he appears to be remembered only for the film *Brief Encounter*'.[19] There were problems leading up to the filming: Wendy Hiller was originally cast as Lucy; a strike at Independent Television cast doubt on the whole project; and Celia Johnson became ill enough for her family to question whether she should go to India where filming was to take place, but her determination prevailed. Filming, not without some inter-personal difficulties, finally took place among spectacular scenery near Simla.

The point of including *Staying On* here is that it is impossible for many to watch this telemovie without being aware of frequent echoes of the previous Johnson–Howard pairing. I don't mean that the director or screenwriter necessarily had such echoes in mind during the making of the film. Some of these are fleeting, such as a photo of Memsahib Lucy in her younger days: it is clearly a photo of Celia Johnson around the time of *Brief Encounter*. When Lucy plays an old 78 record on her ancient HMV radiogram, one thinks at once of Laura's playing Rachmaninoff on her machine; or when she announces 'Tonight I shall go to the pictures', we recall Laura and Alec seated in the balcony and laughing at

Donald Duck. In her final soliloquy following Tusker's death, as she recalls her past with him, she says: 'Then you held my arm for the first time', an almost verbatim repeat of Laura's voice-over response to Alec's performing the same action for her.

On a structural level, the relationship between the bossy Mrs Bhoolabhoy (Pearl Padamsee), proprietor of Smith's Hotel in a 'lodge' of which the Smalleys live, and her put-upon spouse, Frankie (Saeed Jaffrey), who enjoys a drink with Tusker and 'a bit on the side', strikes a kind of parallel with the saucy smack-and-tickle dealings of Myrtle and Albert in *Brief Encounter*. A major structural difference between the film *Staying On* and both its precursor novel and the 1945 film is that it has chosen to proceed linearly. The novel opens with the death of the terminally irascible Tusker, whereas the film elects to make this its penultimate episode, followed only by Lucy's touching soliloquy with its melancholy question for the dead Tusker: 'How could you leave me here alone when you yourself go home.' The word 'home' is of course charged with intimations of the other real world they had so long left behind while 'staying on', as well as with metaphysical implications.

Whether any or all of these echoes were intended and whether audiences unfamiliar with *Brief Encounter* would have a lesser experience when watching *Staying On* is naturally difficult to say. Above all, it is the casting of Johnson and Howard that makes the echoes impossible to ignore. It is almost as if we are given a glimpse of what might have happened to Alec and Laura if they had surrendered to their feelings all those decades ago. What scholarly theory would describe as 'intertextuality' is at issue here: we never come to either novels or films without bringing to them some kind of cultural baggage and, for those familiar with *Brief Encounter*, it is hard to watch *Staying On* without recalling those roles that made Johnson and Howard so memorable.

Notes

1 The relevant links are: www.youtube.com/watch?v=U1dTnq5LUc4 and www.youtube.com/watch?v=0bjcbHbdIaI. Accessed 12 March 2019.
2 Email from Hayley Mills, 23 August 2018.
3 'An Encounter with British Drizzle', *London Evening Standard*, 12 September 2000. (Reviewer's name not given.)
4 Nick Awde, *Theatreguide. London*, Autumn 2000.
5 Emma Rice, *Noël Coward's Brief Encounter*, London: Bloomsbury Methuen Drama, 2013 (reprinted 2015).
6 Ibid, p. 64.

7 Charles Spencer, '*Brief Encounter:* A First-class Return to Romance', *Daily Telegraph*, 18 February 2008.

8 Kate Herbert, 'Theatre Review: *Brief Encounter*, Kneehigh Productions, Melbourne Festival', *Herald Sun*, 13 October 2013.

9 Ben Brantley, 'Arm's-Length Soul Mates, Swooning but Stoically Chaste', *New York Times*, 28 September 2010.

10 *The Times*, 25 October 2017.

11 Robert Dex, *Monday 12 March 2018 www.standard.co.uk* › Go London › *Theatre*. Accessed 16 March 2018.

12 Ibid.

13 Tim Ashley, 'Brief Encounter – Review', *Guardian*, 13 May 2011.

14 Ibid.

15 Mark Swed, 'André Previn's *Brief Encounter* Premieres in Houston', *Los Angeles Times*, 3 May 2008.

16 Chris Mullins, 'Previn and Caird's *Brief Encounter*', www.operatoday.com/content/2011/08/previn_and_cair.php. Accessed 26 July 2018.

17 Paul Scott, *Staying On*. London: Granada, 1978.

18 Kate Fleming, *Celia Johnson*. London: Orion, 1991, p. 270.

19 Vivienne Knight, *Trevor Howard: A Gentleman and a Player* (originally published 1986). London: Sphere Books, 1988, p. 190.

5

Quotations

Some movies seem to have Lean's film in mind as they pursue their central situations – or, at least, I find it hard to view them without the earlier classic in mind – and other films 'quote' directly from it. Among the latter, the one that comes to mind first is Melvin Frank's *A Touch of Class* (UK, 1973); others include David Jones's *84 Charing Cross Road* (UK/US, 1987), Anthony Minghella's *Truly Madly Deeply* (UK, 1992), Sarah Gavron's *Brick Lane* (UK/India, 2007) and Nicholas Hytner's *The History Boys* (UK, 2008) – and, on TV, *Last Tango in Halifax* (2015). By 'quoting' from the film, I mean that scenes from the 1945 black-and-white classic are inserted into the films' narratives or, in the case of *The History Boys*, the last moments of *Brief Encounter* are acted out by some film-mad schoolboys. If the film is being quoted, it is worth noting which excerpts are inserted into the new film – and just how the chosen excerpt bears on the rest of the film. This chapter will consider specific episodes 'quoted' in the films noted above, the point in the narrative of the film concerned at which such episodes are glimpsed on screens large or small, and how this quotation may bear on the film in which it is inserted.

A Touch of Class

In *A Touch of Class*, Vickie (Glenda Jackson), a divorced 'fashion-thief', embarks tentatively on an affair with Steve (George Segal), a married insurance-broker, on the understanding, at least on her part, that there will be no commitment involved. Naturally, what follows proves less than straightforward, but here it is played for comedy. At one point, without warning, we see a scene from *Brief Encounter* playing on the television, with Alec telling Laura he is heading for Africa; 'I've had a job offer. I wasn't going to take it, but it's the only way out.' He asks Laura: 'Do you want me to stay, turn down the offer?' 'Don't be foolish.'

9 George Segal and Glenda Jackson watching *Brief Encounter* in *A Touch of Class*

'Forgive me ...' 'For what?' Then the camera pulls back to reveal Vickie and Steve blubbing as they watch, with Celia Johnson's voice-over about 'our last day together'.

The old film, in the farewell episode chosen here by director–co-screenwriter Melvin Frank, provides a perspective on what was, in the film's advertising line, 'the perfect love affair – until they fell in love'. Steve is a reasonably happily married man, with a beautiful and cultivated wife, Gloria (Hildegard Neil), and two children, but has had affairs in the past and is perfectly ready for a week's holiday in Spain with Vickie. She is equally on for this, provided it takes place in attractive settings. She also makes it plain that it is a no-strings affair, but unsurprisingly, and after a fierce quarrel in a Malaga hotel in which they hurl objects at each other, they are in love.

Back in her London flat, they watch *Brief Encounter* on television, and at the film's end they go their separate ways. There has been a comic complexity of phone calls, of the demands of work and family, and the film ends with Vickie's departure in a taxi as Steve watches from the rain-splashed window of the apartment that has been the scene of their assignations. The film is amusing enough at times but, excellent actress though she is, Glenda Jackson is perhaps somewhat too astringent to leave us finding much poignancy in the film's last moments. Or as the rather sour review in the *Monthly Film Bulletin* claimed: 'Sarcastic rather than wry, brittle rather than suave, Miss Jackson is not equipped for lightness,' and found her 'constrained by a strait-jacket of tame naughtiness and sentimentality.'[1] In fact, the quoted sequence from *Brief Encounter*, in the emotional truth it achieves, may also be seen to 'place' the situation between Vickie and Steve: their response to it *is* sentimental but perhaps it does push them to reassess that situation in the wider context of their lives. The screenplay by Melvin Frank and Jack Rose may be said to invoke the farewell episode from *Brief Encounter* to point to the comparative superficiality of the relationship between Vickie and Steve – and to instigate a more serious appraisal of what has happened between them.

84 Charing Cross Road

By the time *84 Charing Cross Road* appeared as a film, it was already a title to conjure with. In 1973, a lively Jewish bibliophile in New York, Helene Hanff, published *The Duchess of Bloomsbury Street*, a memoir about her visit to London to meet people associated with a Charing Cross Road antiquarian bookshop. She had engaged in a lengthy correspondence with its manager, Frank Doel, and their exchange of letters metamorphosed into book form, bearing the shop's address as its title. In this volume (reprinted many times during the next decade) a very engaging sense of character interplay emerged. Its next incarnation was as a 1975 television production as one in the *Play for Today* series, then as a stage-play (London 1981, Broadway 1982), and then in 1987 as a film whose production was divided between the two relevant countries. This media-flexibility is probably due to the development of its central relationship, which is fuelled by a love of books, is several times on the verge of the consummation of meeting – and is thwarted twice by Hanff's financial problems and then finally by Doel's death shortly before Hanff at last realised her dream of getting to London.

The sequence quoted from *Brief Encounter* is that of Laura and Alec's last meeting as she leans out the window of the train carriage and he asks her to forgive him. 'Forgive you for what?' 'For meeting you, in the first place, for taking a piece of grit out of your eye, for loving you and for bringing you so much misery.' 'I'll forgive you if you'll forgive me.' Throughout the whole episode, Helene (Anne Bancroft) is watching as if stunned by it, the ash on her cigarette by now precariously long as a visual token of her involvement. What is especially striking about the whole sequence, set in a New York cinema, is that there is no lead-up to it. We aren't shown the exterior of the cinema; there is no advertising poster announcing the title; the camera simply cuts to the interior where Helene is found absorbed by what she is viewing. In other words, the audience for David Jones's film is clearly expected to place the black-and-white farewell scene without any further information – a recurring phenomenon among those films that quote such scenes. We assume that Helene is there because she is a devoted

Anglophile, whose passionate interest is in 'the England of English literature', as she writes.

Much of *84 Charing Cross Road* is taken up with Helene and Frank
(Anthony Hopkins) engaged in writing to each other, as she requests
early editions of literary works and he replies about the prospects for
finding these, and while writing they very often address the audience
in a kind of recurring voice-over. In the course of this correspondence,
more personal matters emerge and his later letters are apt to be signed
'Love from us all here, Frank' – or even just 'Love, Frank'. It is not that
Helene constitutes a threat to Frank's marriage to Nora (Judi Dench),
with whom he has two children, but when Helene finally reaches
London, after Frank's death, she meets Nora who says: 'At times, I
don't mind telling you, I was very jealous of you.' Nora is not book-
obsessed and almost recalls Laura's sensible, unimaginative husband
Fred. Just as Laura had found in Alec something missing in her placid
life, so the idea of Helene has meant something new in Frank's. The
film, through having them talk at the camera and in a sort of voice-
over to each other, almost suggests that they are aware of each other's
presence.

The episode from *Brief Encounter* underscores the idea of another
kind of non-consummation: the two who have valued their correspondence, which has created a sense of ongoing warm affection between
them, but sadly never get to meet. Also, the fact of Helene's rapt attitude
in the cinema as she watches Johnson and Howard's farewell suggests an
emotional potential in her that bibliophilia hasn't satisfied.

Truly Madly Deeply

Like *Brief Encounter* and several other films referred to in this book,
Truly Madly Deeply opens at a railway station, this time Highgate
Underground London, from which Nina (Juliet Stevenson) emerges.
The importance of the separations of travel, and especially as depicted
in railway stations (the subject of a later chapter), recurs as images of
meeting and departure. Nina is still in a state of grief over the death of
husband Jamie (Alan Rickman) when he suddenly reappears from the
hereafter, and in very corporeal form, in her flat. The key line may be
Nina's 'Thank you for coming back' – even if he brings along a group
of his friends from the world beyond (leading to Nina's bemusedly que-
rying the notion of 'dead people in my living room watching videos').
But the line referred to above is the one that matters, because one of the
videos they are watching (and Nina joins them) is *Brief Encounter*. The

extract is from the latter's last moments, when Laura's kind husband Fred (Cyril Raymond) initiates this exchange:

> 'Whatever your dream was, it wasn't a very happy one, was it?'
> 'No.'
> 'If there's anything I can do to help …'
> 'You always help me.'
> 'You've been a long way away. Thank you for coming back to me.'

As in *Brief Encounter*, there is an acceptance of what has gone before and a tentative approach to what may lie ahead for Nina and the amiable Mark (Michael Maloney). This may seem a more obvious use of the quoted episode, but it also resonates elsewhere in the film. Nina's colleague Sandy (Bill Paterson) is currently separated from his Spanish wife, who now lives in Spain, and Nina translates his son's postcards to him; and Mark is another father now living away from his child. Jamie's 'return' has helped Nina to come to terms with her loss, and the film ends with her driving away with Mark, as Jamie and his friends watch from a window of the flat. The close-up on Jamie registers a sense of his letting-go of Nina's emotional life: it reveals both a benign blessing as well as a small tear as he watches, another of the kinds of compromise that so many of these films exhibit.

The History Boys

Talk of 'endings' in the senior class in *The History Boys*, adapted from Alan Bennett's play, leads to an impromptu rendering of the final scene in *Brief Encounter*. Preceded by a burst of Rachmaninoff on the class-room piano, one boy, Posner (Samuel Barnett), leaps to his feet and pretends to be Laura teetering on the edge of the station platform – and of suicide – but just 'couldn't do it'. 'I wasn't brave enough. I'd like to be able to say it was because of you [Fred] and the children, but it wasn't … I had no desire ever to feel anything again.' When he has uttered these words, taken from Laura's voice-over in the film, he is joined in the 'performance' by another boy's acting out Fred's comforting words ('Thank you for coming back …' etc., see above). Now this is all done for rather campy satire, but the echo of that unforgettable ending is still almost absurdly moving, especially when we know that Posner nourishes an unrequited passion for another boy – and even when we know it will end in a burst of raucous laughter.

Brick Lane

For a brief moment in Sarah Gavron's touching film, *Brick Lane*, the television is playing but no one is watching. A black-and-white film is screening, and it is the scene from *Brief Encounter* in which Fred, Laura's prosaic husband, is asking her to turn down the music (Rachmaninoff) a little, just after she has recalled the moment when Alec has told her, 'I love you so'. When he goes to kiss her, she says: 'Not here, Alec. Someone will see us' – and this is followed by their first kiss. It is all quite fleeting, but the quotation subtly points us to how we should be reading *Brick Lane*. Is *Brief Encounter*, then, the archetypal film rendering of the unexpected love that surprises the people in the later film, and of a love that they turn away from, as Laura and Alec do?

A young Bangladeshi woman, Nazneen Ahmed (Tannishtha Chatterjee), has been wrenched from an idyllic childhood and sent to London for an arranged marriage with a much older, kind but dull man, Chanu Ahmed (Satish Kaushik). Nazneen, resigned to her life in London's East End, falls tremulously in love with the young man who brings her work as a seamstress. He, Karim (Christopher Simpson), reciprocates her feeling; they make love, which the film records in a sensuous montage at some remove from the usual carnal couplings of contemporary films. Her newfound love means she no longer yearns for the return home that her husband has promised. This situation, with its overtones of *Brief Encounter*, becomes emotionally complex: the film moves to a poignant climax in which a voice-over reflects on being 'torn between two worlds' (Laura might not have expressed it so, but it is true of her as well) and 'different kinds of love'. The film, adapted from Monica Ali's novel by Abi Morgan and Laura Jones, foregrounds Nanzeen's awakening desire for love and independence against a chang ing social scene in which various kinds of racial turmoil are at issue. As always with these 'quoted' passages, there is the assumption that the viewer will pick up the reference and briefly ponder its significance in the new setting.

Once more too, the sheer *range* of films that 'quote' from the 1945 black-and-white classic seems remarkable. By range, I mean in terms of genre, setting and period, and the mere fact of the monochrome filming of the original often seems to cast a resonant light on these later films, as if to say: 'These moral challenges are not new – nor are they any less painful to deal with.'

Last Tango in Halifax

The latest clear-cut 'quotation' I know of is in the TV mini-series *Last Tango in Halifax*, in which Alan (Derek Jacobi), who has had his own (consummated) brief encounter many years before, is slumped on a couch while on television Lean's film is soundlessly playing. In its fleeting way, it offers a comment on Alan's past brief encounters which have recently caught up with him. And can it be a coincidence that one of the women is called Celia (Anne Reid), who has actually been watching the film in the preceding shot? The actual moment from *Brief Encounter* that we first see on Celia's screen involves that by now iconic shot of Laura leaning out of the train window as Alec asks:

> 'You're not angry with me, are you?'
> 'I'm not angry. I don't think I'm anything really. I just feel tired.'
> 'Forgive me.'
> 'For what?'
> 'For meeting you in the first place, for taking a piece of grit out of your eye,
>   for loving you and for bringing you so much misery.'

This episode occurs in *Last Tango* at a time of emotional turmoil and deep unhappiness for Celia, who has failed to attend her daughter's marriage to another woman. She is also unhappy that Alan has not told her about making contact with a son he never knew he had before telling other people. In other words, it is less a matter of exact parallelism than of a comparable bleakness and misery that makes the quoted sequence a potent commentary on the action of the series. The 'quotation' from *Brief Encounter* works here as a kind of shorthand that underscores the emotional content of the *Last Tango in Halifax* while dispensing with the need for more didactic explication

Anna Karenina

In Bernard Rose's undistinguished 1997 version of *Anna Karenina* there is a moment that seems like a direct quote from *Brief Encounter*. *Anna Karenina* is, of course, a sort of ancestor of Lean's film in terms of the conflict between Anna's desire for Vronsky and husband Karenin's wish to hold on to the marriage and the mother of his son. This film version lacks real passion but, in the scene in which Anna is sitting in a train, Rose seems to have drawn on Lean's treatment of a similar scene. Laura, opting out of more chat with gossipy Dolly Messiter, looks out the train window and imagines romantic settings for her and Alec, in a gondola or in an opera box and so on, suggesting she is on the brink of an adulterous affair. Rose's Anna (Sophie Marceau) similarly fantasises, as she also looks from the train window, about what life might be with Vronsky; but, sadly, the comparison does the later film serious disservice by recalling to the cinephile the much more potent sense of private anguish that was the lot of Laura Jesson.

Shameless

Perhaps the quirkiest quotation/echo of all is in the eighth episode of the fifth series of the TV series *Shameless*: the brilliant, anarchic comedy-drama of a family of six kids presided over by shiftless, heavy drinking dad, Frank Gallagher (Mum has left), set in a Manchester housing estate. The synopsis for this 2008 episode begins: 'On the bus to a restart course, Frank has the briefest of encounters with a beautiful stranger, Rosie. Within days, he finds himself falling in love and turning into a new man, but the stage is set for heartache … .' It is difficult (and not very important) to decide whether this episode should be classified as an 'echo' or a 'quotation'. It doesn't 'quote' *Brief Encounter* in the sense of an extract from the original being actually seen on the screen as in the context of other films discussed in this chapter. However, in the unfolding of the episode's main plot it not only follows the famous narrative, but also 'quotes' a good deal of its screenplay, whether in dialogue or voice-over.

By the time of the episode under discussion (2008), Frank's wife, bisexual Monica (Annabelle Apsion), has returned and is pregnant with their eighth child, and Frank (David Threlfall) is doing a 'restart course'. In an early voice-over, we hear Frank anguishing: 'This can't last. This fucking misery can't last', recalling Celia Johnson's almost-identical inner cry of pain. We then go back to 'Four days ago', when Frank boards a bus with his eyes stinging from car fumes, and an attractive woman, Rosie (Esther Coles), asks: 'Can I help?' In further voice-over, he recalls her eyes, her mouth and their promise, and when they meet again in a tea room she appears to be taking the initiative; that is, pursuing the gender-reversal set in motion on the bus. This time it is she who talks enthusiastically about her work, and as he looks at her, enthralled, she echoes Laura's line about how Alec's 'eyes suddenly looked like a little boy's' with: 'You look about ten years old, Frank Gallagher.'

There are other narrative matters going on in the episode, but it is the sense of *Brief Encounter*'s haunting Frank and Rosie's meetings

10 A brief encounter between David Threlfall and Esther Coles in *Shameless*

that commands attention. As Trevor Howard's Alec urged Johnson's Laura to a further meeting, so does Frank urge Rosie, and as he says his farewells to her he tells himself: 'I imagine her going home to her husband, saying I met this bloke on the bus ... Then I knew that she wouldn't – and at that moment I got a tingling in my testicles I hadn't felt since I was a teenager.' The sentiments expressed again and again recall Lean's film, even though some of the language suggests other times and other manners. And of course they do make love back at her home, with Rachmaninoff on the gramophone (and this aged device is another conscious reference).

Their last moments on the bus, when she has decided she cannot desert her ailing husband, are interrupted by a talkative friend and as Frank leaves the bus we expect him to put his hand on Rosie's shoulder – and he does. Back home, Monica comforts him with 'You've been a long way away. Thank you for coming back to us.' And, just as we wonder if this isn't too predictable, and possibly 'heart-warming', she follows it with a warning that: 'If you ever do anything like that again, I'll personally neuter you, like the mangy Tom you are.'

The whole episode is done with remarkable control of tone, drawing on its famous antecedent but not cowed by it. What is really remarkable, in the context of this study at least, is that it was done at all; that sixty-three years on, the relevance of the film is still so potent. It scarcely needed the episode's last voice-over from Frank: 'And just like that, me and Rosie and the tale of our brief encounter was over.' The gender-reversal take on Lean's film and its displacement into a working-class

setting still reinforce the old film's values, even when played for comedy
– and played out in wildly different cultural circumstances.

Note

1   Sylvia Millar, *Monthly Film Bulletin*, July 1973, p. 156.

6

Echoes

As distinct from those films discussed in the previous chapter, which directly 'quote' from *Brief Encounter*, there are many more that seem in various ways to echo the 1945 classic. One can't of course know to what extent the filmmakers involved had *Brief Encounter* in mind, but the fact is that its essential scenario and its moral core still retain their emotional power, despite the shifts in cultural mores, irresistibly suggesting the long shadow it casts. Those titles to be considered here involve – to varying degrees – a relationship whose outcome foregrounds the conflict of desire and – what? – convention, other obligations, decency and other circumstantial and/or moral pressures that one or both protagonists take into consideration. It is not simply a matter of 'duty', but a real concern for the well-being of other people and for one's own self-respect as well, the two being intricately connected in *Brief Encounter* – and, one would hope, in life.

The accounts of the following films are not intended as comprehensive critiques; rather, they are considered chiefly from the perspective of how they seem to echo *Brief Encounter* in diverse ways, such as narrative parallels or the incidence of music or of certain evocative images.

The Fool and the Princess

Maybe the earliest such echo was in an unpretentious British 'B' film, *The Fool and the Princess* (1949), 'a modestly affecting drama of post-war adjustment with a touch of *Brief Encounter* about it' as one reference book's entry on its director/screenwriter, William C. Hammond, has it.[1] Harry Granville (Bruce Lester) is having trouble settling to suburban life with wife Kate (Lesley Brook) after time in Germany. Attached there to a Displaced Persons camp, he had fallen in love with one Moura (Adina Mandlova), whom he erroneously believed to be a princess. When he returns to a post in Germany, he re-meets Moura, who persuades him to go home, urging: 'Our being separated is a burden to be shared by both of us, and, in sharing it, we cannot ever be separated.' After more of such talk, he can at last write to Kate: 'This time, darling, I'm coming home because I want to.'

Based on a story by Stephen Spender, this short film creates a convincing sense of the post-war difficulties in the Granvilles' married life, with Kate trying to ensure domestic harmony in the face of Harry's obvious tension. As in Lean's film, duty and gentler affections win over more passionate demands, and echoes of the 1945 film persist in such matters as the use of music. Here it is Beethoven's 'Appassionata' in the Granville home: as Harry listens, rapt, Kate's face appears, and at this point we realise he is as remote from her as Laura was from Fred while Rachmaninoff was playing. And there is an echo in the brief exchange between Harry and Maura when he returns to Germany. 'Thank you,' Maura says. 'For what?' he asks. 'For being here, for making me happy' – recalling Laura and Alec's 'Forgive me', 'Forgive me for what?' 'For meeting you in the first place … ' and so on. A last and no doubt trivial connection: Irene Handl, the cinema pianist in *Brief Encounter*, here plays a gossiping neighbour who recalls Everley Gregg's Dolly Messiter in the earlier film. Whereas the situation in *Brief Encounter* may have anticipated the post-war need for marital adjustment, in *The Fool and the Princess* this is its explicit narrative spine and context.

The Fool and the Princess was more ambitious than most British 'B' films and attracted some quite favourable notices, such as that by A.E. Wilson who praised it as 'a new approach to the making of the British supporting features, an endeavour to provide pictures of adult interest at modest cost'.[2] The popular journals, *Picture Show* and *Picturegoer*, both commended it as 'unpretentious' and well acted.[3]

Stazione termini/Indiscretion of an American Wife

Vittorio De Sica's 1953 US/Italian co-production, depicting the anguished parting of American Mary Forbes (Jennifer Jones) and the Italian Giovanni Doria (Montgomery Clift) with whom she has fallen in love in Rome, was released in truncated form as *Indiscretion of an American Wife*. Jones's husband, producer David O. Selznick, took the film out of De Sica's hands and the shortened, English-language version emerges as a somewhat stiff and straggling version of the *Brief Encounter* scenario, its antecedence noted often in reference books.[4] The Italian version begins, after a shot of trains steaming through behind the credits, with Mary almost pressing the button of Giovanni's apartment

11 Montgomery Clift and Jennifer Jones in *Stazione termini,* aka *Indiscretion of an American Wife*

before thinking better of it and heading for the Terminal Station; while the US version starts with her writing a letter that asserts that she has experienced with Giovanni 'a happiness I have never known'. Their farewell is first interrupted by the arrival of her nephew Paul (Richard Beymer) with luggage she has asked for, and for the next hour and a bit there are conversations at the station or in a café where they try to come to terms with their relationship. 'I'm a housewife from Philadelphia', she says; she has a husband who has been asking 'When are you coming home?' and a child, 'and I cannot give her up'. There are nuns and priests, Mary's adoring nephew and finally the police, who remove the lovers from an empty stationary train, and these constitute an ongoing reminder of moral and other restraints that precede her final departure and Giovanni's falling from her moving train on to the station platform.

The film is an obvious attempt at reworking some of the *Brief Encounter* terrain, but it stumbles over repetitiveness and moments of near-incredibility in the plotting (e.g., to do with the whereabouts of Mary's luggage or with the wild unlikelihood of the last-minute boarding and Giovanni's still being on the moving train). Nevertheless, *Stazione termini* needs to be noted here as one of the earlier echoes, and the setting of the station for all but the opening minutes is inevitably resonant.

Woman in a Dressing Gown

A British film which despite a very different social setting and the reversal of gender roles in the central situation nevertheless recalls *Brief
Encounter* is J. Lee-Thompson's 1957 domestic drama, *Woman in a
Dressing Gown*, adapted from Ted Willis's play of the same name. One
writer dubbed it 'the *Brief Encounter* of the LCC tenants'.[5] The eponymous 'Woman' is a messy housewife, Amy (Yvonne Mitchell), who
never seems to get properly dressed or to carry out domestic activities
efficiently. Husband Jim (Anthony Quayle) is far from comfortable in
this ill-run home and in fact has a girlfriend, Georgie (Sylvia Syms), who
is everything Amy is not and is fond enough of Jim to be willing to marry
him. When it comes to the crunch, though, Jim cannot bring himself to
leave his wife because 'It's been too long between Amy and me'. She
may be an untidy housekeeper and slovenly dresser, but she *is* his wife of
twenty years and the mother of their teenage son, Brian (Andrew Ray).

The film was a precursor of the British 'new wave' films of the late
1950s, and its mode of social realism makes it as much a film of its time
as *Brief Encounter* was of 1945. Like its predecessor, though without
the same emotional resonance, its central premise does not lose its
potency, and again it is concerned with how such conflict plays out in
'ordinary lives' in which, we recall, Laura Jesson did not believe 'such
violent things could happen'. The word 'ordinary' here is partly a matter
of class: essentially it connotes various levels of middle-class lives as
distinct from the extremes of upper or lower class, as well as differenti-
ating those lives from the starry aura that inevitably surrounds the likes
of Bergman and Bogart in *Casablanca*. *Woman in a Dressing Gown* is
also one of several such films discussed in this chapter in which it is the
man who makes the decision not to sever the ties of some decades. The
Monthly Film Bulletin reviewer seems, at this remove in time, a little too
severe in this summarising sentence: 'The facile ending, with its suggestion of "happy ever after", is in line with the compromising attitude of
the film as a whole.'[6]

Korotkie Vstrechi

The title of Ukranian filmmaker, Kira Muratova's, 1967 romantic
drama was literally translated as *Brief Encounters* when it was shown
in the West. It is not a remake of Lean's film as such, but the fact of its
echoing the latter in its title may well point to the potency of the earlier
film. In fact, there are several moments and plot strands that suggest

such lineage. I have only been able to see the film online, but even so Gennadi Karyuk's eloquent black-and-white cinematography serves Muratova's purpose well as it moves between places and relationships. Muratova was also the co-author of the screenplay, as well as playing the leading role. She was a prolific filmmaker whose productions often met with censorship problems in Russia.

There is no point in a detailed analysis of the film. It is enough to say that it involves a young girl, Nadia (Nina Ruslanova), who leaves her home village, and in another town takes a job as housekeeper to politically active Valya (Muratova), who is a passionate campaigner for better housing projects. What neither woman realises is that they have in common their love for the geologist Maxim (Vladimir Vysotsky). In some ways, Valya's social concern with housing recalls Alec Harvey's dedication to his profession; this time, it is she who tries to imbue him with more enthusiasm for the matter of her concern. An exchange between Nadia and Maxim – 'Come away with me' ,'I will give up everything to go who knows where' – precedes a final one between Valya and Maxim as they appear to settle back into their domestic scene. She asks him: 'Don't you want to rest after your wanderings?' and he echoes this with: 'Don't you want to rest after your daily grind?' In this limited sense, there is almost a reminder of the last moments of *Brief Encounter*, though of course it's hard to know if this is any more than mere coincidence. And there is a moment in a café when Valya and Nadia's serious conversation is interrupted by an over-chatty old man that can't but recall Dolly Messiter's disruption of Laura and Alec's last moments.

But it is the fact of the film's title, perhaps, that makes one susceptible to such echoes, as will be the case with a number of other films which either directly or indirectly invoke the 1945 'classic' as it is now regarded.

Falling in Love

One of the most obvious echoes is Ulu Grosbard's *Falling in Love* (1984, US 1985), described by one contemporary US critic as 'an American *Brief Encounter* that goes on too long. It's about two attractive Westchester commuters, each happily married to someone else, who meet, fall in love and then don't know what to do about it.'[7] He, Frank Raftis (Robert De Niro), is involved in the construction industry, though at what level is never wholly clear, and she, Molly Gilmore (Meryl Streep), is a freelance graphic designer. The film opens (unsurprisingly) on a railway platform, where Molly is waiting for her train, then boards it just as Frank comes racing in and sits behind her. After disembarking, they are later seen at the station of their destination talking into adjacent public telephones, later buying Christmas presents for their spouses, and then on escalators, going in opposite directions, at Manhattan's Grand Central Station.

By this time, the film is beginning to seem somewhat contrived. They each have a friend to whom they talk of their domestic arrangements (and, in Frank's case, also of the friend's), and – not a moment too soon for the film is losing momentum – they both fetch up in Rizzoli's bookshop. Here they bump into each other as they try to exit while improbably laden down with bags of gifts. This is presumably the film's gender-reversed 'grit-in-the-eye' moment, when she comes to his aid by giving him a spare bag. We then see the two families at their Christmas celebrations, when each has found a wrong present, having inadvertently switched bags during the bookshop-door collision. Days after, they are on the same train again, not sure if each remembers the other. Frank talks to colleague Ed (Harvey Keitel) about 'the woman on the train', and Molly tells friend Isabelle (Diane Wiest) about 'the man I met on the train'. Both friends try to persuade Molly and Frank to meet each other again; Ed tells Frank: 'You could take her to my apartment', inevitably echoing Alec Harvey's use of his friend Stephen Lynn's flat in Milford Junction. Flat, trains, hospital, lunch: these sites or motifs, plus images of the protagonists running for trains or sitting down to talk over lunch, can't but recall their black-and-white predecessor of forty years earlier. Pauline Kael was right, if not exactly profound, when she wrote: 'The picture has been called a new *Brief Encounter*, but it's interminable.'[8]

Towards the film's end, Frank leaves a taxi in a traffic jam and goes again to the bookshop, and who should come in but Molly? This is just too much reliance on coincidence, and they engage in a lot of tedious dialogue about which Canby is right to say: 'It's not easy to make a movie about people who initially communicate by making tentative proposals that are answered with tentative "yeahs", "sures", "unhuhs" and "okays".' Streep, especially, is given little to work on by a screenplay with such limitations and a director who encourages too many close-ups that seem devoid of any specific emotional purpose. To be fair, she and De Niro still manage to rise above such deficiencies on occasion, but by the time of their final embrace (improbably located on the train) it is hard to care about the outcome, and the film chooses to end by freezing on their faces as the train runs on.

My overall negative experience of this dawdling, under-nourished piece was not shared by the *Monthly Film Bulletin* reviewer who claimed that the film was 'both modern and nostalgic' as it poses the question: 'how to keep desire alive when sex has become a commodity detached from love? And it has a profoundly moral answer: instead of sex without love, love without sex.'[9] This explanation is ingenious enough without accounting for the film's failing to exert anything like the emotional potency of *Brief Encounter*, which the same review reminds us 'finally returned its heroine to the safety of marriage'. But, as argued in Chapter 2, that is not all – nor even centrally – what is at stake in the 1945 film. And again, as in *Casablanca* (though without the same charismatic effect), the presence of certifiable stars in the leads tends to work against the everyday realities of *Brief Encounter*, as does the sheer improbability of their subsequent meetings.

The Apartment and Billy Wilder

One of the more surprising 'echoes' is Billy Wilder's classic comedy, *The Apartment* (1960). On the face of it, this sharply sardonic piece would not seem to have much in common with *Brief Encounter*. Its scenario revolves around Baxter, a young business executive (played by Jack Lemmon) who cements his position by making his apartment available to his seniors for extra-marital assignations – even to the point of his being left braving the elements because he can't get into his own home. In an essay commissioned for a recent DVD release of the film, Neil Sinyard wrote: 'The inspiration came from an unusual source … His [Wilder's] mind had then turned to a minor film character who had always intrigued him, Trevor Howard's friend in David Lean's *Brief Encounter* (1945), whose flat Howard wishes to use for an affair with a married woman (Celia Johnson).'[10] Of course, the brief encounters in Wilder's film do not remain unconsummated like that in Lean's, but, as Sinyard goes on to point out, there are other moments that recall the earlier film. For instance, that in which Lemmon retrieves the spare key to his apartment, just as Howard's friend, Stephen Lynn (Valentine Dyall), demands the return of *his* key when he realises the purpose to which Howard had been about to put the flat. Further, the insistence of the music in each film is another common motif. Where Lean chose Rachmaninoff for the accompaniment of Celia Johnson's wracked emotional state, Wilder engages in a similar use of music to match Lemmon's varying states of mind and, in the piano piece by Charles Williams – 'Jealous Lover', to underscore some of the most highly charged moments of Fran (Shirley MacLaine), whom Baxter has come to love. And this reminds one that Wilder also 'paid homage to *Brief Encounter* by employing the same concerto on the soundtrack of his earlier film, *The Seven Year Itch* (1955), in a romantic scene in which a middle-aged man (Tom Ewell) attempts to seduce his neighbour (Marilyn Monroe)'.[11] In other words, a director working a decade or more later, and in another cultural context, appears to have been sufficiently struck by aspects of Lean's film to pay passing homage to the latter in very different generic circumstances.

Cairo Time

Nearer to *Brief Encounter* in its overall tone was the 2010 Canada/Ireland/Egyptian co-production, *Cairo Time*. Juliette (Patricia Clarkson), an American women's magazine editor in early middle age, comes to Cairo to join her husband Mark (Tom McCamus), who is detained in Gaza on UN work. He has sent an old friend and colleague, Tareg (*Star Trek* alumnus, Alexander Siddig), to meet Juliette and to look after her till he can get there. She wanders round Cairo, sometimes alone but increasingly feeling lonely, then Tareg joins her and they are almost imperceptibly but inevitably drawn together. When Mark finally returns, there is love and relief in the way she turns to her husband.

This discreetly affecting romance – or near-romance – inevitably reminds one of *Brief Encounter* (and, indeed, of the much more recent *Before Sunrise*, 1995). It recalls *Brief Encounter* in its muted way of suggesting a developing feeling *and* in the fact that this has not been sought and is not about to be gratified at the drop of a hat – or any other article of clothing. It is surely hard to imagine a love story in 2010 in which the protagonists remain dressed throughout, or one in which they don't instantly throw caution to the winds, along with their clothes, and leap straight into bed. And over the course of the burgeoning friendship between Juliette and Tareq there are walks by the river, discussions of different attitudes to life and even telephone calls in which not everything is communicated, which also recall Lean's film.

Director Ruba Nadda makes compelling a love story in which the woman remains in love with her husband, while briefly drawn to the charms of another man. Patricia Clarkson – star of many a US 'indie' drama, here in a more exotic setting – suggests some of the same qualities that made Celia Johnson so moving in Laura's sometimes similar situation. As Juliette, she renders so much of the character's inner life and quiet conflict through a range of subtle gesture, intonation and facial response that one *knows* this woman, as one came to know Johnson's Laura – and as, sadly, one didn't in the case of Streep's underwritten role in *Falling in Love*.

12 Ben Kingsley and Patricia Clarkson in *Learning to Drive*

Learning to Drive

Clarkson is the lead again in *Learning to Drive* (2014), set in New York, in which she plays a writer, Wendy, who has left her marriage and become attracted to her Sikh Indian driving instructor Darwan (Ben Kingsley), whose arranged marriage is also in trouble. The grit-in-the-eye catalyst is here represented by a package she has inadvertently left in his taxi – in which she has been quarrelling with her husband – and which Darwan later returns. This time, though, in a reversal of the *Brief Encounter* situation, it is the man who renounces the possibility of a further relationship, motivated by his sense of commitment to his arranged marriage, recalling the husband's situation in *Woman in a Dressing Gown*. In this matter, it also recalls *Brick Lane*: whatever a Westerner may make of such a marriage, to those involved it is a serious bond, whether or not conducive to lasting happiness. Again, what propels the denouement is the sense that there is more to life than the easy gratification of self, though here, of course, the matter of Darwan's religion is also a key factor in accounting for his renunciation.

Weekend

In the gay romance, Andrew Haigh's *Weekend* (2011), a casual acquaintance made at a gay bar proves to be something more than just a night of sex. As with *Brief Encounter*, the relationship between Russell (Tom Cullen) and Glen (Chris New) will not lead to long-term fulfil-ment. After a good deal of talk about their attitudes to their sexuality and their feelings for each other, Russell finally farewells Glen at the station as he leaves to make his way to Oregon, where he plans to take a course in modern art. Like Alec, he has no prospect of return. There are other echoes of *Brief Encounter* as well as the retreating train and deserted platform: the fact of Glen's going away to pursue his career recalls Alec's decision to go to Africa for the same reason. What was initiated as a very brief – i.e., one-night – encounter impinges more deeply on both men, so that the railway departure resonates poignantly; and Russell recalls a sexual experience he once had with a straight man and wonders if this had ever been revealed to the man's wife. 'Imagine if everyone was open about everything', says Glen, as of course Laura and Alec were never able to be with their spouses. But it's the station farewell that enforces the recollection of the earlier film. And notice how railway stations recur in so many of these films: a station platform can be a very lonely looking setting when a train has just left – especially when one of a couple has gone and the other has been left behind.

The Lunch Box

Young Indian director Ritesh Batra's beautiful first feature film, *The Lunch Box* (2014), kept reminding me so often of *Brief Encounter*, with its account of a love affair that never quite happens, that it was hard to believe the parallels were merely a matter of chance. In each, in terms of overall structure, the protagonists draw back from adultery and settle for other claims on their behaviour. *The Lunch Box* opens on a hazy shot of a city (Mumbai to be exact) and then a crowded train pulls into a station, and the echo of the British black-and-white film of 1945 makes itself heard for the first time; there will be other resonances as well, both in detail and overall structure.

   The film's narrative starter is the apparently very efficient Mumbai lunch-delivery service, in which only one in a million lunch boxes ever goes astray. There are images of men on bikes with boxes tagged for delivery and a sense of teeming crowds with glimpses of boxes of every hue. All this is by way of building up the significance of this service which is taken for granted by, say, the many office workers who simply expect the arrival of their lunch, and offer no acknowledgement, let alone thanks to the deliverer.

   A widower, Saajan (Irrfan Khan), is withdrawn and lonely, as is Ila

(Nimrat Kaur), a beautiful young mother whose marriage to the hand-some taciturn Rajeev (Nakul Vaid) is clearly not a very happy one. She takes a lot of care preparing her husband's lunch box, and when this is wrongly delivered to Saajan the personal drama of the film is set in motion – and proceeds with a quiet subtlety and poignancy.

At one point, Ila is seen listening to music played on a neighbour's tape-deck and the film cuts to Saajan who hears children singing the same song. The importance of music as a way into the protagonist's life is felt, in their different ways, in both films. There is even an equivalent of Lean's gossipy Dolly Messiter (Everley Gregg), who ruins the last meeting for Laura and Alec, in the incessant cheeriness of Saajan's colleague who bears down on his wish to be left to himself. In this matter, Batra's screenplay offers a small parallel of unwanted intervention in Ila's case when her unseen aunt in the apartment floor above shouts down instructions to her niece about her husband's diet. At the time of the film's release, the *Guardian* critic began his review with: 'Already a huge success in its native India, Ritesh Batra's Mumbai-set romance arranges a tender marriage of *Brief Encounter* with Ernst Lubitsch's *The Shop Around the Corner*.'[12] Yet more evidence of Richard Dawkins' 'cultural transmission'?

Carol

Four minutes into Todd Haynes' 2013 film, *Carol*, adapted from Patricia Highsmith's 1952 novel *The Price of Salt*, two women who have been engaged in a love affair are having what they believe will be a final meeting in a café. They are middle-class and unhappily married Carol (Cate Blanchett) and young would-be photographer Therese (Rooney Mara). When their meeting is interrupted by the arrival of Therese's former boyfriend, Carol makes her excuses and stands to leave, placing her hand firmly on the younger woman's shoulder – recalling of course how Dolly interrupted the last moments together for Alec and Laura, when he performed exactly this action of farewell. This meeting pro-vides a sort of bookend for the film, repeated as it is at the film's end, and there are many other direct parallels with Lean's film. Between the two episodes, the story of how the two women came together and the ways in which their meeting has shaken the texture of their lives is unfolded, in what one reviewer described as *Carol*'s 'borrowing a key framing device from the 1945 masterpiece *Brief Encounter*'.[13] However, at odds with the latter, *Carol* does not end without any hope of the two lovers' being reunited, recalling the novel's last sentences: '[Carol's] hand waved a quick, eager greeting that Therese had never seen before.

13 Cate Blanchett reassures Rooney Mara in *Carol*

Therese walked towards her.'[14] And Carol has been able to secure regular time with her young daughter while her divorcing husband has been granted custody.

Unlike some of the other films referred to above – films that seem to echo *Brief Encounter* – in relation to *Carol* director Haynes specifically acknowledged the 1945 film as a starting-point for his own film in an interview in the Melbourne newspaper, *The Age*.[15] It's not just the key device that invokes *Brief Encounter*; rather, the whole film offers a poignant study of emotions that have a hard time expressing themselves, especially in public places, and it is this fact that allows it to be recreated in very different restrictive circumstances. In *The Age* a week later, another writer casually describes Highsmith's own background and how it informed her novel: 'Although the encounter had been so brief, [the vision of] "Carol" continued to haunt her.'[16] In a subsequent interview Haynes claimed: 'David Lean's *Brief Encounter* was a seminal point of reference for me when making *Carol*. The intense subjectivity in that movie, for instance, of the Celia Johnson character. It's her recounting this episode and it's all being remembered on the night it ends as she sits quietly with her husband in the living room.'[17]

About that last meeting of Carol and Thérèse that is interrupted by a third person: there is incidentally an echo of this (and of Alec and Laura's spoiled last moments) in *Testament of Youth* (2105). Here, the chattering of Aunt Belle (Joanna Scanlan) spoils the last farewell, again in a café, of Vera (Alicia Vikander) and Rowland (Kit Harington) before he goes off to war and death.

Yanks

I haven't read any reviews of John Schlesinger's *Yanks* (1979) that refer
to *Brief Encounter*, but inevitably, when one comes across a situation
in a film that seems to draw on the renunciation of a possibly rewarding sexual liaison in the interests of matters and persons other than
such gratification, it is hard not to remember what happened at Milford
Junction – and especially in its railway station. When the eponymous
troops arrive at their army base in a Lancashire town in 1943, the sheer
disruptiveness of different temperaments and values seems likely to
cause problems in marriages and other relationships, as well as in larger
cultural matters. When army captain, John (William Devane), advises
Helen (Vanessa Redgrave) to allow her son to leave the boarding-school
at which he is very unhappy, she replies ironically: 'Do what you feel?
Never mind duty?' She will become drawn to John, goes for a flight to
Ireland with him for luxury supplies, but is finally unable to engage in
the sexual relationship he has in mind. Desire is there, but she withdraws
as she realises other claims on her loyalties. His wife back in the US
wants a divorce, but her naval officer husband is coming home on leave
and she has two children to consider. The only love affair that seems to
run happily is that between Molly (Wendy Morgan) and soldier-boxer
Danny (Chick Vennera), but they have less of the film's limelight than
the other two – and less in the way of conflicting demands on their moral
sense.

The other main plot strand involves Matt (Richard Gere), a sergeant
from Arizona, who is attracted to Jean (Lisa Eichhorn), daughter of a
local storekeeper, as she is to him. They make it to a hotel room, but she
significantly says: 'I'm feeling strange about coming here. Do you understand? Perhaps I'm not a woman of the world.' Surprisingly though,
just short of consummation, it is Matt who turns away, admitting he is
unready to commit to their relationship. Echoing *Brief Encounter*, the
film ends at the railway station from which the troops are leaving – and
there is a moment of joyful farewell as Jean's wave to the departing train
is returned by Matt. Again, the setting of the station with the characteristic clock and subways, along with the importance of music (both clas-
sical and popular) and a scene in a cinema, keep nudging recollections
of the 1945 film. One reviewer commented rather curiously: 'The course
of the three love affairs … is worked out with dispassionate neatness.
John and Matt behave with perfect propriety towards their absent rivals,
and in doing so seem unconsciously to devalue the authenticity of their
own needs',[18] thus hinting at a critical point of view not to be found in
writing about *Brief Encounter*.

Mademoiselle Chambon

Perhaps the most poignant revisiting of *Brief Encounter* territory is a French film, Stéphane Brizé's *Mademoiselle Chambon* (2011), and the connection was noted by reviewers at the time. For instance, the London daily the *Independent* wrote: 'Stéphane Brizé, who made the superb *Not Here To Be Loved* (2005), presents another study in thwarted love that relocates the spirit of *Brief Encounter* to provincial France.'[19] The film's last two episodes would have been enough to stress this parallel: the second-last is set on an empty railway platform, from which Véronique (Sandrine Kiberlain) has just boarded the train that will take her away from the town where she has fallen in love with Jean (Vincent Lindon); and the last finds Jean returned home to take his place at the kitchen table with wife Anne-Marie (Aure Atika). As in most of the films echoing the famous forerunner, someone will have to leave the scene of unsought passion, and nowhere is this more affecting than in *Mademoiselle Chambon*. And in perhaps no other echo is music so crucial: ordinary working-man Jean is entranced by Véronique's violin playing of Elgar's '*Saut d'amour*', and we recall how potent the Rachmaninoff was in the earlier film. The film's review in *Sight & Sound* was accompanied by a still of Véronique, alone on the railway platform, with the caption: 'Brief encounter: Sandrine Kiberlain.'[20]

From the outset, director Brizé makes clear an ordinariness and decency in this couple. He is a capable builder/mason; she is a respected

14 Sandrine Kiberlain in *Mademoiselle Chambon*

teacher. He is happily married to Anne-Marie, who works in a factory, and they have a likable small son Jérémy who is being taught by Véronique. Jean is established as a good husband, father and son (to his aged father), and she is clearly conscientiously engaged by her work. When he goes to repair a window at her flat, he is taken by the Elgar she plays for him and the music echoes with him as he drives away – recalling the way the Rachmaninoff is heard over Laura's pensiveness during her train journey home. As in all of these films, one of the protagonists has to make a decision to leave or the other to settle for return to domestic obligations, and the image of a retreating train so often precedes that of a return to the scene of those obligations. The partner to whom this return is made will be aware of and will adjust to the knowledge of the others having been 'a long way away'. These recurring images of trains, tunnels and platforms are so common in the films considered here that the incidence of railway stations warrants further consideration – and will be given this in Chapter 9.

Lost in Translation

Many reviewers, including those for the *Guardian*, the *Independent* and the *Daily Telegraph*,[21] and the American journal *Rolling Stone*[22] and the *New York Times*,[23] among others, evoked *Brief Encounter* in their review of Sofia Coppola's *Lost in Translation* (2003). This delicate romance (sort of) involves two people at a loose end in Tokyo: Bob Harris (Bill Murray) is a somewhat faded film star doing whisky advertisements there; and Charlotte (Scarlett Johansson) is there with – or mostly without – her photographer husband John (Giovanni Ribisi). Bob has a demanding wife back home who persists in phoning about pressing domestic matters such as colour choice for a new carpet; Charlotte is left alone much of the time while John goes off on shoots.

Bob first registers Charlotte in a crowded lift, an incident he later doesn't recall, but subsequently they keep running into each other sitting solitarily in bars. They exchange views on what each other is doing or expects of life, and moments of *Brief Encounter* are recalled on several occasions. Their time together is once interrupted by Bob's over-chatty friend Kelly (Anna Faris), recalling Dolly Messiter's similar function in Lean's film; at a later moment Charlotte is left looking solitary on a railway platform (again, what is it about station platforms that can make them look so bleak?). Along the way, though, they spend time in each other's hotel rooms, even lying platonically on the same bed; but in the end they kiss goodbye, each agreeing 'I miss you', and then go their separate ways, aware of the separate claims on them. Bob has slept with the hotel's lounge singer, but his and Charlotte's relationship remains a friendship that might have been more but isn't. *Sight & Sound* took the line that Bob's one-night stand had 'polluted a delicate love story that might have taken its place alongside similar assignations in *Brief Encounter*, *The Clock* (both 1945) and *Before Sunrise* (1995)'.[24]

Shane and George Stevens

British film scholar, Neil Sinyard, preparing a book on US director George Stevens, drew my attention to still further American films that in certain key moments seem to have drawn their inspiration from *Brief Encounter*. The idea of Stevens' majestic western, *Shane* (1952), seemed improbable in this context, but on re-viewing the film I could only agree with Sinyard's comment that 'The last, beautifully acted, scene between Alan Ladd and Jean Arthur is pure Noel Coward on the range; the final handshake as powerful and poignant as Trevor Howard's squeeze of Celia Johnson's shoulder' as he leaves the refreshment room.[25] Shane (Ladd), the wanderer who has had a taste of domestic life with Joe and Mary Starrett (Van Heflin, Arthur) and helped sort out the threats to their homestead, rides off after that handshake and after a number of mutually appreciative glances during the film. In riding off, he renounces the possibility of anything further between him and Mary, out of respect for what he has observed of her family life.

Sinyard also drew my attention to two further films that seem to echo Lean. The first of these echoes is in a scene from John Stahl's *Walls of Jericho* (1948) that is 'almost an homage to *Brief Encounter*: an emotional farewell between two secret lovers on a station platform, interrupted by a friend of the heroine, which ruins their goodbye. There's no equivalent scene in the novel.'[26] The other resonant narrative thread is to be found in George Stevens' *Something to Live For* (1952), in which an unhappy actress (Joan Fontaine) has become an alcoholic and falls in love with the former alcoholic (Ray Milland) who has been deputed to help her. He returns her feeling for him, but ultimately returns to his devoted wife (Teresa Wright). Perhaps Stevens had an unusually serious regard for *Brief Encounter* that manifested itself in several of his films. There's a section in a book by Mandy Merck called *Hollywood's American Tragedies*, which also argues its influence on *A Place in the Sun* (1951).

The Judge Steps Out

Another American film, which was made quite soon after *Brief Encounter* and reminds one of the essential return to obligations beyond the self that is its moral centre, is Boris Ingster's *The Judge Steps Out* (March 1947, but re-titled in the UK as *Indian Summer*). Judge Thomas Bailey (Alexander Knox) is bored with the routines of his life and feels at odds with his rather difficult wife Evelyn (Frieda Inescort). On his way to Washington to discuss an appointment, he becomes ill, takes time out, and falls in love with Peggy (Ann Sothern), who runs a roadside café. He helps the unmarried Peggy to adopt a child, is clearly attracted to her, but in the end returns to his role as judge and to the wife who has mellowed during his absence. He and Peggy, in another *Brief Encoutner* echo, say their farewells on a railway station. Tom has been forced to reappraise his life and, in following the dictates of conscience and decency, returns to take up the reins again, knowing also that Peggy has found happiness with her child.

Nashville and Robert Altman

Given Robert Altman's early besottedness with *Brief Encounter* and Celia Johnson, it is tempting to ponder whether his glorious *Nashville* doesn't echo them both. When Haven Hamilton (Henry Gibson) sings: 'I can't leave my wife and there's three reasons why/There's Jimny and Kathy and sweet Lorelei/ For the sake of the children I must say goodbye.' A little later, Linnea Reese (Lily Tomlin), after an enjoyable sexual encounter with singer Tom Frank (Keith Carradine), quietly quits his bed and heads for home with Delbert (Ned Beatty) and her deaf child. These moments recall that Altman was on record as having found his way into filmmaking after viewing *Brief Encounter*: 'The first film that made a difference in my mind between a movie and a film … was *Brief Encounter*… I remember thinking, "What is this about?" This girl, Celia Johnson, was not pretty. She wore those sensible shoes. And suddenly I'm in love with her.'[27]

Brooklyn

A much more recent film whose denouement recalls Laura's love/home conflict and its resolution is John Crowley's exquisite *Brooklyn* (2015), adapted from Colm Tóibín's novel. Here, Eilis (Saoirse Ronan) has left her native Ireland, gradually settled into Brooklyn, fallen in love with and quietly married Italian Tony (Emory Cohen), when a family death sends her back to Ireland. She is torn between 'home' (i.e., Ireland) and love for Tony. While in Ireland, and not having revealed her marriage, she is much attracted to Jim Farrell (Domhnall Gleeson), but tells a friend she is going 'home' (i.e., Brooklyn). 'I want to be with him [Jim]. I want to be with my husband [Tony].' Following the latter course, she meets a girl on deck and in their conversation comes the line about Brooklyn: 'So many Irish people there, it's like home.' In other words, she has accepted the greater claims of husband and home over that of sexual attraction – and as always there are other contributing factors, in this case to do with religion, distance from home and all that is involved in the matter of immigration.

Call Me by Your Name

One of the latest echoes is Luca Guadagnino's *Call Me by Your Name* (2017), in which Elio (Timothée Chalamet), the son of a Lombardy-based professor, becomes sexually obsessed with the handsome young American researcher, Oliver (Armie Hammer), who has come to work on his manuscript with the professor (Michael Stuhlberg). The relationship between the two young men becomes overtly sexual, but when Oliver returns to the US he telephones Elio to say he is getting married. It is not wholly clear, or even perhaps important, whether Oliver is being true to a previous relationship, but what, for the umpteenth time, recalls Lean's film is Elio and Oliver's farewell at the local railway station.

Very recently, the British Film Institute produced an article entitled '10 Great Films about Brief Encounters'. Several on this list have been discussed in this chapter, including *Lost in Translation*, *Weekend* and *Call Me by Your Name*, but the others named offer further examples of the way the old film continues to make its presence felt, not only in the films named in the article itself but also in the way this draws on the familiar title.[28] The subtitle of the piece is: 'From *Before Sunrise* to *In the Mood for Love*, there's nothing so achingly romantic on screen as a brief encounter'. *Casablanca*, which preceded *Brief Encounter*, is one of the films listed, but the insistence of the 1945 title is in itself indicative of its evocative power.

Of course, there is more to these films and those others cited in this chapter than the narrative twist of renunciation displacing self-gratification, or of images of departures from railway stations: the wide range of cultures and ideologies involved ensures this, but the echoes of Lean's classic remain to haunt these films.

* * *

Former *Sunday Age* critic Tom Ryan added three more echoes to my list: *The End of the Affair* (1999), *Intimacy* (2001) and *Mrs Palfrey at the Claremont* (2005), his reviews of which had each alluded to *Brief Encounter* parallels.[29] Those titles discussed above all involve a relationship whose outcome foregrounds the conflict of desire and those other obligations suggested above that weigh on the protagonists' sense of what is right. This has been the case with virtually all the films considered in this chapter of 'echoes'.

The End of the Affair

The End of the Affair is the second adaptation of Graham Greene's novel,[30] in which Sarah (Julianne Moore), married to decent but dull civil servant, Henry (Stephen Rea), falls passionately in love with a writer, Maurice (Ralph Fiennes). Five years later, in 1944, fearing Maurice has been killed during a bomb raid, she pledges to God that she will renounce him if God will let him live. There are some obvious echoes of *Brief Encounter*; for example, the flashback framework in which Maurice comes to terms with the affair and, above all, Sarah's renunciation – though God, not Henry, is the other protagonist here. The film is framed by Maurice's recording of his feelings at his typewriter, to which he returns intermittently, reminding one of Celia Johnson's intermittent voice-over as her way of coming to terms with her situation. The film has other moments that evoke Lean's film: for instance, when Sarah and Maurice go to the cinema together (actually watching a love scene from *21 Days*, a 1939 release with a screenplay by Greene), followed by a visit to a restaurant where their hands touch and he pronounces: 'I'm in love you know' and she replies: 'Me too', recalling the comparable moment for Laura and Alec. And, as with Lean's couple, nothing lasting will come of this mutual realisation.

Intimacy

The reviewer's casual reference to Lean's film suggests that reviewers can take for granted the persistence of the scenario and values of the 1945 film as a recognisable point of reference for their readers. Patrice Chéreau's *Intimacy*, with its scenes of uninhibited nudity and sexuality, may seem a long way from the restrained kisses exchanged by Celia Johnson and Trevor Howard (Celia never gets beyond removing her scarf), but there is again the powerful sense of a relationship at odds with the rest of their lives as played out by Mark Rylance (Jay) and Kerry Fox (Claire). Again, it is the woman who walks away finally from the affair and, again, she is married to an amiable husband whom she has been deceiving on a weekly basis and to whom, and to their son, she returns. It is essentially sexual gratification that she is renouncing, but renunciation it certainly is. Perhaps the contrast here is more potent than the parallel: whereas Alec and Laura love each other but are denied sexual fulfilment, Chérou's lovers have a regular and vigorous sexual relationship but otherwise know nothing about each other. When the film leads them to confront other aspects of their lives, Claire will return to her likable husband Andy (Timothy Spall), resisting Jay's plea of 'Come back – stay'.

Mrs Palfrey at the Claremont

Dan Ireland's *Mrs Palfrey at the Claremont*, derived from Elizabeth Taylor's novel, doesn't deal in narrative parallels with the old classic. However, it is explicitly raised in an exchange between the eponymous Mrs Palfrey (Joan Plowright) and the young writer, Ludo (Rupert Friend), who comes to her aid (Alec-like) when (in her grit-in-the-eye moment) she slips on the pavement outside his flat. The plot involves a deception – she passes Ludo off as her grandson (cf. Laura's being led into deceiving husband Fred) – and at one point he asks her what her favourite film is and she replies, '*Brief Encounter*. I saw it when I was eighteen and at the end was weeping shamelessly. There was nothing left for us [her and husband-to-be] to do but fall in love.' Later, Ludo goes into a DVD shop to buy the film and meets a young girl, who, in a nice cross-generational touch, says: 'It's one of my favourites.'

It's not that all these films mirror *Brief Encounter* in narrative or character detail, but the fact that the film critic of a popular, non-specialist newspaper feels able to refer to the old film surely points to its ongoing place in popular culture. And this reviewer's references are by no means unusual: it seems widely accepted that readers will 'get' the allusion and associate it with the points being made about emotional involvement and the difficulties that may frustrate its fulfilment. Sometimes, though, it is enough merely to name the film as someone's favourite, as above, to establish the echo.

* * *

An echo in another medium occurs in an exchange between two lovers in Madeleine St John's *A Stairway to Paradise*.[31] This time it is the man who says: 'I have obligations … You know my situation as well as I do … I have a wife and two children and a household to maintain: those are the givens.' Whereas the woman involved had expected them to run away together and cannot make do with intermittent – and clandestine – meetings. There are no doubt plenty of other novels, as well as films, in which comparable scenarios can be found; my point here is that they now inevitably bring a black-and-white 1945 film to mind.

Notes

1 *The Encyclopedia of British Film*, 4th edition, Manchester: Manchester University Press, 2013, p. 325.
2 Quoted in a digest of reviews in the *Cinema Studio*, 12 January 1949, p. 14.
3 *Picture Show*, 8 January 1949, p. 11; *Picturegoer*, 29 January 1949, p. 15.
4 For example, Derek Winnert's *Radio Times Film & Video Guide*, London: Hodder & Stoughton, 1993, p. 523; John Walker, *Halliwell's Film: DVD & Video Guide 2007*, London: Harper Collins, 2006, p. 573.
5 Edward Goring, *Daily Mail*, 5 October 1957.
6 B.D., *Monthly Film Bulletin*, November 1957, p. 137
7 Vincent Canby, *New York Times*, 21 November 1984.
8 Pauline Kael, *State of the Art*, Boston: Dutton, 1985.
9 Pam Cook, *Monthly Film Bulletin*, May 1985, p. 153.
10 Neil Sinyard, 'SWEET AND SOUR: The Greatness of Billy Wilder's *The Apartment*', Arrow DVD, December 2017. Quoted from Ed Sikov, *The Life and Times of Billy Wilder*, New York: Hyperion, pp. 429–30; and Cameron Crowe, *Conversations with Wilder*, London: Faber & Faber, 1999, pp. 136, 292, 347.
11 Gene Phillips, *Beyond the Epic: The Life & Films of David Lean*, Lexington: The University Press of Kentucky, 2006, p. 89.
12 Xan Brooks, 'The Lunchbox Review – "A Quiet Storm of Banked Emotions"', *Guardian*, 13 April 2014.
13 Mike D'Angelo, 'Todd Haynes Goes Back to the '50s with a Rapturous New Romance, *Carol*', *AVI Film*, 19 November 2015.
14 Patricia Highsmith, *Carol* (originally *The Price of Salt*, 1952), London: Bloomsbury, 2015, p. 307.
15 Stephanie Bunbury, 'Risking All for Love', *The Age*, 9 January 2016 (*Spectrum*, p. 12).
16 Jane Sullivan, 'Turning Pages', *The Age*, 9 January 2016 (*Spectrum*, p. 29).
17 As told to David Jenkins, http://lwlies.com/interviews/todd-haynes-carol-interview/. Accessed 9 February 2019.
18 John Pym, *Monthly Film Bulletin*, October 1979, p. 214.
19 Anthony Quinn, *Independent*, 22 September 2011.

20 *Sight & Sound*, October 2011, p. 70.

21 All three reviews 4 January 2004.

22 *Rolling Stone*, 8 September 2003.

23 *New York Times*, 12 September 2003.

24 Ryan Gilbey, *Sight & Sound*, January 2004, p. 52.

25 In correspondence with Neil Sinyard, 2017.

26 Ibid.

27 Michael Zuckoff, *Robert Altman: The Oral Biography*, New York: Alfred A. Knopf, 2009, p. 55.

28 David Morrison, 'Ten Great Films about Brief Encounters', www.bfi.org.uk/news-opinion/news-bfi/lists/10-great-films-about-brief-encounters. Accessed 17 March 2018.

29 These reviews appeared in the *Sunday Age*, 5 March 2000; 27 January 2002; 29 October 2006.

30 The earlier version, directed by Edward Dmytryk and starring Deborah Kerr and Van Johnson, was released in 1955.

31 Madeleine St John, *A Stairway to Paradise*, Melbourne: Text Publishing, 1999, p. 64.

7

From big screen to small – and elsewhere

Apart from the disastrous 1974 telemovie remake discussed in Chapter 3, there has been a remarkable incidence of television references to the title, and often to aspects of the narrative and thematic elements, of *Brief Encounter*. When last checked, the Internet Movie Database (IMDb) listed no fewer than 96 television episodes, short films and other programmes that feature or call up the film's title. Now, the phrase had been in very modest use since the 1860s, according to one source, but in the same source's graphing of the usage it was seen to soar from the mid 1940s, and then reached another high peak as late as 2010.[1] No doubt many of these usages are trivial, but the fact that, since 1945, the title has been invoked so often points to its potency in public awareness at large. And not just in the UK: the US, Australia and even Hong Kong have drawn on the resonant title for TV items

One of the earliest such occasions was the 1954 US-based *Producer's Showcase* in which Otto Preminger directed several episodes derived from Coward's compendium, *Tonight at 8.30*. What matters here is the fact that Trevor Howard repeated his role of Alec Harvey, this time opposite Ginger Rogers – somewhat unusually cast as Laura – in *Still Life*, or as it was now known, *Brief Encounter*. Howard's relations with Preminger were strained to say the least, but it is significant that he chose Howard to repeat the role that he would always be associated with. The director's advice to Howard regarding the role and his co-star was: 'You must pick her up with you, take her to the counter for coffee and pinch her ass.'[2] Given Howard's original failure to understand the delayed consummation for Laura and Alec when Lean was directing him, Preminger's instruction may well have chimed more with his view of their situation. Not only was restraint not a commonly recurring motif in US television or screen fare, but Howard, despite the sensitivity of his playing of Alec in Lean's film, was from all accounts (e.g., biographies of both him and Celia Johnson) not greatly given to it in real life.

Among the many TV episodes, fortunately some of them still available for viewing online, some do no more than use the title – or a punning version, or other variant of it – secure in the knowledge that it will ring some sort of bell with viewers. The punning usages can be dismissed quickly for the most part. There are episodes with titles such as (UK-based unless noted): *Aunt Bee's Brief Encounter* (in US comedy series *The Andy Griffith Show*, 1961); *Thelma's Brief Encounter* (an episode in US series *Good Times*, 1977, set in an impoverished black community in Chicago); *Beef Encounters* (twice – in US comedy series, *Szyszmk*, 1977, and UK comedy-drama crime series *Boon*, 1986, starring Michael Elphick); *Briefcase Encounter* (twice – in Australian series *Kingswood*, 1982, and UK series *About Face*, 1989, with Maureen Lipman and Robert Bathurst); *Briefless Encounter* (in US series *Who's Boss?*, 1984); again *Briefless Encounter* (in *The Upper Hand*, 1990, starring Honor Blackman); *Grief Encounter* (in series *Goodnight Sweetheart*, 1993), which is one to which I'll need to return; *Reef Encounter* (in a David Attenborough series, *Wildlife on One*, 1997); *A Very Brief Encounter* (in comedy series *My Family*, 2009); and *Encountered Briefly* (in *Doctors*, 2003, starring Christopher Timothy).

That, along with numerous minor variants of the title, such as *A Brief Encounter* and *Brief Encounters*, is enough to indicate the prolificacy of this particular phenomenon. It seems unlikely that any other film title has given rise to such seemingly endless repetition. As recently as 2017, a UK/Ireland short simply entitled *Brief Encounter* was in production. What strikes one again and again is the casual way in which potential viewers (and, as will be later seen, readers) are meant to take the title in their stride, as if it refers to an aspect of our cultural baggage with which we all should be familiar.

I don't propose to work my way through the ninety-odd television usages of the famous title – not here, at any rate – but enough checking of the individual items listed on the internet has revealed that some deserve more attention here than others. By this I mean that these seem to have drawn something more than just the title from the celebrated original. Some are actually made in reference to Lean's film. For instance, in Episode 26, Season 5 of the NBC's *Dinah Shore Chevy Show* (1961), Shore and Ralph Bellamy actually play characters called Laura Jesson and Alec Harvey in this adaptation of Coward, set in 1908 Boston, and a half-dozen of the other key characters from the film also appear. In Episode 5, Season 1 of *Big Screen Britain* (2003), a documentary series about classic British films, Margaret Barton, Beryl in *Brief Encounter*, is interviewed about her experience by Ben Fogle, presenter of ten such episodes in the series. In 2011, there was a short film (directed, shot and edited by Charles Leek) simply entitled *Brief Encounter*, which adapted the grit-in-the-eye narrative starter to a contemporary setting, but filmed in Carnforth Station where the original grit made its presence felt in the lives of Laura and Alec.

The 1984 episode of *Fresh Fields*, entitled *A Brief Encounter*, offered a comic variant on the notion of the housewife who is tempted by a man she meets in the course of her daily life. Her 'daily life' is less common than that of many housewives because it includes fencing classes. Hester Fields' (Julia McKenzie) enthusiasm for this pursuit, when she comes home after a 'marvellous' session, leads husband William (Anton Rodgers) to become a bit suspicious of Hester's fencing instructor, Mr Frobisher (Terence Hardiman). During one lesson, Frobisher, with his arm around Hester so as to guide her, says: 'Just relax and let your body move with mine.' A little later he tells her that she's 'the most exciting woman I've ever taught'. He wants to kiss her neck, and she lets him – 'Just this once'. From this we cut to Hester and William in bed, she knitting and he reading. When next time he comes home, he finds Frobisher 'coaching' Hester in their sitting-room; he gestures with a duelling pistol, which, in comic anti-climax, proves to be an elaborate cigarette lighter. The episode makes quite good comic capital out of its brief encounter, and perhaps, partly because it is very middle-class in its setting, does more than most to earn its right to the ubiquitous title (and McKenzie and Rodgers know how to maintain the comic tone).

One of the television versions or borrowings of more than passing interest is the 1999 *Grief Encounter* episode of the UK television series *Goodnight Sweetheart*, which ran for six seasons from 1993 to 1999. Protagonist of the series is television repairman Gary Sparrow (Nicholas Lyndhurst) who has become a time traveller and who moves between the 1990s and the wartime days when *Brief Encounter* was being filmed. In the episode relevant to this study, in the later period he is married to his somewhat formidable wife Yvonne (Emma Amos), while back in 1945 he is taken with barmaid Phoebe (Elizabeth Carling). There is no need to go into the (mildly ingenious) plot manoeuvres by which he finds himself involved in these two worlds; it is enough to say here that Noël Coward and David Lean are filming *Brief Encounter*. Coward wants a nightclub scene with Phoebe, along with Gary (who has an unearned reputation as a songwriter) accompanying her on the piano.

The episode contains two excerpts from the film: the first is the tilted shot of Laura's rushing out on to the platform (a television watcher says: 'I thought she was going to top herself' – as indeed many viewers may have feared in the case of Laura); and the second is the film's last scene with Gary's thanking her for 'coming back', just as Fred had done. There are perhaps not many moments in film history as recognisable or

15 David Benson as Noël Coward, with Nicholas Lyndhurst and Elizabeth Carling in *Goodnight Sweetheart*

as often quoted as these. When Gary comes into the studio, he is jealous when he sees Phoebe sitting in the 'Milford Junction' refreshment rooms with composer Anthony Blair, who says to her 'I've never met anyone like you – tender and rare'. Though the hat she's wearing is somewhat reminiscent of the one Celia Johnson wore, her reply is less so: 'You make me sound like a piece of steak,' following this more in character with 'Please, Tony, I'm a married woman.' Gary mistakes their dialogue for the real thing as he rushes in, only to find that the proposed nightclub scene has been abandoned at the request of Celia (sitting nearby and wearing the iconic hat) because she doesn't believe Laura would go to a nightclub.

The outcome of this episode of the once-popular series can't matter much now. It's enough to say that Gary is married to each of the women in the appropriate time period. But the overtones of Lean's film keep making themselves felt, as often for comic as for serious echoes. In the 1990s, the show's producers were obviously confident that these would resonate sufficiently with viewing audiences to underpin the action of the episode. As indeed were the producers of the similarly entitled Episode 7, Season 2 of the comedy series *Birds of a Feather* (18 October 1990) in which the eponymous meeting takes place – unsurprisingly – on a railway station platform. Sharon (series star Pauline Quirke) has just been the subject of verbal abuse from a young layabout when she sees further along the platform a middle-aged man, Don (Mark Kingston), being mugged and robbed. She goes to his assistance and assures him 'I'm used to violence. I'm a married woman.' But this shouldn't lead anyone to think the episode is about to become politically correct about women's lives. This is a comedy in which she can meet him for a thank-you date, when she reveals: 'I'm married to a Greek, the only thing I've got in common with the Queen.' They meet several more times (five, to be exact, her sister reminds her) and she goes to bed with him, though he has no plan to leave his wife. At their last meeting, he gives her a Sergeant Pepper record as a souvenir of the 1960s and she evokes the same period with a gift of drugs. A police officer (standing in for Dolly Messiter??) interrupts this meeting in Don's bedroom – not to arrest Sharon for drug-supplying but to return Don's wallet that his mugger had made off with. The network of marriages (Sharon's husband is in prison on drugs charges), the use of the station setting to initiate the central relationship and the final interruption were no doubt seen as justifying the title of the episode, even though its tone is entirely one of the broad comedy that characterised the popular series. For those in the know, at least, these allusions were presumably an added ingredient in the episode's texture.

The *Brief Encounter* episode of the mid-1990s cult series *This Life* is about as diametrically opposed to the prevailing morality of Lean's film as it could be. In this sharply written and acted episode the brief encounter is essentially for the purpose of sex, taking its start from the point the original never reached. Beautiful but currently depressed young lawyer, Anna (Daniela Nardini), goes on a drinking date with junior colleague Jo (Steve John Shepherd). Both more than half-cut, they return from the bar to the legal office they work in and throw themselves enthusiastically into semi-drunken sex. When, next evening, back at the flat she shares with four other young lawyers, Anna makes clear to Jo that last night was 'just a bit of fun. I thought you understood this', telling him 'You and I could never have a serious relationship', Jo is furious at having been used as 'just a bit of rough'. There are other relationships at work in the episode, but this is the one that earns the title of the episode: for Anna sex was enough and, without meaning to be callous about it, she has to set Jo to rights. For her, last night was absolutely nothing more than a brief encounter, and she can't help it if he wanted something more.

The relevant episode in the US series *Some of My Best Friends* (2001) does no more than pun on the title. Episode 4 of Series 1 is a mildly amusing gay-focused comedy about a guy who wonders if his flatmate has designs on him when he thinks the flatmate may have made off with his boxer shorts. There is speculation about Frankie's sexual preferences, with another flatmate saying: 'No straight man is that good at picking out clothes.' And so on. The brief episode, as it were, moves to an amusing anti-climax, but it is really only the title that connects it to the 1945 film. Another episode in a US series, *Beverly Hills Bunz*, again seems to have little do with Lean's film apart from the title. The encounter between an LA detective and visiting journalist ends with the two in bed, the climax to a tedious comedy-drama: but the persistence of the title, this time in 1988, maintains its claim on viewer attention.

Despite its being titled *Briefest Encounter*, the following Granada TV item, first screened 27 May 1998, might be more aptly labelled the 'Bizarrest Encounter'. Incidentally, it is listed as a 'TV movie' lasting one hour on IMDb,[3] but when viewed online it seems to have been a series of episodes. Whichever was its origin, its content renders it a very strange descendant of Lean's film. Directed by Nick Hamm, it is a two-hander, co-starring Rik Mayall as party-crasher Greg and Amanda Donohue as fashion journalist Siobhan. They have met at a party of someone called Stefano, and have gone from it to Siobhan's flat where Greg is looking forward to sex, of which, as he explains, he has had none since his wife died. Well, things do not go as he hopes, partly because her dog attacks him and he later appears to have killed it. This is all done for comedy, as is his lie about how he went to the party because he knew Stefano was gay and has lived with another man for seventeen years, and his repeated inability to remember how to pronounce her name (he tries 'Shoveen' and, even, Shirley). The increasingly outrageous scenario involves bits of bloodshed, smashing items of furniture and ultimately setting fire to the apartment. Their brief encounter is quite often wittily written (by Peter Learmouth) and performed; there are bursts of Rachmaninoff on the soundtrack (music director is Barrington Pheloung); and the dog could be seen as a sort of Dolly Messiter, except that it intervenes before a relationship has started. But it is so removed in spirit from *Brief Encounter* that one can only surmise that the old title is so embedded in culture that any meeting and potential relationship between two strangers seems inevitably to be some sort of descendant – or that the episode's makers counted on the title adding a resonant touch that would attract knowledgeable viewers?

That last phrase is probably more than can be said for the similarly titled Episode 2 of Season 1 in the US series *Brothers & Sisters*, aired on 3 October 2010. In the frayed relationships between siblings, children and parents, and others, there are moments that might be described as brief encounters, ensuing from a launch party for a friend's underwear advertising campaign, but otherwise it's just one among many examples of the resonance of the original title in the popular culture across the decades. There are some attractive performances from the likes of Sally Field, Matthew Rhys and Rachel Griffiths, and some preoccupation with the idea of people being honest with each other, but essentially the title is just a hook on which to hang the rest.

That last comment is no doubt true of many other of the items that recycle the title, often in punning form and often with no other visible connection to the original. Two others not available for online viewing which invoke the title straightforwardly are first a US seven-minute short film of 2003, set in a laundromat.[4] Here, a young man is attracted to a good-looking women who smiles at him but without serious promise of more. She leaves, and when he finds a pair of her underpants have become mixed up with his laundry he races after her. A lot seems to have been going on in seven minutes, but my sources aren't clear about the outcome. And an even shorter (i.e., five minutes) US film is called simply *A Brief Encounter* (2009), the plot summary for which informs us that 'Gia, a temptress residing in New York City, stalks and kills the men she's had illicit affairs with'.[5] Such short features have come a long way from Milford Junction, in terms of both continent and sexual dealings.

One of the more recent examples of playing on the title is the 2016 miniseries *Brief Encounters*, starring Penelope Wilton, Peter Wight, Sophie Rundle and Karl Davies. This series, strongly cast and with impressive production values, ran to six episodes. It involves a network of relationships that leads to a group of women demonstrating and selling Ann Summers lingerie and sex aids in private houses as a means of making some extra money when the factory-worker husband of one of them loses his job. The series, now available on DVD, is not without some substance on the matter of women's roles and some of the reactions of their husbands, and in these ways perhaps it reflects not only the title but some of the issues raised by the 1945 title it invokes. There are in fact numerous underwear or 'lingerie' retailers in both the UK and the US that advertise their wares in stores bearing the name of the film, in either singular or plural form. Even a household name like Calvin Klein has made explicit use of the film's title.[6]

To end this account on a light note, I draw attention to Victoria Wood's *Brief Encounter* parody, presented by BBC Tea-Time in May 2007. It opens in the Milford Junction tea room, with Albert Godby getting his hand smacked for trying to pinch one of Myrtle's mince pies when she is about to serve, not Laura, but Dolly Messiter (Celia Imrie). Dolly snatches her plate and goes to her table just as Laura enters, wearing Celia Johnson's famous hat. When Laura (Victoria Wood) gets a crumb in her eye, a doctor, Bob (Bill Paterson), comes to the rescue of course, and Dolly has rushed out for her train. Their subsequent dialogue parodies the original to comic effect:

'Are you married Bob?'
'Yes, my wife's bit of an old trout, I'm afraid. We're very devoted … It's just that she can be rather vicious – and she takes drugs.'

And later, when he asks if she could come to the pictures with him, and she replies: 'I couldn't possibly', he follows this with:

'Here's another suggestion. I'm leaving for a leper colony tomorrow on the boat train to Nairobi from King's Cross. Could you leave all this and start a new life with me?'

When he goes, Dolly comes running back in and we are left with Laura's voice-over saying:

'Such a silly story but I can't explain how I came to run away with Dolly.'

Apart from the famous hat, the film parodies the original in the sheer speed with which their brief encounter hurtles through the narrative matter of the film: in the way it demolishes the married lives of the pair (hers is merely 'humdrum' compared with his!); in its playing with class (Myrtle offers pekoe tea 'which I keep for the middle classes'); and in Myrtle's refrain of 'There's a war on, you know'. The latter, of course, reminds us of when the original was made, of how it never referred to the war and yet how its scenario no doubt resonated significantly with audiences at the time, as Ken Puckett's *War Pictures*, discussed in Chapter 2, argued. But this is making Wood's dealings with the original sound solemn, which it is emphatically not.

As will be apparent, some of the many TV episodes and short films that make use of the title (or variants of it) have more points of contact, narrative and emotional, with the original than others. However, even when there seems to be no more than a punning or facetious allusion to it, there is still the *fact* of its invocation to be contended with, and this usage is undoubtedly an ongoing phenomenon of the seventy-odd years since Trevor Howard removed the grit from Celia Johnson's eye.

Notes

1 *New York Times Chronicle*, 'Visualizing Language Usage in New York Times News Coverage Throughout History'. Accessed 10 May 2016.

2 Vivienne Knight, *Trevor Howard: A Gentleman and a Player*, London: Sphere Books, 1988, p. 85.
3 www.imdb.com/title/tt0106482/?ref_=fn_tt_tt_12. Accessed 10 January 2018.
4 Filmed in the 'Suds & Comfort Laundromat, Somerville, Massachusetts', according to www.imdb.com/title/tt0437110/locations?ref_=ttfc_ql_5. Accessed 19 August 2018.
5 www.imdb.com/title/tt1700713/. Accessed 12 January 2018.
6 See, for instance, Calvin Klein Underwear Brief Encounters Hipster Briefs, SHOPBOP. www.shopbop.com/brief-encounters-hipster-calvin-klein/vp/v=1/845 524441948057.htm. Accessed 12 March 2019.

8

Odds and ends

If it were just a matter of how often *Brief Encounter* had been remade for film, stage or television, this would be remarkable enough to warrant attention, but I am amazed at the way the title and the aura surrounding the film have so insistently infiltrated the culture at large. That letter headed 'Brief encounter?' quoted at the beginning of this study is but one of dozens, possibly hundreds, of instances that invoke what has been called the most famous love story in cinema history. This chapter aims to give further ideas on the eclectic nature of its inheritance.

Four visual promotions

G.E. Refrigerators Commercial

In 1958, celebrated US comedy duo Elaine May and Mike Nichols appeared in a very funny parody of *Brief Encounter*, again suggesting that the film's *réclame* had already gone beyond domestic borders.[1] May, lavishly attired in furs, enters the improbably elegant showrooms of General Electric, and tells the salesman – Nichols in morning dress – that she 'has come to say goodbye'. He details the many remarkable features of the refrigerator (e.g., an ice-tray that effortlessly spills its products into a waiting dish). He asks her: 'Why are you doing this?' (i.e., 'saying goodbye'), in reply to which she tells him: 'Because I must. I can't ask you to give up all this.' He acknowledges that: 'Refrigerators are my life' (his version of Alec's preventive medicine?). She 'has always known that' and is sacrificing her own feeling for him, in return for which he gives her a product that means she'll 'never have to defrost again'. It is wittily loaded with echoes of the film it parodies, and that last phrase of Nichols' about defrosting is no doubt intended as a reminder of the sort of restraint that was always being called into play in contemporary accounts of the film. Such a faux-advertising short is lampooning the famous film, but the fact of its invoking the latter is further argument for its secure place in film – and inter-cultural – history at large.

Student's trailer for a remake

In 2009, Patrick Tan, a Melbourne student, received a High Distinction for directing and editing a video which depicted a preview, or 'trailer', of a remake of *Brief Encounter* – an assignment for his Master of Multimedia Design at Monash University.[2] His 3-minute, 24-second black-and-white video captures the spirit of the film – and the hyperbolic language so characteristic of previews. It begins with the title A VERY MOVING LOVE STORY and an image of Alec (John Rickard) and Laura (Patsy King) embracing on a bridge against a background of wintry trees. This is followed by another title: VOTED BEST ROMANTIC BRITISH FILM EVER! A close-up of Laura is accompanied by her voice-over reflecting ruefully: 'I'm a happily married woman – or rather I was till a few weeks ago.' After highlighting the crucial grit-in-the-eye moment, there are glimpses of the pair walking in the street, talk of going to the pictures and of spouses, before returning to the opening embrace and to Alec's eliciting the promise to meet again next Thursday. Along with A MOVING LOVE STORY, the trailer also promises DELIGHTFUL COMEDY, illustrating this with Myrtle's 'banburies' upset all over the floor.

The whole thing is done with real feeling for the film, and, though its Alec and Laura appear perhaps a decade older than their forebears, suggests some of the – for them – cataclysmic effects of falling so unexpectedly in love. But equally remarkable is that an Australian student sixty-odd years later should have so immersed himself in this film. I have found students also absorbed by it at a similar remove in time, and these seem powerful pieces of evidence for the view that *Brief Encounter* somehow gets to the heart of certain human experiences. It was no doubt a film of its time, as Margaret Barton said[3] (and as many writers, such as Ken Puckett in *War Pictures*, discussed earlier, have claimed), but the very existence of artefacts such as Patrick Tan's 'preview' seem to insist that it is also a film for other times and places.

As does an anecdote Renee Glynne, production secretary on *Brief Encounter* when she was just 18, recalled among other information about the film's making. Years later, she'd gone to a friend's graduation ceremony in an art gallery in Bethnal Green.[4] The friend was involved in costume design and at the ceremony he and several others performed scenes from the film, presumably drawing on the dress of the film's period.

16 Stills from the short film 'Keith Encounter', promoting the ceramics of Keith Brymer Jones

'Keith Encounter': a potted version

An attractive couple (i.e., 'Laura' and 'Alec') is sitting in the refreshment room, looking sad and drinking coffee in large cups designed by potter Keith Brymer Jones. They raise their cups between snatches of dialogue, revealing, as they do so, a key word embossed on the cup, each time advancing to comic effect the trajectory of their relationship. It opens with:

'Are you all right darling?'
'Yes, I'm all right' [she replies as Alec's raised cup says 'repressed'].
'I wish I could think of something to say.'
'It doesn't matter, not saying anything' [Laura says as her raised cup says 'depressed'].

As the 'Myrtle' and 'Albert' characters hover in the background, the conversation continues:

'Won't your wife be lonely if you're late home?'
'Don't worry about Susan. She's very busy with her W.I. meetings or washing her hair'
['frigid' is the word on Laura's cup].

'Will your husband mind?

'Oh no, he works late. I'm sure he won't notice' ['moron' is the word on
Alec's cup, while a dog and Albert and Myrtle are behaving in an unre-
strained manner].

After this there is no further dialogue, just a succession of cups being
raised, bearing words such as 'tease', 'desire', 'love', 'need'; ending with
'quick', 'together', 'now' and 'mine', and a cut to the train arriving and
an exchange of lips and eyes in close-up.[5]

All this happens in 1.36 minutes, and what is odd is that the unnamed
actors playing their versions of Laura and Alec might easily have played
the real thing! The wife of Brymer Jones's business partner, Dominic
Speelman, had been directing a group of actors at the Edinburgh fringe
in a play called *The Fitzrovia Hour*, based on a 1950s radio programme.
These actors agreed to appear in a short promotional video drawing on
Brief Encounter, which the potters planned to use to market their ceramics in the US, believing that the 1945 film's 'quintessentially British' qualities would help their sales.[6] It was filmed in Whitstable in a restaurant
that, for Brymer Jones, 'had all the attributes for the aesthetic feel of a
railway station waiting/tea room'. This is a clever satirical take on the
original that works well by never seeming to exaggerate anything. The
tone is quiet and lethally comic, as it deals with 'repression, duty and love
not fully fulfilled'. And again, what strikes one is that *Brief Encounter*
should have been called on to do duty in this situation, playing on the
kinds of reserve displayed in the original incarnations of Laura and Alec.

Making a meal of – or from – it

In 1970, director Alan Parker made a 45-second video commercial
called 'Bird's Eye Roast Beef Dinner for One – *Brief Encounter*'.[7] It
opens on a station platform, with a replica of the famous clock, and with
'Alec' farewelling 'Laura' who is hanging out the train window in a shot
that recalls one of the most famous framings of the film:

LAURA: 'I won't say goodbye.'
ALEC: 'No, don't say goodbye. It sounds so permanent.'
LAURA: 'It's only for a very short time.' [i.e., till next Thursday]

As Alec watches her leave, Rachmaninoff swells on the soundtrack, and
he walks away. He is actually going home, where he opens a pre-cooked
meal of Bird's Eye Beef, with mashed potatoes, peas and Yorkshire
pudding. 'Specially for people who aren't used to being on their own',
as it says on the packet – and as Alec's eye turns to a photo of Laura.

Perhaps the very English meal is the reason for evoking what is often seen as a very English film. The video is in black-and-white, with 'Alec' looking a bit like Trevor Howard, while 'Laura' looks more seriously middle-aged than Celia Johnson.

So, a ready-to-serve meals company obviously felt there was mileage in invoking the old film twenty-five years after its first appearance. Social historian David Kynaston records a commentator, Lynn Barber, as insisting that in a 'worst of times' decade 'the most exciting event of the Fifties ... [was] the advent of the Birds Eye Roast Beef Dinner for One',[8] surely one of the more bizarre settings for the citing of the famous film.

On the page

There are many references to the film, or its title, in novels, in reviews of other films or novels in which the reviewers have found echoes or, indeed, parallels with *Brief Encounter*.

Casual allusions

To give some idea of these eclectic usages, here is a sample of books and articles that draw on the title, whether as a title or as a verbal echo.

In his memoir, actor-director Bryan Forbes wrote of a short film he and a colleague were making in the early days of his career. Called *Saturday Night*, and perhaps never released, it concerned 'a young man who finds himself bored and alone in London, wanders the streets, visits a café and there has a chance meeting with a girl his own age. The teenage brief encounter provides no solution and they part again.'[9]

In Kate Atkinson's *One Good Turn*, she wrote of a character, Martin, whose 'books were set in the Forties, just after the war. It was an era of history Martin felt particularly drawn to, the monochrome deprivation of it, the undertow of seedy disappointment in the wake of heroism. The Vienna of *The Third Man*, the Home Counties of *Brief Encounter*.'[10] In a later book of Atkinson's, *Life After Life*, an actor says, 'Millie was using a funny clipped accent, either trying not to give way to emotion or imagining herself to be a character in a play or film, one who was putting on a stiff upper lip – Celia Johnson in *Brief Encounter* came to mind. The call of duty, the moral imperative of doing the right thing.'[11] This comes from a section of the book set in 1960. Actually, the use of 'stiff upper lip' rather underestimates the emotional complexity of Johnson's Laura: there is more at stake there than just the restraint implied by the cliché.

The psychiatrist obsessed with his wife's death in Sebastian Barry's novel, *The Secret Scripture*, writes in his 'Commonplace Book': 'Every day I feel compelled to go up to her room, often I hurry, as if there is an urgency, like at the end of that old film, *Brief Encounter*. As if, should I delay, she would not be there. As indeed she may not.'[12]

Robert Harris's novel, *The Ghost*, makes passing reference to the film title during an episode in which a bomb has gone off in central London, with people surging up from the Underground. 'A loudspeaker said something about an "incident at Oxford Circus". It sounded like an edgy romantic comedy: *Brief Encounter* meets the War on Terror.'[13]

Australian novelist Steven Carroll in *A World of Other People*, set in late wartime England, writes of 'this meeting, this brief encounter – as the phrase goes – has prompted these speculations' and a little later 'His world has shifted; hers was merely interrupted. She will return to hers; he will not to his. If that brief encounter has done anything, it has done that.'[14] And they go their separate ways as Laura and Alec did.

In her prize-winning novel, *The Dark Circle*, Linda Grant twice makes explicit reference to the film. The first occurs during a post-war meeting between a former serviceman, now an MP, and a woman he hasn't seen for some time and who has now become a television producer. 'She had, he thought, cheekbones like apples that pushed up when she smiled, a Celia Johnson face, not bad-looking, but she brushed men off, she froze them out with her eyes. If it hadn't been for the war, he thought, she would have become one of those unhappily married women who had read everything in the local lending library and drank too much sherry before her husband came home from work.' Much later in the novel, another couple 'had seen *Brief Encounter*. "Why don't you just fuck her?" a voice from the row behind had jeered and the sight of the stolid husband in his armchair had made Miriam snort through her nose.'[15] The latter reference recalls not just the film but also the audience reaction to its earliest screening – and, indeed, Trevor Howard's own insensitive off-screen response to the lovers' hesitations.

In an account of her Italian mother's adaptation to Englishness, novelist Marina Warner wrote: 'In Cairo many people spoke in different tongues, and Ilia was among them. Her Italian receded, though later she began teaching it for A-level: when she went back to Italy for holidays, younger people congratulated her on her perfect command of the language – theirs had moved on. Maybe her delivery had become old-fashioned, the Italian equivalent of Celia Johnson's English in *Brief Encounter*.'[16]

Jane Gardam, in her novel *Faith Fox*, refers to a woman wearing a hat in Fortnum & Mason: 'So sweet the little diamond brooch in the lapel (she loved a diamond). She smiled up at the deadpan waitresses who said to each other, "Isn't she like *Brief Encounter*, and yet she can't be more than, say, thirty-five? "Or *Mrs Miniver*," they said.'[17]

In her recent biography of Anthony Powell, Hilary Spurling twice invokes the film title. First, she records Powell's sparse career in Hollywood as 'a handful of brief encounters'. Later, she writes of Alan Bishop, prototype for Powell's famous egoist Widmerpool, as one 'whose own impact on readers' minds, in his lifetime or afterwards, probably depends on that single brief encounter in 1939 when Tony recognized him as a character waiting to be put back into a book'.[18]

Jane Mills's study of what makes popular film tick, *The Money Shot*, introduces a section of a chapter headed 'Not a Dry Eye in the House' with: 'Have you ever dreamed of taking off for a *Brief Encounter* with that drop-dead gorgeous man you met on the train?' She goes on to write: 'Another form of punishment took the form of being brought to heel, with the husband re-established as lord and master. In *Brief Encounter* the rather plain housewife (played by the exquisitely English Celia Johnson) with a very suburban taste in hats can't hack it in the world of adultery. She decides to stay with terribly tedious hubby, allowing herself only the occasional escapist memory when the BBC symphony orchestra happens to play something as bold as Rachmaninov on the wireless.'[19]

A very recent novel, Dennis Glover's *The Last Man in Europe*, writes of his protagonist's meeting with a bootblack in Spain during the Civil War. 'A gentleman and a bootblack on equal terms! Brothers! In that brief encounter, his understanding of his surroundings suddenly became complete.' It may be said of this reference that the period in which the meeting is set precedes the Lean film (the same may be said of the quoted passage in Steven Carroll's book), but the point is that the two authors concerned were decades later, and it is they who use the phrase, presumably aware of its provenance.[20]

The list of references never seems to run dry. A review in the Melbourne newspaper *The Age* of the British comedy, *Man Up*, wrote of two people who 'meet by chance under the clock at Waterloo Station, which might be a nod in the direction of the wartime British classic *Brief Encounter*'.[21] The critic writing about Thomas Dixon's *Weeping Britannia: Portrait of a Nation in Tears* in the *London Review of Books* drew attention to the way the author 'reminds us of the great tearjerkers of English culture – Sydney Carton's imagined speech from the scaffold, Nurse Cavell's last words, Celia Johnson's return to her husband in *Brief Encounter* – ... enough to start my eyes pricking'.[22] The film is in good company here, even if 'tearjerker' does rather undervalue the emotional

power of the examples quoted. In March 2017, Jane Wheatley wrote
an article about London-based, Sydney-born author and film producer
Robin Dalton. Dalton claimed that her first husband 'had employed
private detectives to follow his young wife and a diary was discovered
in which she described various brief encounters',[23] a reference at a
somewhat indecorous distance from the 1945 film! And in *Prospect
Magazine*, there is a regular interview feature with prominent public
figures, including archbishops and authors, entitled 'Brief encounter'.[24]

Most recently, at the time of writing anyway, the actor Domhnall
Gleeson was interviewed by Kevin Maher about the making of the film
Goodbye Christopher Robin. Maher wrote: 'He [Gleeson] portrays
[A.A.] Milne's emotion as something buried and inaccessible, with only
the slightest facial flickers hinting at limitless pain beneath. "The classic
template for this is *Brief Encounter*," he explains. "Where you're not
trying to express yourself throughout, but when you do, even in a small
way, it breaks your heart."'[25] Again, as in so many of these allusions,
there are implied aspects of so-called British reserve, ideas of duty,
resolve, selflessness, often suggesting that such notions belong essentially
to a conventional middle-class sensibility.

Books

The cover of a theoretical book about what cinema 'means', *The Power
of Movies*, is adorned with two stills of Celia Johnson and Trevor
Howard from the film.[26] The book is not about *Brief Encounter* (or
about any other individual film) but the shots of Johnson's somewhat
anxious expression and Howard's apparently comforting warmth are
evidently held to be adequately suggestive of what the book has in store.

Stephen Bourne's *Brief Encounters* carries the subtitle of *Lesbians
and Gays in British Cinema* and, like several gay authors, Bourne sees
the film as having 'a gay subtext which comes from Coward's own
gay sexuality'.[27] This point of view may well have some credence, and
Emma Rice, author of the 2013 Kneehigh production based on the film,
supported the notion in the Foreword to the print edition, writing that
Coward knew what he was writing about because of the furtiveness
required in being gay in the 1930s.[28] Or as Richard Dyer wrote in his
monograph on the film: 'The subject matter – forbidden love in ordinary
lives – makes an obvious appeal to gay readers, as do fear of discovery
and settling for respectability.'[29] The keyword may be 'subtext', in the
sense that we will never be certain how far Coward saw the challenges
of his sexuality as feeding into either the preceding play, *Still Life*, or to
its film successor. Along with all those comments about how the film

is really most concerned with English 'restraint', the insistence on gay resonance seems to shy away from what seems to me the nub of the film's moral understanding. By this I mean again that exchange quoted in Chapter 2 of this book:

ALEC: 'We know we love each other. That's all that really matters.'
LAURA: 'It's not all that really matters. Other things matter too, self-respect matters, and decency. I can't go on any longer.'

In other words, there is something more basic about the film's emotional and moral charge than either the 'restraint' idea or the gay subtext allow for: that is, the notion that, for people of all persuasions, there is always more at stake than mere self-gratification. The poet William Blake wrote: '*Those who restrain desire do so because theirs is weak enough* to be restrained',[30] but even so great a poet may have missed the notion of restraint's being called into play because of a concern with lives beyond the protagonist's own, because of an unwillingness to cause pain to others.

Past Encounters

This novel by Davina Blake, self-published in 2014, is set for much of its length in Carnforth, or nearby Lancaster, with major inserts in wartime Germany. Around Carnforth Station, along with other posters to do with *Brief Encounter*, are posters depicting the cover of Blake's book.[31]

The novel covers the years from 1939 to the end of the war in 1945, then leaps to 1955. A young woman, Rhoda, works in the Carnforth Station bookshop and falls in love with a teacher, Peter, to whom she becomes engaged before he goes off to the war. While he spends a lot of time as a prisoner of war in Germany, she becomes infatuated with Matthew who has come to Carnforth as part of the unit shooting David Lean's film *Brief Encounter*. The asthmatic Matthew dies just before the end of the war, and Rhoda tries to readjust to the idea of marrying Peter. Ten years later, she discovers that he has been visiting Helen, widow of his wartime buddy, Archie. He has never told Rhoda about these visits and she has never told him about Matthew's: these are the 'past encounters' at the heart of the novel, and each involves an element of lying that recalls Laura's situation when she finds herself lying to her husband Fred in Lean's film.

It recalls the film in so many ways in the telling of this story, in matters large and small. Obviously in terms of the narrative at large, Blake draws on the idea of a relationship, then a marriage, put under strain by an unsought passion (on Rhoda's side) and a secret friendship growing out of wartime stress (on Peter's). But there are innumerable smaller echoes of the film: the insistence on the station clock (so vividly present in the film); Rachmaninoff on the wireless; Patty as Rhoda's yappy friend and Peter and Helen's lunch spoilt by another chatty friend (c.f. Dolly Messiter); the 'Royal Scot' rushing through the station, which, of course, is a major setting in the novel, as it was in the film; Peter, running late to meet Rhoda, takes her to the cinema where *Goodbye Mr Chips*, rather than *Flames of Passion*, is playing; and so on.

But what links the novel to Lean's film is the fact that threading its way through it is the actual filming of *Brief Encounter* in Carnforth. As we know, the night sequences were shot there to avoid the threat of air attacks down south where the lighting necessary for these sequences could have attracted enemy fire. Rhoda takes on extra work in the catering services for the film crew, expressing surprise at food items Londoners have been able to procure in war-straitened 1945. She is fascinated by glimpses of Celia Johnson ('Her big doe eyes were even more striking in reality … She's sort of mesmerising'), by the fake clock the crew has put up with 'hands they can move around', and by the 'flattage' the crew has constructed to represent the exterior of the refreshment room. When she sees the film, she feels that 'The re-creation of the refreshment room at Carnforth was too clean and tidy.' This room was built in the studio at Denham – and, in a case of life imitating art, which in its turn was originally imitating life – the Carnforth rooms in real life were rebuilt to copy the film's version of it.

Knowledgeable as Blake is about the film, it is surprising to find a few 'errors', such as referring to the film's producer Anthony Havelock-Allan as Havelock Ellis. Perhaps the spirit of the famous scholar of human sexual behaviour hangs over many a film, but he did not have a screen credit on *Brief Encounter*. Also, she writes about Trevor Howard as if he were already a box-office idol whom the girls in the canteen would be mad about, whereas he was scarcely known at the time, having made only two very small prior film appearances – and even less likely is Rhoda's saying: 'Now Dirk Bogarde, I wouldn't mind serving him the tea.' Apart from an uncredited teenage appearance in *Come On George!* in 1939, he appeared in no feature until 1947. Perhaps these details are of no consequence to Blake's readers, and in fact the book's overall quality is of no real relevance here, where what does matter is simply that she provides another – and extended – example of the way *Brief Encounter* continues to infiltrate the wider society, in this case almost seventy years later.

By contrast, Julian Clary's *Briefs Encountered* merely draws on the famous title for his often amusing, bawdy novel that purports to make its readers privy to Noël Coward's love life as conducted in an old Kent manor house, called Goldenhurst. The novel moves between the present and the days of Coward's supremacy in the 1920s and 1930s. It is mildly entertaining in its dealings with gay relationships but is of no consequence here except in its smartly suggestive variant on the old title.

Other snippets

Brief Encounter crops up in conversation early in Jonathan Teplitzky's 2013 film, *The Railway Man*. A traumatised Second World War soldier, Eric (Colin Firth), jumps on the Manchester–Edinburgh line train and takes a seat opposite an attractive young woman, Patti (Nicole Kidman), who begins to talk to him. He gives information about railway stations they pass through – Warrington, Lancaster and so on – indicating Carnforth in the distance. 'That's Carnforth where they filmed *Brief Encounter*, but you're too young to know about that.' Her reply is: 'My aunt went to see it with a couple of girlfriends', recalling that, whenever Celia Johnson (Eric has filled in the name) got tearful, a sailor in the audience would call out, 'Come on Trevor! Give 'er one!' This snatch of conversation again reminds one of David Lean's own recollections of the film's first screening in Rochester.

'Visiting Rocky', an episode of *As Time Goes By*,[32] opens with Jean Pargetter (Judi Dench) and Lionel Hardcastle (Geoffrey Palmer) rowing on a lake. Or rather, Lionel is doing the rowing and doing it rather incompetently as Trevor Howard did, eliciting from Jean: 'You're not very good at this are you?' – inevitably recalling Celia Johnson's (somewhat less acerbically rendered) 'You don't row very well do you?' Whereas Howard accepts Johnson's appraisal with a laugh, Lionel insists that they are not changing places – and the boat has to be towed in. A day or so later, Jean and Lionel are on their way to visit his father, Rocky, in Hampshire. They stop for tea on their way – it is served in plastic cups with ditto spoons – and Jean, a little nervous of meeting Rocky, stands for this exchange:

JEAN: 'Shall we go?'
LIONEL: 'What about your tea?'
JEAN: 'I gulped it.'
LIONEL: 'Lucky Celia Johnson and Trevor Howard didn't meet in a buffet like this. Their brief encounter wouldn't have lasted five minutes.'

One of the more bizarre references to the film occurs in the comic the *Beano*, in which a televiewing woman and child are watching onscreen a man dancing on a railway platform. He goes on to say: 'The theme of this performance is *Brief Encounter*, a 1945 film about two people who fall in love waiting for a train.' The family dog is asleep, the child lying upside down on the couch says: 'Urgh! I must give that a watch … Not!', while the woman (grandmother?) wipes her eyes as she contributes: 'It's a classic.'[33] Will this encourage a new generation to seek out the source of the reference? I wonder, too, how many generations were expected to be able to answer this quiz question in *The Times* Daily Quiz, 18 October 2017: 'Q 4. Dr Alec Harvey and Laura Jesson fall in love in which 1945 film?'[34]

In Emily Barr's novel *The Sleeper* (2013), she tells the story of two strangers meeting on an overnight train with dramatic consequences. And in an article she wrote about films that significantly feature trains, she describes *Brief Encounter* as 'my favourite film', citing it as 'a big part of the inspiration behind *The Sleeper*'.[35] Accounting for the film's appeal, she goes on to say: 'Celia Johnson and Trevor Howard portray the couple as good people, simply swept up in a romance beyond their control. While the dialogue is clipped and twee, the trains rushing dramatically through tunnels, and the Rachmaninov soundtrack, leave the viewer in no doubt as to the wild passion that is boiling beneath.' I may quibble with the use of 'twee' in relation to the dialogue, but otherwise Barr's account calls up much of the film's ongoing appeal.

As well, it is surprising how often the term appears in reviews of other films and novels. For instance, two recent reviews of John Banville's novel, *Mrs Osmond* (derived from Henry James's *The Portrait of a Lady*), invoke it: the *Financial Review*'s contains the phrase 'brief encounters' in its heading;[36] and Brenda Niall, in the *Australian Book Review*, wrote how Isabel Osmond 'relives her past in a series of brief encounters'.[37] In an online reappraisal of Elizabeth Bowen's *The Heat of the Day* (1948) can be found the following: 'Bowen's attempt to widen the scope beyond the middle classes she's most comfortable with. A lot of it ends up reminding me of the railway and station tea-room workers in *Brief Encounter* (1945). The scene in which Connie is first introduced, with her groceries bouncing down the stairs is broad comedy, and at first I took it to be no more than comic relief while the posh characters get on with the important stuff.'[38]

And so the never-ending list goes on. In 1984, an Australian book of amusing satirical sketches by columnist Ron Saw and illustrated by artist Donald Friend was simply titled *Brief Encounters*.[39] The *Australian* newspaper, headlined a review of a popular TV comedy: 'Brief encounter with fresh comedy: Pick of the day: Almost Midnight, Goober, Lost in Pronunciation, Streaming on ABC iView.'[40] An online article reflecting on the film *Toni Erdmann* was titled 'Brief Encounters: The pleasures of being lost in translation'[41] and goes on to describe '*Toni Erdmann* as a comedy about these encounters: the fleeting, ephemeral moments that spring from the messy ether of life, and dissolve before we even recognize them as memorable'. The heading 'Brief Encounters' appears below the regular 'On Television' pages in an edition of the *New Yorker* in which Emily Nussbaum reviews the series *The Night Manager* and others, with no apparent special reason to use the title and making no reference to the film.[42] To end this eclectic selection of pieces highlighting the 1945 film's name, even if that's the extent of the articles' concerns, an editor gave the following title to an essay of mine on the incidence of British film in Australian cinemas: 'Brief encounters: British cinema in Australia'.[43] Historically, it belonged to the period when 'a good British film' was a popular alternative to all-conquering Hollywood – and perhaps less demanding than the rarer foreign-language movies. In capital cities there were cinemas devoted to the screening of British films, often regarded as 'more natural' than their Hollywood counterparts: many of these are now long-forgotten, but as to *Brief Encounter*, both the title and what it evokes remain across a surprisingly wide-ranging demographic.

At the time of writing, this last – and one of the most unusual – reference to the film came to me. 'Two Australian academics[44] are researching the idea that the character of Alec Harvey was based on a real doctor at the London School of Hygiene and Tropical Medicine. The field of social medicine and epidemiology (recognising disease patterns in populations) was coming into prominence in the 1930s. Alec is a character who loves his work. When he first talks about his work is when Laura first falls in love with him. The academic pair's search is for the man who inspired Coward, reckoning he possibly once heard a similar speech across a dinner table in Bloomsbury.'[45] If medical researchers are now inspired by an aspect of *Brief Encounter*, one begins to wonder if there is any field that is wholly immune to its influence!

Notes

1 G.E. Refrigerators Commercial with Mike Nichols & Elaine May, 1958. www.youtube.com/watch?v=ZPGHQYutitY. Accessed 12 March 2019.

2 See www.patricktan.com.au/component/k2/item/64-brief-encounter.html?Itemid=135&check_fullwidth=yes. Accessed 11 November 2017.

3 Interview with author, November 2017.

4 Author interview with Renee Glynne.

5 See www.youtube.com/watch?v=8gfTUgFzP1M. Accessed 29 January 2018.

6 This information came by email from Keith Brymer Jones, 10 November 2017.

7 See www.youtube.com/watch?v=fABzM0lPhsM. Accessed 12 March 2019.

8 David Kynaston, *Family Britain 1951–57*, London: Bloomsbury, 2001, p. 530.

9 Bryan Forbes, *Notes for a Life*, London: Collins, 1974, p. 179.

10 Kate Atkinson, *One Good Turn*, London: Transworld Publishers (2006), republished 2011, pp. 24–25.

11 Kate Atkinson, *Life After Life*, London: Doubleday, 2016, p. 293.

12 Sebastian Barry, *The Secret Scripture*, London: Faber & Faber, 2008, p. 191.

13 Robert Harris, *The Ghost Writer*, London: Arrow Books 2008, Film tie-in edition, 2010, p. 12.

14 Steven Carroll, *A World of Other People*, Sydney: Harper Collins, 2013, pp. 82, 86.

15 Linda Grant, *The Dark Circle*, London: Virago, 2016, pp. 75, 174.

16 'Those Brogues: Marina Warner on her Parents and Other Travellers', in the *London Review of Books*, Vol. 38 No. 19, 6 October 2016, p. 29.

17 Jane Gardam, *Faith Fox – A Nativity*, London: Sinclair-Stevenson, 1996, p. 8.

18 Hilary Spurling, *Anthony Powell: Dancing to the Music of Time*, London: Hamish Hamilton, 2017, pp. 216, 372.

19 Jane Mills, *The Money Shot: Cinema, Sin and Censorship*, Annandale, NSW: Pluto Press, 2001, p. 189.

20 Dennis Glover, *The Last Man in Europe*, Melbourne: Black Inc, 2017, p. 45.

21 Paul Byrne, 'Friends but Few Benefits as Rom-com Pairing Fails to Gel', *The Age*, 5 November 2015, p. 21.

22 Ferdinand Mount, 'Lachrymatics', *London Review of Books*, 17 December 2015, p. 31.

23 Jane Wheatley, 'Robin Dalton', *The Age: Good Weekend*, 4 March 2017, p. 7.

24 See prospectmagazine.co.uk. Accessed 20 August 2018.

25 Kevin Maher, '"The Truth is Worth Telling" – How I Discovered the Real AA Milne', *The Times*, 26 September 2017, p. 8.

26 Colin McGinn, *The Power of Movies: How Screen and Mind Interact*, New York: Vintage Books, 2005. Cover design by Brian Barth.

27 Stephen Bourne, *Brief Encounters: Lesbians and Gays in British Cinema*, London: Cassell, 1996, p. 77.

28 Emma Rice, *Noël Coward's Brief Encounter*, London: Bloomsbury, 2013, p. 1.

29 Richard Dyer, *Brief Encounter*, London: BFI Publishing, 1993, p. 11.

30 From William Blake's 'The Marriage of Heaven and Hell: The Voice of the Devil'.

31 Davina Blake, *Past Encounters*, Self-published, 2014.

32 *As Time Goes By*, Series 2, Episode 3, aired 24 January 1993.

33 The *Beano*, 30 September 2017.

34 *The Times* 18 October 2017: The Times Daily Quiz (by Olav Bjortomt), p. 16 (*Times 2*. Q 4).

35 Emily Barr, 'Trains Just Got Cool', *Cosmopolitan*, 4 July 2013.

36 'John Banville, *Mrs Osmond – Brief Encounters*', *Financial Times*, September 2017.
37 Brenda Niall, 'No closure for Isabel: *Mrs Osmond*', *Australian Book Review*, January–February 2018, p. 25.
38 https://wecanreaditforyouwholesale.com/1946–1989/the-heat-of-the-day-eliza beth-bowen/, 5 July 2013. Accessed 12 March 2019.
39 Ron Saw, *Brief Encounters*, Cammeray, New South Wales: Richard Griffin, 1984.
40 Justin Burke, *Australian*, 5 January 2017.
41 Article by John Semley, www.salon.com/2017/02/12/brief-encounters-the-pleasures-of-being-lost-in-translation/?source=newsletter. Accessed 12 February 2017.
42 Emily Nussbaum, *New Yorker*, 30 May 2016, p. 78.
43 Brian McFarlane, 'Brief Encounters: British Cinema in Australia', *Island*, Issue 60–61, Spring/Summer 1994, pp. 60–64.
44 Professor Alan Shiell, LaTrobe University and Professor Penny Hawe, University of Sydney.
45 Information sent by email from Penny Hawe, 11 January 2018.

9

What is it about railway stations?

Trains can give the promise of new scenes as well as a return to old ones. They are dominated by timetables and departures and a curious sense of an individual's being sealed off from the outside world. They can promise new experiences; or rigidly timed daily journeys, as Fred reminds Laura when she expresses doubts about Bobby's joining the navy and thus rarely seeing him. Fred's comic reply is: 'All right old girl. We'll put him in an office and you can see him off on the 8.50 every morning.' Fred, of course, has no idea of how disruptive trains and stations have been for Laura.

The idea of the railway *station* as a place of meetings and departures has figured in many of the films referred to in this book, especially in Chapter 6. More so than airports or bus stops, railway stations allow close-ups of those meetings and, especially, departures, after which there is a curious sense of desolation when the person farewelling is left on the empty platform. As Raymond Durgnat wrote of railway stations: 'From the platform the rails stretch away. Even when the terminal is a bustle of arrivals and departures, the mood is one of routine, separateness, greyness. Hence they recall the renunciation of passion: Lean's *Brief Encounter*, de Sica's *Indiscretion*.'[1] Or perhaps, now, they carry with them a nostalgic charge that the other sites of coming and going don't: they've been around so long and they are apt to have architectural and catering associations that recall days long gone.

I want to draw attention here to four stations (there may well be more) for their varying connections with *Brief Encounter*. As Jeffrey Richards wrote: 'The poignancy of Alec and Laura's situation is enhanced by the station setting, in particular the prosaic buffet, with its polished tea urns, Bath buns under glass domes, and coal-fired stove ... The express racing through is their passion. She plans to throw herself under it but pulls back to resume her life. The stopping trains going in opposite directions, taking her to Ketchworth and him to Churley, represent the humdrum reality of their normal lives.'[2]

Four stations

Langwatby

The station, which was opened in 1876 and now services the village of Langwatby in Cumbria, is no longer staffed, train tickets having to be purchased in advance. However, the station building has now been converted into the 'Brief Encounter Tea Rooms' and an antique shop, while a shelter has been built for passengers awaiting trains.[3]

Reading

In 2015, to mark the 175th anniversary of Reading's railway station, the Museum of Reading announced plans for a year-long programme of research into the past, present and future of the railways in Reading, culminating in an exhibition set to open in 2016. Museum manager, Matthew Williams, explained: 'The new station with its European style architecture gives a real glimpse of the future but the railway has long been at the heart of Reading's life and livelihood. It's a place of goodbyes and hellos, lost luggage, missed connections [could there be a touch of irony here?] and brief encounters.'[4] Now, it is just that last phrase that is of any consequence here, but two other stations need to be noticed for more substantial reasons.

Wymondham

The Wymondham Station Bistro was known until 2011 as the '*Brief Encounter* Refreshment Rooms', and a placard announcing this is still to be found on the platform. The former owner, David Turner, had done a lot of house-building and restoring. He struck a deal with British Railways in the late 1980s and refurbished the former tea rooms in the style of those in *Brief Encounter* and, under the name of the film, the restaurant was opened by actor Bill Pertwee in 1989. He gave it this name because he'd copied it from the film, with railway carriage seats for the restaurant. He'd also met Joyce Carey (Myrtle Bagot in the film) and, with such contacts, he generated publicity for the whole venture. He recalled that the site was often visited by actors (including Dora Bryan), and attracted the attention of Michael Portillo for his *Great British Railways* television series. In 2000, there was a celebration of the first ten years of the renovated site, attracting about 1500 visitors, including Margaret Barton – the last surviving credited cast member of the film – and with the express to Edinburgh running through from King's Cross

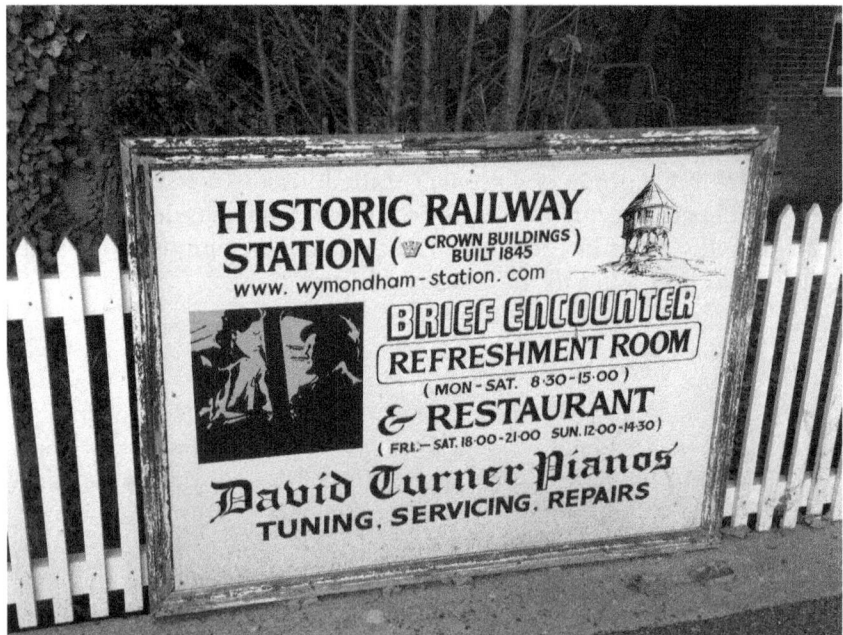

17 A sign advertising the 'Brief Encounter Refreshment Room' at Wymondham Station, Norfolk

to Norwich.[5] This occasion was recorded on *Anglia News*, in which Ms Barton was seen – echoing Beryl – serving tea to customers.[6]

Turner retired in 2011 and the restaurant name was changed, but it is still possible to have lunch in the 'Brief Encounter Room', where one sits on seats modelled on a railway carriage in a room decked out with photos of trains of various periods and the odd shot of the film.

Carnforth

This, of course, is the 'real thing' in the sense that it is here, as reported earlier, that the night scenes of *Brief Encounter* were shot, in February 1945, to avoid the danger of bombing that the required lighting might have attracted down south. Carnforth Station has since become a tourist attraction for those interested in the film. When I visited the station, the actual platform on which the Scottish express train hurtled through was not in use because of repairs. In any case, a fence had been erected along the edge of the platform. The tea rooms were not used in the film but recreated at Denham Studios; since then, the original refreshment centre has been redesigned to replicate the studio set, the former marble counter now replaced by wood, and the large water and coffee urns are now in place as they were in the film. Kyle Burford, who works the tea room with his sister Rhian, told me how a sign giving information about a Leeds train appears wrongly in the film – it belonged to Carnforth but was *not* right for Milford Junction. Also, he told how the famous station clock (built in the early nineteenth century by Joyce of Whitchurch)[7] was scrapped after the filming, but, when word came of its being in London, a local man long associated with the railway, Jim Walker, reassembled all the parts and subsequently maintained the clock. A wooden pendulum needed much care. For the filming, a canvas clock-face was used to avoid having a 24-hour wait for successive takes of the same episode. Knowledge of such detail indicates how central the film is to the town's tourist trade. There is even a poem about how the clock was manipulated with moveable hands:

Then the film crew came along
And muzzled it, fitting it out with hands
They could twirl at will, making it blind
As a lover and giving the lie to time.

Only after the lovers parted forever
And the camera shot the engine's final
Mushroom-cloud blast, could the clock
Be unmasked and time returned to itself.

A copy of the poem is now to be found on one of the station's walls. That phrase – 'giving the lie to time' – could almost be read as a comment on how film goes about its dealings with the realities of time.

There's also a 'heritage centre' dealing with aspects of the film which screens continuously from 10am to 4pm every day, with comfortable seats for viewers and a shop from which I bought a few artefacts that are illustrated in this book. These include numerous postcards, drinks coasters bearing the film's poster (larger versions of which are to be found around the station, on the platforms, in subways and in the various rooms devoted to the film and David Lean), cylindrical biscuit tins similarly decorated, fridge magnets and elegant boxes of chocolates, fudge, etc. each with a famous shot from the film on its lid.

Scattered around are many shots from the film, a replica of a train door through the window of which addicts can have their photos taken, and heaps of luggage of the kinds belonging to the film's period. During my visit on a Monday morning, visitors/tourists kept winding their way through the centre, and several settled in to watch the film.

As well as all the aforementioned visual reminders of the film, there

10 The Carnforth Station clock

were a number of posters with verbal information about matters relating to it, including some useful ones about the film's locations. From one of these I discovered that the daytime street scenes were actually shot in Beaconsfield, Buckinghamshire – where the 'Five Ways Café' became the exterior for the film's Kardomah Café – and that the interior scenes of the cinema attended by Alec and Laura were shot on the balcony of the Metropole, Victoria.

19 A display about the film at Carnforth Station, Lancashire

The amount of information available at Carnforth, valuable as it is in itself, is a really significant indicator of the way the film has retained its drawing power over the seven decades since it first appeared. There is indeed a booklet called *A Brief Encounter with Carnforth Station*, and the station was brought to still wider attention in an episode of

20 *Brief Encounter*-themed memorabilia on sale at the Carnforth gift shop

Great British Railway Journeys. In Series 7, Episode 2, 'Windermere to Carnforth', Michael Portillo continued his journey through the Lake District, visiting the homes of Beatrix Potter and John Ruskin on the way, and finishing his journey with what is described as 'a brief

21 The author's grandson poses behind the replica train door at Carnforth Station, Lancashire

encounter on Carnforth Station'.[8] The episode is currently unavailable for re-viewing online, but part of its interest was, as I recall, in Portillo's conversations with tourists who had come to the station because of its association with *Brief Encounter*.

In 2016, the BFI posted a short film online (5.50 minutes) entitled 'Could You Really Say Goodbye? *Brief Encounter*'s Carnforth' in which Heritage Centre manager John Adams discusses how the film is shown continuously to visitors on nine rather luxurious chairs that came from the Winter Gardens in Morecambe. He also draws attention to the David Lean exhibition, which had the support of the Lean Estate and the BFI. The owner of the refreshment room, Andrew Coates, recalls the setting up of the room thirty years earlier when he'd been a little worried that the *Brief Encounter* connection might fade and customers decline. So far, he says, this is not a worry, with visitors across a wide age spectrum, and including university students who know the film from their courses, maintaining a steady stream of clients.[9]

A documentary on *Brief Encounter* made as part of The Carlton Film Collection opens on the railway farewell ('Forgive me … etc.'), and involves interviews with Ronald Neame, Anthony Havelock-Allan, Margaret Barton, Sheridan Morley, Lucy Fleming and John Sessions. The final credits include: 'Thanks to the Friends of Carnforth Station'.[10] Anyone interested in the film might well become a 'friend' of Carnforth Station, grateful for the material it preserves for cinema archaeologists.

Notes

1 Raymond Durgnat, *Films & Feelings*, London: Faber and Faber, 1967, p. 232.

2 Jeffrey Richards and John M. Mackenzie, *The Railway Station's Social History*, Oxford: Oxford University Press, 1986, p. 362.

3 www.tripadvisor.com.au/Restaurant_Review-g2331291-d2470563-Reviews-Brief_Encounter_Coffee_Shop_Restaurant-Langwathby_Eden_District_Lake_District_Cu.html. Accessed 24 August 2018.

4 'Reading Station: 175 years to be marked by a museum exhibition', by Linda Fort, in GetReading, 27 March 2015. www.getreading.co.uk/news/local-news/reading-station-175-years-marked-8928946. Accessed 18 August 2018.

5 Information provided from Lisa Groom, current staff member at Wymondham Station Bistro, 15 October 2017, and interview with David Turner, 18 October 2017.

6 The DVD kindly given to me is undated. The reporter commenting on the occasion was called Malcolm Robertson.

7 See *A Brief Encounter with Carnforth Station*, brochure published by I.D. Promotions, p. 5.

8 Viewed on Australian television channel SBS, 2 March 2017. First aired in the UK in January 2016.

9 'Could You Really Say Goodbye? *Brief Encounter*'s Carnforth, BFI, posted 15 February 2016.

10 The Carlton Film Collection, 2000. Screened on Australian television, Foxtel channel 133, on 19 September 2016.

Conclusion: *Brief Encounter* in the twenty-first century

There seems to be no sign of a slowing down in references to the 1945 classic. Not merely those allusions in other people's fictions across a media range, but in the ongoing discussion that can be found in newspapers and other journals, discussion that over seventy years after the film's first appearance still finds it worth attention. Other films come and go – 'franchises' such as *Star Wars* or *Harry Potter* – and they give rise to sequels, become household names, especially with younger filmgoers – but none seems quite to outdo *Brief Encounter* in the sheer eclecticism of its surfacing in so many diverse cultural circumstances or in its seeming to 'speak' to succeeding generations. Less reliant on star power or obvious genre affiliations, it has now long outlasted Coward's original play, or such other films derived from his plays, including *Private Lives* (1931), *This Happy Breed* (1944), *Blithe Spirit* (1945) or *Relative Values* (2000). The film clearly touched on matters of human significance in such ways as account for the longevity of its place in the culture.

What, then, is it about this black-and-white film of seventy years ago that has given it such a life? What are the kinds of values it enshrines and how have these been rendered in films and TV productions made in such different eras and for such different audiences? It is one thing to insist on the timelessness of its central moral view – that there is more to life than the satisfying of desire, whatever the changing mores – but this alone would not be sufficient to account for the film's amazing afterlife. Being morally unimpeachable doesn't necessarily ensure the making of a great film. What also, and obviously, matters is that its moral conflicts are incarnated in remarkable performances that grow out of actors so perceptively understanding what they are rendering, what they are making of a major director working on a screenplay that gives them that scope, and on the contributions of other collaborators such as the cinematographer and music director.

By coincidence, the day after I had written the above paragraph, I had an email from Celia Johnson's daughter, Lucy Fleming, making virtually the same point. I'd asked her what she thought was the explanation for the film's long life, and she replied:

> Your question is … one I get asked a lot. I am not sure I know the answer. I would say firstly that the film is good and has become a classic because it has a truth in the playing, a script that is beautifully written and a skill in the photography, design and editing that work together in a very special way. Noel, David and Ronnie Neame [producer] were at the top of their game and it all gelled to make a memorable film. Trevor Howard and Celia were well cast and both played their characters beautifully and with a clarity and simpleness that worked so well. Much of the film shows Coward's skill in writing lines that say one thing and emotions that say another. I think your thought about the morality of the film is quite right and so very different from today. It tells the story of a time and values that have now disappeared.[1]

As to Lucy's last sentence, I'd agree that the values may well have changed but suggest that the central truth that I characterise above as: 'there is more to life than the satisfying of desire' will always be important, however much or little it guides us at any given time. It is not, then, just a matter of nostalgia for that 'time and [its] values', but of something more basic about human life, motivation and behaviour; about contradictory impulses.

As mentioned in the Introduction, I was always impressed by how moved my university students were by a film made at least twenty years before they were born. Certainly, they still enjoyed the comedy: this can seem slightly patronising, but it can also make a case for a less-restrained approach to human relations as it offers a lower-orders parallel to the pain of Alec and Laura's affair. And, one might add, the contrast intensifies the poignancy of the situation in which the protagonists have found themselves.

Not many films as old as *Brief Encounter* – or, indeed, even much younger – keep turning up for comment in a variety of publications. Of course, it is forever being written about in books exploring aspects of British cinema: some of these are essentially academic in their preoccupations, such as Ken Puckett's *War Pictures* (1917), discussed in Chapter 2, and some – like my own *Twenty British Films: A Guided Tour* (2015) – are intended for a more general readership, to give two recent such books. An interesting title directed towards a more broadly cultural examination, Alison Light's *Forever England: Femininity, Literature and Conservatism between the Wars*, reminds us in its Afterword of the place the film holds in a changing society. Light writes of Laura as 'the last of the wartime heroines', going on to say: 'With its sympathy for middle age and affectionate scenes of home comforts, the film is as much an infatuation with a fading image of national life as it is an exposure of its stifling conformity.'[2] In relation to such notions, the film has acquired further status as a sort of historical document of its times.

It is, of course, not surprising to find the film included in books with titles such as *The Great British Films*,[3] but it is perhaps more unusual to come across articles recalling it in the daily press. Margaret Barton, Beryl in the film and 91 at the time of writing, has been and still is in steady demand for talks to various groups and television interviews and newspaper articles. One of the latter was titled: 'Last surviving cast member of *Brief Encounter* on the film's enduring appeal', and in it she described how she came to be cast – Lean and Coward having seen her in several London plays during the war – and how she came to value Celia Johnson: 'There was something that captured you when you saw Celia close up.'[4] A few months later, in 2016, she was interviewed for BBC News on the occasion of her 90th birthday, and this was reported in an article headed '*Brief Encounter*'s Margaret Barton: "I was never a film star"'. In the report of the interview, she comments on the pleasures of working with David Lean who 'would ask me on the set sometimes, even when I wasn't needed, to come and watch from behind the camera … He wanted me to see the two main characters working their scenes.'[5] Because the refreshment room's interior was built on a set at Denham Studios, she didn't need to go to Carnforth, though she is photographed decades later at Carnforth's Heritage Centre.

Another actress who would later work with Celia Johnson in the 1971 BBC production of *The Cherry Orchard*, Gemma Jones, reported in the *Daily Telegraph* in 2011 how 'every time it [*Brief Encounter*] comes on TV, I feel I mustn't watch it again, but I always end up getting hooked and watching it all the way through'. She goes on to express her delight in working with Johnson, who she felt had 'an innocent quality about her'.[6]

In 2015, an article in the *Guardian* headed '*Brief Encounter*: Is It Still Relevant at 70?' found its author, John Patterson, in a state of complete reversal about the film.[7] The piece began with: 'For most of my life I have utterly scorned *Brief Encounter*. I hated its emotional constipation, its plummily accented, almost-adulterous middle-class lead characters … and their exasperating inability to throw caution to the wind, bite the bullet, and just get it on.' While he has retained his dislike of Lean's 'epics of the 1960s', he has so completely changed his mind about *Brief Encounter* to write: 'now I admire it beyond measure', finding that its 'displaced hysteria' in matters like the movie trailer for 'Flames of Passion' or the Rachmaninoff make the film 'a rollercoaster of social and emotional horrors'. He now quite sees why it led Robert Altman to become a director and 'For that alone, it deserves our gratitude.'

Four days later in the same year, *The Times* listed *Brief Encounter* as the 'Classic film of the week' to mark its 70th anniversary, and drew attention to the way Todd Haynes's *Carol* (discussed in Chapter 6) offers a parallel structural element in its opening and ending scenes to the old film's tea room in two similarly set episodes.[8] Still later, in 2015, another article, by Michael Newton, appeared in the *Guardian* with the headline: 'Loved But Not Lost: David Lean's *Brief Encounter* and *Dr Zhivago*'.[9] He cites these as 'surely two of the greatest love stories committed to film', and, though some, myself included, find the latter guilty of dawdling pictorialism, Newton made some interesting comparisons between the two. He argues: 'Both films demonstrate the impossibility of an illicit love finding a place in the world. In *Brief Encounter*, social convention and decency prevent it ... [whereas] In *Doctor Zhivago*, it is history and the political realm that prove to be love's enemy.' A little later, in paying tribute to Celia Johnson, he writes: 'Her voice softly breathes diffident desire: here, emotion lies in the experience of its suppression.'

Are there many other films whose 70th birthday has given rise to such speculation? Probably not, but then are there any others whose entrenched place in the business of everyday living keeps manifesting itself in so many diverse ways? This is not to undervalue the place of such titles as, say, *Casablanca* or *Gone with the Wind* in the collective memory, but simply to note the ways in which Lean's film, whether just the title or other aspects of its texture, makes such repeated appearances in the life of the times since 1945.

Three last – somewhat contrasting – accounts of the film appeared in the popular press in recent years. Or rather, two are contrasted with the third, a piece in the *Daily Mail* which sported the heading: 'The Truth About *Brief Encounter*: SHE Had No Teeth – And HE Was a Psychopath!' Well, that's a provocative start to another article published in the wake of the film's 70th birthday. In the not unusual way, it describes the film as 'a tale of forbidden love and doing the right thing in an era of British stiff upper lips and high moral standards', and is actually one of the few accounts that ventures to add that 'it struck a chord with many who were struggling with their consciences over an illicit wartime romance'.[10] While comparing Celia Johnson with the character of Laura, the writer, Marty Greene, goes on to undermine any idea of the actress as a glamorous movie star, telling us that 'Celia wore thick-lensed spectacles and false front teeth', having knocked out her own in a teenage swimming accident. But that, unnecessary as it may seem,

22 Celia Johnson gazes out of the train window

is nothing to what Greene tells us about Trevor Howard's 'lifetime of heavy drinking' and 'reinventing himself as a war hero'. Those who have read his biography[11] may well have caught a whiff of the roistering side of the actor, but Greene's revelations about War Office records claiming 'he had a psychopathic personality and was considered unfit for military service' don't really add much to our understanding of the film. They may, however, increase respect for his performance as Alec in a film whose moral constraints he apparently never really grasped!

The other two articles offered very different headlines. Noted British-born, American-based film critic and historian, David Thomson's, piece in the *Guardian* is simply titled: '*Brief Encounter*: The Best Romantic Film of All Time'.[12] This precedes a convincing account of what has helped it to endure in spite of a changing world, settling finally for Celia Johnson with: 'it is largely due to her that the film is still so moving … Her voice is measured but the eyes are desperate. That she holds the film together is beyond doubt.' The article in the *Daily Telegraph* is an echo of Thomson: '*Brief Encounter* is Named "Most Romantic Film" of All Time',[13] with the author announcing the results of a vote by a panel of actors, directors and critics.

As late as 2017, *Time Out* magazine also found it in No. 1 place in a poll seeking out the '100 best romantic movies', and as with several other such polls it found *Casablanca* in second place. Could it be that it is the sheer ordinariness of the lives of Alec and Laura that gives *Brief Encounter* the edge in these surveys? One might expect high-minded renunciations by such glittering stars as Bogart and Bergman, but in that much repeated, nay, even 'iconic' image of Johnson leaning out of the train window to say goodbye to Howard, it may be that we can all more easily imagine ourselves behaving as they do. Perhaps, as Hayley Mills suggests, it comes down to this: 'you see two conventional, married middle-class people fall madly in love with each other … And you know it can't be, they're too nice, too decent, they have to do the right thing. And you wonder, would I do the right thing?'[14] Is it, then, not just a matter of recognising a kind of truth in what we've been watching but as well then relating it to ourselves? It would be good, if unlikely, to be around for the film's centenary: it will probably, at core, still be relevant and painful in what it suggests about human lives.

Notes

1 Email from Lucy Fleming, 1 February 2018.
2 Alison Light, *Forever England: Femininity, Literature and Conservatism between the Wars*, London: Routledge, 1991, pp. 208, 209.
3 Jerry Vermilye, *The Great British Films*, Secaucus, New Jersey: Citadel Press, 1978.
4 Darren Slade, *Northern Echo*, 7 February 2016.
5 Reported by Tim Masters, Entertainment and Arts, 27 May 2016.
6 'Gemma Jones interview with David Gritten', *Daily Telegraph*, 28 April 2011.
7 John Patterson, *Guardian*, 2 November 2015.
8 Kate Muir, 'Classic film of the week: *Brief Encounter* (1945), *The Times*, 8 November 2015.
9 Michael Newton, *Guardian*, 14 November 2015.
10 Marty Greene, *Daily Mail*, 11 December 2015.
11 Vivienne Knight, *Trevor Howard: A Gentleman and a Player, The Authorised Biography*, London: Sphere Books Ltd, 1986.
12 David Thomson, *Guardian*, 16 October 2010.
13 Hannah Furness, *Daily Telegraph*, 23 April 2013.
14 Hayley Mills, email, 23 August 2018.

Cast and credits, *Brief Encounter* (1945)

Cast

Laura Jesson (Celia Johnson), Dr Alec Harvey (Trevor Howard), Albert Godby (Stanley Holloway), Myrtle Bagot (Joyce Carey), Fred Jesson (Cyril Raymond), Dolly Messiter (Everley Gregg), Mary Norton (Marjorie Mars), Beryl Waters (Margaret Barton), Stanley (Dennis Harkin), Stephen Lynn (Valentine Dyall), Mrs Rolandson (Nuna Davey), Organist (Irene Handl), Bill (Edward Hodge), Johnnie (Sydney Bromley), Waitress (Avis Scott), Policeman (Wilfred Babbage), Margaret Jesson (Henrietta Vincent), Bobbie Jesson (Richard Thomas), Clergyman (George V. Sheldon), Doctor (Wally Bosco), Boatman (Jack May).

Credits

Production company: A Noël Coward-Cineguild Production

Producer: Noël Coward

In charge of production: Anthony Havelock-Allan, Ronald Neame

Production manager: Ernest J. Holding (assistant Renee Glynne, uncredited)

Director: David Lean

Screenplay: Noël Coward, David Lean, Anthony Havelock-Allan

Cinematography: Robert Krasker

Editor: Jack Harris

Art direction: L.P. Williams

Music: Rachmaninoff Piano Concerto No. 2, played by Eileen Joyce, with the National Symphony Orchestra, conducted by Muir Matieson

Sound editor: Harry Miller

Select bibliography

Blake, Davina, *Past Encounters* (Self-published, 2014).

Bourne, Stephen, *Brief Encounters: Lesbians and Gays in British Cinema 1930–1971* (London: Cassell, 1996).

Brief Encounter With Carnforth Station (Designed and published by I.D. Promotions, n.d.).

Brownlow, Kevin, *David Lean* (London: Richard Cohen Books, 1996).

Clary, Julian, *Briefs Encountered* (London: Ebury Press, 2012).

Coward, Noël, *Still Life* (1936), in *Play Parade: Vol. 1V* (London: William Heinemann, 1954).

Coward, Noël, *Brief Encounter* (1974; reprinted London: Faber and Faber, 1990).

Dawkins, Richard, *The Selfish Gene* (Oxford: Oxford University Press, 2006).

Drazin, Charles, *The Finest Years: British Cinema of the 1940s* (London: André Deutsch Ltd, 1998).

Durgnat, Raymond, *Films & Feelings* (London: Faber and Faber, 1967).

Dyer, Richard, *Brief Encounter* (London: BFI Publishing, 1993).

Fleming, Kate, *Celia Johnson: A Biography* (London: Orion Books, 1991).

Knight, Vivienne, *Trevor Howard: A Gentleman and a Player* (1986; reprinted London: Sphere Books Ltd, 1988).

McFarlane, Brian, *An Autobiography of British Cinema* (London, Methuen/BFI Publishing, 1997).

McFarlane, Brian, *Twenty British Films: A Guided Tour* (Manchester: Manchester University Press, 2015).

McFarlane, Brian, 'The *Brief Encounter* That Goes On and On ...', *Inside Story*, 3 May 2016.

Murphy, Robert, *Realism and Tinsel: Cinema and Society in Britain 1939–48* (London: Routledge, 1989).

Neame, Ronald, *Straight from The Horse's Mouth* (Lanham, Maryland: Scarecrow Press, 2003).

Phillips, Gene, *Beyond the Epic: The Life & Films of David Lean* (Lexington: The University Press of Kentucky, 2006).

Puckett, Kent, *War Pictures: Cinema, Violence, and Style in Britain 1939–1945* (New York: Fordham University Press, 2017).

Rice, Emma, *Noël Coward's Brief Encounter* (London: Bloomsbury Methuen Drama, 2013).

Richards, Jeffrey, *Films and British National Identity* (Manchester: Manchester University Press, 1997).

Scott, Paul, *Staying On* (London: Granada, 1978).

Index

CORNWALL T

GUIDE 2025

THE ULTIMATE GUIDE TO STUNNING LANDSCAPES, LOCAL DELIGHTS, AND SEASIDE ADVENTURES"

KATHY M. MORRIS

TABLE OF CONTENTS

INTRODUCTION

A Journey Through Cornwall: A Trip to Remember.

From the time I arrived in Cornwall, I knew I was about to embark on an adventure that would leave an everlasting stamp on my soul. The salty Atlantic breeze met me as I stepped off the train in St. Ives, the golden sands and turquoise waters unfolding like a dream in front of me. I had read innumerable travel books, seen stunning images, and heard stories of Cornwall's charm—but nothing could have prepared me for the beauty I was about to witness.

A Castle in the Clouds: The Legend of Tintagel

My first trip was Tintagel Castle, which is steeped in history and legend. Standing on the clifftop, the remnants of the castle spread out in front of me, its ancient stones whispering stories of King Arthur and Merlin. As I crossed the dramatic footbridge, the wind howled about me, transporting memories of a bygone period. The wave slammed against the cliffs with rhythmic, almost mesmerizing force. I went around the ruins, envisioning knights and kings traveling these same routes centuries before. It felt like I'd stepped into a mystical universe, where history and legend blended flawlessly.

The Eden Project - A Green Wonderland

I traveled from ancient traditions to the Eden Project, a masterpiece of ecological innovation. As I entered the distinctive biomes, I was taken to different parts of the world—the humid, lush rainforest teeming with exotic flora, and the Mediterranean biome, bursting with vivid colors and the aroma of citrus. It was more than just a botanical garden; it was a real, breathing reminder of our planet's wonders. I sat on a bench inside the Rainforest Biome, closed my eyes, and listened to the gentle flow of water and distant calls of tropical birds. It was an event that heightened my respect for nature in ways I had never known before.

St. Michael's Mount, A Fairytale Tidal Island

One morning, I got up early to explore St. Michael's Mount, a tidal island that looked like something out of a fantasy story. Timing was everything: the water was low, revealing the ancient stone causeway that linked to the island. Walking across seemed like going back in time. I climbed the steep path to the castle, pausing to enjoy the panoramic views of the sea and the mainland. Inside, I went through huge rooms decorated with armor, tapestries, and antique treasures. The view from the summit was breathtaking—a mix of ocean blues and rolling green hills, with the Cornish coast stretching indefinitely into the distance.

A Taste of Cornwall: Pastry Perfection and Cream Tea Controversy

Of course, no trip to Cornwall is complete without partaking in the region's famous cuisine. My first proper Cornish pasty was from a little bakery in Padstow, where the flaky crust gave way to a warm, properly seasoned filling of meat, potatoes, and swede. "It was love at first bite."

Then came the great debate: cream or jam first? In a beautiful small tearoom overlooking the sea, I meticulously assembled my scone. I followed the Cornish tradition and spread a large layer of jam before topping with a dollop of thick, creamy clotted cream. As I took my first bite, I knew one thing for certain: no matter how it was prepared, this was a divine experience.

A Sunset Performance at the Minack Theatre.

One of the most amazing experiences of my vacation was watching the sun set beyond the horizon at the Minack Theatre. Carved into the cliffs, this open-air theater provided a panorama that was almost as captivating as the concert itself. As the performers entered the stage, the waves smashed against the rocks below, merging in with the sounds of the play. The sky glowed in hues of orange, pink, and purple, casting a golden glow over the area. It was an experience that no words could adequately convey—a time when art and nature danced in perfect harmony.

Hidden Beaches and Coastal Hikes

I embarked on the South West Coast Path, eager to discover Cornwall's rough beauty. The walk took me past magnificent cliffs, isolated coves, and gorgeous beaches that felt like hidden jewels. I gazed in astonishment at Kynance Cove, where the emerald-green seas glittered in the sunlight, contrasted with the dark, jagged rocks that formed the shoreline. I kicked off my shoes and let the chilly water lap at my feet before taking a long intake of salty air.

A farewell, but not goodbye.

As my adventure drew to a close, I found myself lingering at Land's close, watching the waves crash against the cliffs for the final time. Cornwall had given me more than just memories; it had given me a strong sense of connection, wonder, and an insatiable need to return.

I boarded my train with a grateful heart and a vow to myself: this would not be the last time I walked these seaside trails, tasted Cornwall's rich flavors, or lost myself in its history and stories. Cornwall had captured a bit of my spirit, and I knew I'd be returning. Until then, I'd keep its power with me, a reminder that some locations are more than merely visited; they're felt, treasured, and longed for.

CHAPTER 1

Why Visit Cornwall in 2025?

Cornwall, the jewel of England's southern coastline, continues to enchant visitors with its magnificent scenery, rich history, and vibrant culture. Whether you're a first-time visitor or a returning traveler, 2025 is an especially exciting time to visit this legendary site. With new attractions, enhanced infrastructure, and changing travel preferences, there are more reasons than ever to put Cornwall on your itinerary.

A timeless destination with fresh experiences.

Cornwall has long been a popular destination for nature lovers, adventurers, and those searching for a quiet coastal escape. While its timeless attraction remains—dramatic cliffs, beautiful beaches, and tiny fishing villages—the region is also changing. In 2025, visitors may expect refurbished cultural sites, eco-friendly activities, and an increase in sustainable tourism efforts to preserve Cornwall's natural beauty.

The year also represents key milestones for various historical sites, including improved visitor experiences, interactive exhibitions, and special events commemorating Cornwall's rich history. Cornwall in 2025 gives a unique perspective on its iconic sights, whether you're walking through the remnants of Tintagel Castle, discovering the subtropical gardens of Trebah, or watching a play at the Minack Theatre.

Ideal for all types of travelers.

Cornwall is a destination that appeals to a diverse range of interests. Adventurers can enjoy world-class surfing conditions in Newquay, stunning hiking paths along the South West Coast Path, and exhilarating watersports in St. Ives. Cornwall's castles, ancient stone circles, and Arthurian legends bring history and mythology to life for those who enjoy both. Meanwhile, families will enjoy the abundance of kid-friendly activities, including the Eden Project's futuristic biomes and the interactive exhibitions at the National Maritime Museum Cornwall.

Cornwall's coastline is filled with calm bays, lovely beach communities, and secret gardens, all of which beckon leisurely exploration. Whether you want to relax in a traditional tea shop, take in the calm views from a cliffside café, or walk around art galleries in St. Ives, Cornwall's laid-back vibe makes it the ideal escape from the hustle and bustle of everyday life.

A Culinary Hotspot With Unique Flavors

Foodies will find 2025 an excellent year to visit Cornwall's thriving culinary scene. While the county has long been known for its characteristic Cornish pasties and excellent fish, it is increasingly becoming recognized for its Michelin-starred restaurants, innovative farm-to-table eating experiences, and craft breweries. Traditional favorites, such as freshly caught fish from Padstow's renowned seafood scene and homemade clotted cream for the perfect cream tea, are still must-try delights. Visitors will, however, notice an increase in the number of vegan, vegetarian, and eco-conscious restaurants that use locally sourced ingredients.

Sustainable and Pet-Friendly Travel

Cornwall will be at the forefront of sustainable travel in 2025, because to its strong emphasis on eco-tourism. Many accommodations now provide eco-friendly initiatives such as plastic-free policies, solar-powered energy, and locally sourced food. The region has also implemented new conservation initiatives to safeguard its rich fauna, so that future generations can enjoy its breathtaking vistas.

Cornwall is one of the UK's most dog-friendly destinations. Many beaches, hiking routes, and even cafés welcome four-legged companions, making it an ideal vacation destination for those who do not want to leave their pets behind.

An Unmissable Year to Discover Cornwall

Cornwall in 2025 is a must-see destination, offering a variety of cultural events, natural attractions, and new travel experiences. Whether you come for the magnificent beauty, the rich heritage, or the superb food, this enchanting region has something for every traveler.

A BRIEF HISTORY WITH CULTURAL HIGHLIGHTS

Cornwall's history is as dramatic and captivating as its rugged coastline. For centuries, this southwestern tip of England has been a land of myths, maritime legends, and industrial significance. Its unique Celtic past, seafaring traditions, and deeply ingrained cultural identity continue to influence the Cornwall we see today. Understanding its history allows tourists to appreciate its charm beyond the magnificent scenery and sandy beaches.

Cornwall's Ancient Origins and Celtic Roots

Long before England became a single kingdom, Cornwall existed as a separate territory, inhabited by early hunter-gatherers and then by Bronze Age and Iron Age populations. By the first millennium BC, Cornwall had established itself as a Celtic cultural bastion, sharing a legacy with Wales, Scotland and Ireland. The Cornish people spoke their own language, Cornish, which is a member of the Brythonic Celtic family, and upheld distinct traditions that can still be heard today.

The arrival of the Romans in Britain around AD 43 altered the landscape throughout the country, but Cornwall, due to its remote location, largely escaped their dominance. While the Romans had an impact on trade, particularly in the mining of tin—a major mineral used in bronze production—Cornwall remained a land of independent tribes that preserved its ancient traditions.

The Age of Legends: King Arthur and Tintagel Castle.

No account of Cornwall's history is complete without including King Arthur, one of Britain's most well-known mythical figures. Many think that Tintagel Castle, positioned majestically on a clifftop overlooking the Atlantic Ocean, was Arthur's birthplace, making it a must-see destination for fans of myth and history both. Though historians doubt the veracity of Arthur's existence, the legend is strongly rooted in Cornish culture. Visitors to Tintagel may explore the castle ruins, walk across the stunning footbridge connecting the mainland to the island, and immerse themselves in the Arthurian legends that continue to enchant imaginations.

Another Arthurian connection can be discovered at Dozmary Pool, a small, isolated lake on Bodmin Moor, which is claimed to be the last resting place of Excalibur, the mythical sword bestowed upon Arthur by the Lady of the Lake. Even today, the moor's hazy sceneries create an atmosphere reminiscent of the stories of Camelot and its knights.

Medieval Cornwall's Saints, Smugglers, and Mariners

By the early medieval period, Christianity had taken hold in Cornwall, resulting in the construction of numerous churches, monasteries, and pilgrimage sites. St. Michael's Mount, an island connected to the mainland by a tidal causeway, rose to prominence as a holy destination, with the Archangel Michael claimed to have visited it himself. Cornwall's religious past is also seen in the countless old crosses and holy wells dotted around the countryside, many of which date back to the early Christian period.

Cornwall's shoreline, while breathtakingly beautiful, was known for shipwrecks, piracy, and smuggling. The dangerous waters around Land's End and the Lizard Peninsula resulted in numerous wrecks, and local people frequently practiced "wrecking"—salvaging cargo from ships that ran aground. Smuggling was common in the 18th and 19th centuries, with illicit products like brandy, tea, and tobacco being brought in from France to dodge high taxes. Many of Cornwall's fishing villages, including Polperro and Mevagissey, have deep-rooted smuggling histories, and visitors today can explore hidden tunnels and coves that once served as secret storage sites for contraband.

The Mining Boom and Cornwall's Industrial Legacy

The 19th century saw Cornwall ascend to global prominence as one of the world's premier mining regions. The county's large reserves of tin, copper, and arsenic powered the Industrial Revolution, and Cornish miners became highly trained workers in demand around the world. The term "Cousin Jack" referred to Cornish miners who emigrated to countries such as Australia, South Africa, and the United States, carrying their knowledge with them.

Today, the remains of Cornwall's mining past can still be studied. The Cornwall and West Devon Mining Landscape is a UNESCO World Heritage Site that protects the towering engine houses, deep mineshafts, and industrial artifacts that formerly powered the region's economy. The Geevor Tin Mine, now a museum, allows visitors to explore a genuine mine and learn about the difficult yet interesting lives of Cornish miners.

Cornish identity and the revival of the Cornish language

Despite centuries of external influence, Cornwall has maintained a strong sense of identity based on its history, language, and traditions. Though the Cornish language dropped greatly after the 18th century, a revival effort in the twentieth century restored its use. Visitors can now see multilingual signs in both English and Cornish, and some people speak both languages fluently. Cultural events, music, and teaching are all part of the ongoing effort to preserve the language.

The Gorsedh Kernow, an annual celebration of Cornish heritage, is one of the most important events promoting the language revival. Established in 1928, it honors those who contribute to Cornwall's cultural preservation, sustaining the region's particular character within the United Kingdom.

Cornwall's artistic and literary influences

Cornwall's natural beauty and evocative vistas have long influenced painters, writers, and filmmakers. St. Ives, a picturesque fishing town, became a hub for artists in the twentieth century, attracting figures such as Barbara Hepworth and Benjamin Nicholson. The Tate St. Ives, an extension of London's Tate Gallery, honors Cornwall's artistic tradition by displaying works influenced by the sea, light, and rough landscapes.

Literature plays an important role in Cornwall's cultural history. Daphne du Maurier, one of Cornwall's most famous writers, frequently depicts the region's gloomy landscapes and untamed beaches in her books. Her novel Rebecca, set in the fictional Manderley, was inspired on Menabilly, a Cornish estate where she had lived. Visitors can visit several areas associated with her paintings, such as the stunning cliffs at Polridmouth Cove and the enigmatic Bodmin Moor.

More recently, the popular television series Poldark has renewed interest in Cornwall's past by depicting the challenges of 18th-century miners as well as the breathtaking beauty of the county's surroundings. Fans of the program can visit filming locations such as Charlestown's historic port and the windswept cliffs of Porthcurno.

Cornwall in the Modern Era: Preserving Heritage and Embracing the Future

Today, Cornwall embraces modern tourism while remaining firmly rooted to its historic heritage. The county's dedication to conserving its heritage is reflected in its well-kept historic sites, lively arts scene, and cultural events celebrating everything from traditional music to Cornish pasties. Sustainable tourism initiatives ensure that future generations can experience Cornwall's rich history while protecting the environment and authenticity.

For visitors, understanding Cornwall's past entails more than just seeing castles and museums; it's about feeling the echoes of history in every seaside village, old ruin, and community festival. Whether meandering through the medieval alleyways of Truro, discovering the depths of a tin mine, or standing atop the cliffs of Tintagel, Cornwall's history is a living, breathing aspect of the journey, making each visit a step back in time.

CORNISH TRADITIONS & LOCAL ETIQUETTE

Cornwall is more than just a beautiful destination; it is a land with deep-rooted traditions, a strong sense of identity, and a unique culture that distinguishes it from the rest of England. From ancient customs and festivals to daily social conventions, understanding Cornish traditions and etiquette improves the visitor experience and promotes a greater appreciation for the local way of life.

Cornish Identity and Community Spirit

Cornish people are quite proud of their past and generally identify as Cornish rather than English. Cornwall has its own flag, the black-and-white cross of Saint Piran, the patron saint of tin miners, which is prominently displayed on buildings, cars, and clothes throughout the province. Cornwall has a strong feeling of community, and visitors who interact with the residents will notice a friendly and welcoming atmosphere.

While tourism is an important sector, Cornwall is a working town that values fishing, farming, and local craftsmanship. Respect for the local way of life is valued, particularly in rural areas and tiny communities. A cordial welcome, as basic as "hello" or "how are you?""When visiting businesses or cafés, goes a long way towards establishing a favorable impression.

Traditional Cornish festivals and celebrations.

Cornwall has an extensive festival calendar that honors its Celtic traditions, marine history, and seasonal changes. These events allow visitors to experience true Cornish traditions, ranging from folk music and dancing to centuries-old ceremonies.

One of the most well-known events is St. Piran's Day, which takes place on March 5th. This day celebrates Saint Piran, the patron saint of Cornwall and tin miners, with parades, music, and gatherings throughout the county. The largest celebrations are held in Truro, Penzance, and Perranporth, where people wave the Cornish flag, sing traditional songs, and drink pasties and local ale.

Another strongly entrenched celebration is Padstow's Obby Oss, a May Day ritual that involves dancers and musicians marching through the streets with two adorned "osses" (hobby horses). The origins of this celebration are unknown, however it is said to be related to ancient fertility rituals. The event's hypnotic drum beats, laughter, and revelry captivate visitors, making it one of Cornwall's most immersing cultural experiences.

For tourists coming in late June, the Golowan Festival in Penzance is a spectacular exhibition of Cornish culture, with bonfires, parades, and performances that bring the town to life. Golowan began as a midsummer fire festival and has since expanded into a week-long celebration of Cornwall's artistic and cultural history.

During the winter, the Montol Festival in Penzance revives Cornwall's pagan practices with masked processions and fire-lit performances, providing a unique view into the region's folklore and ancient belief systems.

Cornish Cuisine and Dining Etiquette

Food is an important part of Cornish culture, with several distinctive dishes originating in the region. The Cornish pasty is the most well-known, a hearty, crimped pastry stuffed with beef, potatoes, swede, and onions. Pasties were traditionally created for tin miners, with one end left unfilled so they could hold it with unclean hands and throw away the contaminated crust. Pasties are now a must-try for any tourist to Cornwall, and they can be found in bakeries and cafés around the county.

Another delicacy is Cornish cream tea, which is made up of scones, clotted cream, and jam and is usually served with tea. However, in Cornwall, cream is spread first, followed by jam—in contrast to adjacent Devon, where the order is reversed. While this may appear to be a minor element, it is a source of pride and dispute among residents, and tourists should expect lighthearted discussions about it.

When dining out, especially in traditional pubs and tea houses, it is normal to make your order at the bar or counter rather than wait for table service. Tipping is appreciated but not required, and a 10% gratuity is usually sufficient in restaurants. In smaller restaurants and cafés, rounding up the bill is a courteous way to express appreciation.

Social Customs and Local Etiquette

The Cornish are famed for their warmth, but they also value civility and respect for their surroundings. A casual, welcoming demeanor is appreciated, but it is usually best to avoid drawing parallels between Cornwall and other parts of England. Some Cornish people feel themselves culturally separate from the rest of the UK, therefore referring to them as "English" rather than "Cornish" may not be well welcomed.

Respecting nature is an important aspect of local etiquette. Cornwall's coastline, moorlands, and historic monuments are its pride and pleasure, and visitors must adhere to the "leave no trace" policy. Littering, damaging coastal paths, and disturbing wildlife are all strongly discouraged. Many localities, notably cultural sites such as Tintagel Castle or St. Michael's Mount, have restrictions prohibiting people from climbing on ruins or removing stones in order to safeguard these relics for future generations.

Beach etiquette is also important. While Cornwall's beaches are popular for sunbathing, surfing, and dog walking, visitors should be aware of designated swimming zones and seasonal dog restrictions at some beaches. In addition, several beaches prohibit barbecues and bonfires due to environmental concerns. Checking local regulations before putting up a picnic or fire guarantees a trouble-free vacation.

Respecting local traffic restrictions and being aware of restricted parking places is critical in villages and fishing ports. Many Cornish roads are tiny, so driving into small communities takes patience and caution. Giving way to oncoming vehicles on single-lane roads and being courteous to pedestrians contributes to a great experience for both visitors and residents.

Cornish Language and Its Revival

While everyone speaks English, Cornwall has its own language, Kernewek, which was once widely spoken but declined in the 18th and 19th centuries. In recent decades, there has been a resuscitation movement, with street signs, place names, and even some establishments using Kernewek alongside English. Visitors may see greetings like "Kernow a'gas dynnergh" (Cornwall welcomes you) on signage or hear the occasional "Dydh da" (good day) from excited locals.

While it is not compulsory for tourists to learn Kernewek, attempting to understand and appreciate its presence demonstrates respect for Cornwall's cultural heritage. Learning a few phrases or inquiring about the language can frequently lead to amicable talks with locals who are passionate about preserving their heritage.

Cornwall's Marine Traditions & Seafaring Heritage

As a county surrounded by the Atlantic Ocean, Cornwall has a deep affinity to the sea. Fishing has been a way of life for years, and towns such as Newlyn, Mevagissey, and Padstow rely on it. The annual Looe Lugger Regatta, held in Looe, commemorates Cornwall's fishing past by displaying traditional sailing boats, and the Newlyn Fish Festival (when hosted) emphasizes the importance of seafood in Cornish cuisine.

Cornish fishing communities continue to have strong superstitions and marine culture. Many locals believe in lucky charms, and it is considered bad luck to bring bananas aboard a fishing boat. Visitors who take boat tours or go fishing may hear intriguing stories about Cornwall's seafaring past, including brave smugglers and legendary marine animals.

Surfing is another important part of Cornwall's seaside culture. Towns like Newquay are well-known for their surfable waves, and the Boardmasters Festival, which combines music and surfing events, is a highlight of the summer calendar. Even if you don't surf, witnessing the experienced wave riders on the beaches is an exhilarating aspect of the Cornish experience.

Embracing Cornish Culture as a Visitor

Understanding and honoring Cornish traditions enhances the enjoyment of any visit. Travelers can immerse themselves in

Cornwall's rich cultural fabric by participating in community activities, learning about local customs, and sampling traditional foods. Whether celebrating St. Piran's Day, eating a pasty by the sea, or simply enjoying the slow-paced lifestyle, tourists will depart with a greater understanding for this exceptional county's distinctiveness.

ESSENTIAL TRAVEL TIPS & BEST TIME TO VISIT

Planning a vacation to Cornwall entails more than just selecting a destination; it also necessitates an awareness of the region's seasonal changes, transport logistics, and insider suggestions for making the most of your stay. Whether you're drawn to Cornwall for its spectacular beaches, beautiful fishing villages, or rich history, knowing when to go and how to get around will make your vacation even more enjoyable.

Best times to visit Cornwall.

Cornwall's attraction varies with the seasons, providing a range of experiences all year. The optimum time to come is determined by the type of experience you seek, which could be sun-soaked beach days, rough coastline walks, or bustling local festivals.

Spring (March-May) is one of the most lovely periods to visit Cornwall. The landscape comes to life with blooming wildflowers along seaside walkways and gardens, such as the Lost Gardens of Heligan and Trebah Garden. The weather are pleasant, and there are less people, making it an excellent time for leisurely hikes and sightseeing. This is also when Cornwall's festivities begin, with St. Piran's Day in March and the Flora Day celebration in Helston in May, all of which provide unique glimpses into the local culture.

Summer (June to August) is Cornwall's most popular and busiest season, enticing visitors with its warm weather, extended daylight hours, and vibrant atmosphere. The beaches in St. Ives, Newquay, and Perranporth become popular sites for sunbathing and surfing, while coastal towns hold a variety of festivals such as Boardmasters in Newquay and Falmouth Week. However, this is also the peak season for tourists in Cornwall, resulting in crowded beaches, fully booked lodgings, and higher rates. It is strongly advised to plan hotels and attractions in advance while going during the summer.

Autumn (September to November) is an excellent time to visit for individuals who like a more relaxed atmosphere with pleasant temperatures. The summer crowds begin to leave, while the sea remains warm enough for swimming and surfing until September. The autumn colors make places like Bodmin Moor and the coastal trails even more picturesque. This season also features local culinary events, such as the Newquay Fish Festival and Truro's Great Cornish culinary Festival, where tourists may experience fresh seafood and local specialties.

Winter (December–February) is the quietest and most rugged season, ideal for those who enjoy stormy seascapes and cozy pub evenings by the fire. While some attractions and accommodations are closed for the season, winter has its own appeal. Truro's Christmas markets, Mousehole's iconic harbor lights, and Penzance's Montol Festival all offer one-of-a-kind seasonal activities. Though the weather can be unpredictable, with heavy rain and severe winds, it's an ideal time for individuals seeking seclusion, dramatic coastline scenery, and lower lodging costs.

Getting to Cornwall.

Cornwall is accessible via a variety of forms of transportation, although due to its remote position, travel requires some forethought.

Cornwall Airport Newquay serves as the primary gateway for air travel, offering local and some international flights. Cornwall is connected to major hubs via flights from London, Manchester, Edinburgh, and Dublin, making it a convenient option for those looking to avoid long trips. Car rentals are available at the airport, while taxis and buses provide onward transportation.

The Great Western Railway (GWR) operates trains from London Paddington to Truro, St. Austell, and Penzance. The trek takes about five hours and includes magnificent rural and sea views. An alternative is the Night Riviera Sleeper Train, which allows passengers to wake up refreshed in Cornwall following an overnight journey from London.

Cornwall is accessible by car via the M5 motorway, then the A30 or A38 roads that lead into the county. While driving allows for more flexibility, keep in mind that Cornwall's roads, especially in rural areas, can be narrow and winding. During peak summer months, traffic congestion is prevalent, especially around major tourist attractions.

Bus services are available, with National Express and Megabus operating long-distance routes to Cornwall from major UK cities. Local bus services, provided by First Kernow, provide transit within Cornwall, but schedules can be rare in outlying locations.

Ferries also give access to Cornwall, with lines connecting the county to the Isles of Scilly and across the River Fal, joining Falmouth and St. Mawes. The ferry ride to the Isles of Scilly from Penzance is a picturesque alternative to flying.

Getting Around Cornwall.

While public transportation is available in Cornwall, hiring a car is generally the best option to explore the area at your own leisure. Many of Cornwall's attractions, including secluded coves, old ruins, and lonely moorlands, are not easily accessible by bus or train.

Driving in Cornwall takes patience because many roads are narrow and passing lanes are popular in rural regions. Parking in attractive places like St. Ives and Padstow can be difficult during peak season, therefore park-and-ride services are recommended.

For individuals who do not own a car, Cornish branch line trains, such as the beautiful St. Ives Bay Line and the Looe Valley Line, provide stunning coastline vistas and convenient access to major towns. Local buses are another alternative, albeit they may necessitate advance preparation due to limited timetables in some places.

Cycling is a popular way to explore Cornwall's countryside, with routes such as the Camel Trail, which connects Bodmin and Padstow and offers a traffic-free scenic experience. Bike rentals are provided in various towns.

Walking is a fantastic way to experience Cornwall's stunning landscapes, and the South West Coast Path provides some of the best coastal excursions in the UK. Walking, whether for a short stroll or a multi-day trek, allows visitors to get up close to Cornwall's breathtaking cliffs, secluded beaches, and historic sites.

Where to stay in Cornwall?

Cornwall provides a wide selection of accommodations, from luxury hotels and boutique B&Bs to charming cottages and budget-friendly hostels.

For those wanting a seaside vacation, St. Ives, Falmouth, and Padstow provide attractive harborside lodgings with access to beaches and superb dining options. If you're seeking for a serene countryside retreat, Bodmin Moor and the Roseland Peninsula provide tranquil locations and breathtaking scenery. Adventurous travelers may enjoy camping or glamping in gorgeous areas such as Treen Farm or Gwithian Towans.

Booking accommodations well in advance is strongly advised, especially during busy summer months and festival seasons.

Practical Travel Tips:

When visiting Cornwall, it's important to be prepared for the unpredictable weather. Even in the summer, sea breezes can make temperatures feel cooler, and rain showers can occur suddenly. Those planning outdoor activities should pack layers, waterproof clothing, and sturdy walking shoes.

Respect for local customs and the environment is essential. Cornwall's natural beauty is one of its most notable attractions, so responsible tourism is encouraged. Littering, disturbing wildlife, and removing stones from historic sites are all discouraged, and visitors should adhere to the "leave no trace" principle when exploring.

Mobile phone reception can be spotty in some remote areas, particularly on the moors and along certain coastal stretches. Offline maps or a physical guidebook can be useful for navigating these areas.

Many shops and small cafés operate seasonally, with some closing throughout the winter. Checking opening hours in advance ensures that you don't miss out on local experiences.

Cornish people value politeness and friendliness from visitors. Engaging with locals, supporting independent businesses, and showing respect for the region's heritage and environment contribute to a more enjoyable and immersive travel experience.

UNDERSTANDING LOCAL LAWS & TOURIST SAFETY

Cornwall is a safe and welcoming destination for tourists, but like any travel experience, it is essential to be aware of local laws, regulations, and safety considerations. Whether you are exploring coastal trails, driving through narrow lanes, or enjoying the nightlife, understanding the rules and best practices ensures a smooth and enjoyable visit.

General Laws and Regulations

Cornwall, as part of England and the United Kingdom, operates under British law. Tourists are expected to follow national regulations regarding public behavior, alcohol consumption, and traffic laws. One of the most crucial parts of travel in Cornwall is road safety, as the region has numerous small, twisting roads that require additional caution.

Public behavior is typically relaxed, although respect for local norms and traditions is highly prized. Anti-social behavior, such as excessive noise in calm residential neighborhoods, littering, or public drinking, can lead to penalties or exclusion from particular venues. The UK has tight prohibitions against drug possession and use, with severe punishments for anybody caught in violation.

Smoking is prohibited in indoor public spaces, including restaurants, pubs, and hotels, unless designated outdoor smoking areas are provided. To protect the environment, many beaches and natural reserves ban smoking and littering.

Alcohol use is permitted in most public locations, unless specifically prohibited by local councils. Some towns may have designated "alcohol-free zones," where drinking in public settings is prohibited. Purchasing alcohol is only allowed for people above the age of 18, and bars and pubs need identification for age verification if requested.

Wild camping, while popular among outdoor enthusiasts, is normally not allowed in Cornwall without the landowner's permission. However, there are several authorized campsites giving scenic accommodations with required utilities.

Beach and Coastal Safety

Cornwall is famous for its magnificent coastline, but the sea can be unpredictable, and safety should always be a priority. The county has several lifeguarded beaches, particularly during the summer months. Beaches such as Fistral Beach near Newquay, Perranporth, and Polzeath are well-monitored, and visitors should always heed the lifeguard flags and cautions.

Strong tides and rip currents are typical, especially on the Atlantic-facing beaches. Swimmers should stick to designated safe zones and avoid swimming alone. Surfing and water sports are popular hobbies, but beginners should receive instruction from qualified instructors and wear proper safety equipment, such as wetsuits and surfboard leashes.

Rock pools, cliffs, and caves can be intriguing to explore, but proceed with caution. Cliffs can be unstable, and falling rocks endanger those who stand too close to the edge. Tide times should always be confirmed before visiting caverns or wandering along the shoreline, as the tide can come in suddenly and cut off access. Tide timetables are frequently available in tourist information centers and local stores.

Jellyfish and weever fish stings are occasionally dangerous in Cornish waters. Most stings are not harmful, but they can be painful. Rinsing the affected area with seawater and applying heat can help to relieve discomfort. If you experience a significant response, seek medical help.

Hiking and Outdoor Safety

Cornwall's landscapes provide some of the most spectacular walking paths in the UK, including sections of the South West Coast Path and rough inland routes like those on Bodmin Moor. However, hiking in Cornwall necessitates preparation because weather conditions can change quickly.

Proper footwear is required because many trails have uneven ground, steep climbs, and rocky paths. Weather-appropriate clothing, including waterproof layers, is recommended, even in the summer months. Many areas have weak mobile phone signals, so carrying a paper map or downloading offline navigation tools can be beneficial.

Visitors should follow marked paths and respect the local wildlife and livestock. Many trails pass through farmland, so it's important to close gates behind you and avoid disturbing animals. Dogs should be kept on leashes in areas where livestock are present, as loose dogs can startle sheep and cattle, resulting in dangerous situations.

If you're hiking alone, let someone know your planned route and estimated return time as a precaution. Mist and fog can quickly settle over remote areas like Bodmin Moor, reducing visibility and making navigation difficult.

Driving in Cornwall.

Driving in Cornwall can be an unforgettable experience, particularly for visitors who are unfamiliar with the narrow country roads and steep coastal routes. The speed restrictions vary by area, although in many rural areas, the national speed limit of 60 mph (96 km/h) does not always imply that driving at that pace is safe. Slower speeds are often necessary, particularly on blind turns and single-track roads.

Many roads in Cornwall require the use of passing places, where one driver must pull over to allow another vehicle to pass. Drivers should be prepared to reverse if necessary and always show patience with other road users. In tiny communities, parking can be scarce, and it is often advisable to use park-and-ride services where available.

Fuel stations can be few and far between in some rural areas, so it is advisable to fill up before embarking on long journeys. Electric vehicle charging stations are becoming more common, but availability should be confirmed in advance, particularly in more remote areas.

Those inexperienced with driving on the left side of the road should exercise particular caution near roundabouts and crossroads. Pedestrians and cyclists share many of Cornwall's roads, so extra awareness is required, particularly in tourist-heavy areas.

Wildlife and Environmental Protection

Cornwall is home to a rich diversity of species, including seals, dolphins, and uncommon seabirds. Many areas, such as Lizard Point and St. Agnes Head, are designated nature reserves, and visitors are encouraged to respect these protected habitats.

Disturbing wildlife is discouraged, and feeding wild animals, particularly seabirds, is not recommended as it can disrupt their normal activities. Some beaches enforce dog restrictions during peak months to protect nesting birds and local ecosystems.

Littering is treated seriously in Cornwall, and tourists are asked to take their rubbish with them or use designated containers. Many areas participate in "Plastic-Free Cornwall" initiatives, aiming to reduce the impact of plastic waste on marine environments. Recycling bins are widely available, and reusable water bottles and shopping bags are encouraged.

Medical and Emergency Services

Cornwall has a network of medical facilities, with major hospitals located in Truro (Royal Cornwall Hospital) and Penzance (West Cornwall Hospital). Minor injury units are offered in towns such as St. Austell, Falmouth, and Bodmin for less serious medical difficulties.

For emergency situations, visitors should dial 999 for ambulance, police, or fire services. For non-urgent medical concerns, calling

111 gives access to medical advice and support. Pharmacies are available in most towns, offering over-the-counter medications and minor health consultations.

Travel insurance is highly recommended, particularly for international visitors who may not be covered by the UK's National Health Service (NHS). Many outdoor sports, such as surfing and hiking, have inherent hazards, and having coverage for accidents or emergency medical procedures is advisable.

Respecting Local Culture and Community

Cornwall has a strong local identity, and visitors are encouraged to respect and appreciate its culture. Many locals are proud of their Cornish history, and while English is the prevalent language, Cornish (Kernewek) is still spoken and celebrated in specific regions. Learning a few simple words, such as "Kernow" (Cornwall) or "Dydh da" (Good day), can be a fun way to participate with the local culture.

Local businesses and independent stores are the heart of many Cornish towns, and supporting them by purchasing local produce, handmade crafts, and traditional delicacies helps preserve the region's economy.

Visitors to Cornwall may have a fulfilling and worry-free trip by adhering to local regulations, being safe, and respecting the region's distinctive heritage.

Exploring Tintagel Castle: The Legend of King Arthur

Tintagel Castle, perched spectacularly on Cornwall's craggy northern coastline, is one of the area's most famous and fabled landmarks. This mediaeval fortification, steeped in myth and history, is forever tied to King Arthur's legend, making it a must-see for history aficionados, literature lovers, and adventurers alike. Tintagel Castle, with its stunning coastline backdrop, amazing archaeological artefacts, and rich storytelling, provides a remarkable voyage through Cornwall's history.

The legend of King Arthur and Tintagel Castle

Tintagel Castle's reputation originates from its connection to the legendary King Arthur. Tintagel was the birthplace of King Arthur, according to Geoffrey of Monmouth's 12th-century book Historia Regum Britanniae (The History of the Kings of Britain). Arthur's father, Uther Pendragon, is said to have fallen in love with Igraine, the Duke of Cornwall's wife. Uther was magically disguised as Igraine's spouse by the wizard Merlin, allowing him to enter the castle and give birth to Arthur.

Tintagel Castle has become a pilgrimage destination for those who are attracted by Arthurian legends. While historians question the veracity of these stories, there is no denying that the castle's stunning setting and old ruins evoke a profound feeling of mystery and romance.

Best Visiting Times and Ticket Prices.

Tintagel Castle is open all year, but the ideal seasons to visit are spring and early fall, when the weather is good and the crowds are lighter. Summer is peak season, attracting a big number of people, but it also provides more daylight hours for exploring.

Ticket rates vary according on the season, but as of 2025, the normal adult entrance is approximately £16, with discounts available for children, families, and seniors. English Heritage members can attend for free, and pre-booking online typically results in small reductions. It is recommended that you check the official English Heritage website for current pricing and any temporary closures due to weather.

Accessibility and Pet Policies

Tintagel Castle's rough seaside position presents certain obstacles for guests with mobility issues. The castle ruins are accessible by a steep walk and a new footbridge, which provide breathtaking views but require a good level of fitness. The bridge, which replaced the old land connection, improves access, but there are still steps and uneven terrain throughout the property.

Wheelchair access is limited, however the visitor centre and certain vistas provide accessible spaces for individuals who are unable to complete the entire climb. Visitors with limited mobility can also take use of shuttle services from the ticket office to the base of the cliffs.

Tintagel Castle welcomes pets, making it an ideal destination for dog owners. However, dogs must be kept on a leash at all times due to the sheer cliffs and wildlife in the region. There are several dog-friendly walking trails nearby, and water bowls are available at the tourist centre.

What To Expect: Coastal views and historical insights.

A visit to Tintagel Castle is more than just the mythical connection to King Arthur; it is also an opportunity to see one of Cornwall's most spectacular coastal landscapes. The site is divided into two sections: mainland ruins and island ruins, which are connected by the striking Tintagel footbridge.

The Mainland Ruins

Before crossing to the island, visitors can explore Tintagel's mainland section, which includes the remains of a mediaeval courtyard, chapels, and fortifications built by Richard, Earl of Cornwall, in the 13th century. These ruins provide insight into mediaeval life in Cornwall and offer breathtaking views of the Atlantic Ocean.

Footbridge and Island Ruins

The modern footbridge, completed in 2019, spans the dramatic chasm between the mainland and the island, providing an exciting entrance to the castle's main section. Once on the island, visitors can wander through the castle's ruins, imagining how it would have looked in its prime. The views from here are breathtaking, with sheer cliffs descending into the turquoise waters below.

Merlin's Cave

One of Tintagel Castle's most fascinating attractions is Merlin's Cave, which is located beneath the castle cliffs on Tintagel Beach. At low tide, visitors can enter this sea cave, which is claimed to have been the abode of Merlin the Wizard. The cave's mysterious atmosphere, mixed with the sound of waves echoing down its chamber, make it a must-see for visitors looking to experience the true essence of Arthurian legend.

Gallos Statue and King Arthur's Footprint

Another highlight is the Gallos Statue, a stunning bronze monument of an armoured King Arthur standing majestically atop the cliffs. The statue, installed by English Heritage, adds an extra element of myth and drama to the landscape. Near the statue, visitors will find the "King Arthur's Footprint", a mysterious rock formation shaped like a foot, which some believe marks where Arthur once stood.

Wildlife and Nature

Beyond the history, Tintagel Castle is a haven for nature lovers. The cliffs surrounding the location are home to seabirds, including peregrine falcons and razorbills. Wildflowers bloom in the spring and summer, providing beautiful color to the landscape. Dolphins and seals are occasionally sighted in the waters below, making for an especially unique sight during a visit.

Practical Tips for Visiting Tintagel Castle

- Wear sturdy footwear: The terrain is uneven and features some severe rises.
- Check the tidal schedule: If you want to explore Merlin's Cave, visit at low tide, as it becomes inaccessible when the tide rises.
- Arrive early or late in the day: This helps avoid peak crowds, especially in summer.
- Bring a camera: The vistas are some of the most stunning in Cornwall.
- Dress in layers: The weather can change fast, and strong coastal breezes are usual.

A journey through time and myth.

Tintagel Castle is more than just a historical landmark; it is a spectacular setting where history, legend, and nature all come together. Whether you come for the Arthurian connections, the mediaeval legacy, or the breathtaking coastline scenery, this ancient fortification creates an impression. As you stand atop the ruins, looking out over the thundering waves below, it's easy to see why this location has inspired stories for generations.

Tintagel Castle is a must-see destination in Cornwall for anyone looking for adventure, history, and folklore.

THE EDEN PROJECT: A FUTURISTIC GARDEN WONDERLAND.

The Eden Project is one of Cornwall's most impressive attractions, attracting tourists from all over the world with its beautiful architecture, immersive ecological experiences, and dedication to sustainability. Located in a reclaimed china clay pit near St Austell, this futuristic botanical paradise provides an incredible voyage through some of the world's most beautiful ecosystems, all contained under massive, strange biomes. Whether you are a nature lover, a science enthusiast, or a family seeking for a fun day out, the Eden Project offers a unique combination of education, conservation, and adventure.

A Vision for Sustainability and Conservation.

The Eden Project began as a pioneering attempt to raise environmental awareness and inspire people to care for the earth. The complex, which opened in 2001, has transformed a bleak industrial area into a lush and healthy ecosystem, showcasing the potential of ecological regeneration. Today, it is a symbol of sustainability, demonstrating cutting-edge techniques in green building, renewable energy, and climate education.

The Eden Project is much more than a botanical garden. It functions as a global research hub, working with scientists, environmentalists, and educators to find solutions to major environmental concerns including deforestation, climate change, and biodiversity loss. Visitors not only enjoy a visually breathtaking experience, but they also learn how they may help to create a more sustainable future.

Iconic Biomes: Rainforests and Mediterranean Wonders

One of the most striking aspects of the Eden Project is its two massive biomes, which house ecosystems from all over the world. These futuristic geodesic domes are among the world's largest greenhouses, providing an environment for plants from various climates to thrive.

Rainforest Biome: A Tropical Escape.

Stepping inside the Rainforest Biome is like travelling to the heart of the Amazon or the depths of Borneo. The biome resembles a hot, humid jungle, complete with towering trees, gushing waterfalls, and diverse plant life. Lush green ferns, gigantic bamboo, and cocoa trees create a rich, immersive experience, while elevated walkways provide a treetop view of the jungle canopy.

One of the Rainforest habitat's features is the Canopy Walkway, which takes visitors to the top of the habitat for a bird's-eye perspective of the tropical ecosystem. The air is dense with moisture, and the aroma of damp earth and flowering orchids pervades the space, providing a sensory experience unlike any other in the UK. The biome also highlights the role of rainforests in regulating global temperature, as well as the issues of deforestation and conservation efforts worldwide.

The Mediterranean biome is a sun-drenched paradise.

In sharp contrast to the steamy rainforest, the Mediterranean Biome transports visitors to a world of sun-kissed vineyards, fragrant herbs, and olive groves. The air is warm and dry, with scents of lavender, citrus, and rosemary. Inspired by the landscapes of southern Europe, California, and South Africa, this biome provides a peaceful and visually attractive experience.

Visitors can explore vivid floral displays, such as Bougainvillaea, lemon trees, and bright pink oleanders, which thrive in the carefully managed atmosphere. Sculptures and art pieces integrate harmoniously with the natural surroundings, creating a calm ambiance suited for leisurely exploration. The Mediterranean Biome also showcases sustainable agriculture and the ways in which people have adapted to arid conditions over the years.

Other Attractions Inside the Eden Project.

Beyond the biomes, the Eden Project provides a variety of interactive exhibitions, outdoor gardens, and adventure activities, making it a popular destination for people of all ages.

The Outdoor Gardens, which span over 30 acres, offer native Cornish plant species as well as carefully designed landscapes that benefit pollinators and wildlife. Visitors can walk through the gardens to see wildflower meadows, sensory trails, and a heritage apple orchard.

For thrill seekers, the Eden Project features England's longest zipline, the SkyWire. This thrilling ride takes you high above the biomes, providing breathtaking views of the entire site. The Eden Project also includes rock climbing challenges, a giant swing, and adventure trails, making it both exciting and educational.

The Invisible Worlds Exhibition is one of the most fascinating exhibits, delving into the unseen forces that shape our planet, from microscopic organisms to cosmic energies. Visitors can learn more about the interdependence of all life on Earth by participating in hands-on displays and multimedia installations.

Entry fees and seasonal discounts.

The Eden Project admission fee varies based on the time of year, with peak season costs being higher. As of 2025, standard adult tickets cost around £35, with discounts available for children, seniors, and families. Those who book online in advance frequently benefit from lower rates, and annual passes are available for those who plan to visit multiple times.

Special incentives, such as winter reductions and off-peak prices, make the Eden Project more reasonable during the calmer months. Many visitors also use the local resident passes, which provide unlimited entrance for a year at a fraction of the cost.

Accessibility and Family Friendly Amenities

The Eden Project is one of Cornwall's most accessible attractions, designed to welcome people of all abilities. The pathways throughout the property are wheelchair accessible, and mobility scooters are available for rent. Assistance dogs are welcome, and staff are trained to provide further assistance as needed.

For families, the Eden Project is a terrific destination, with plenty of interactive activities, playgrounds, and educational sessions to keep children involved. The site hosts seasonal events, such as Easter egg hunts, summer science festivals, and winter light displays, ensuring there is always something new to experience.

The Eden Project also features a range of dining options, offering sustainable, locally sourced food. The on-site Mediterranean Terrace Café offers exquisite wood-fired pizzas and fresh salads, while the Rainforest Biome café serves tropical-inspired cuisine utilising ingredients produced on-site. There are also picnic spaces for people who wish to bring their own meals.

Why should you visit the Eden Project?

The Eden Project is more than just a tourist attraction; it is also a living laboratory, conservation project, and educational hub. Visitors leave with not only memories of breathtaking landscapes, but also a greater understanding of our planet's fragility and beauty.

With its magnificent biomes, interactive exhibits, and commitment to sustainability, the Eden Project is an important stop on any vacation to Cornwall. Whether you are captivated by nature, wanting to learn about climate change solutions, or simply looking for a stunning day out, this world-renowned destination offers an experience like no other.

Few sites in Cornwall captivate the mind like St. Michael's Mount, a breathtaking tidal island off the coast of Marazion. This stunning island rises from the seas of Mount's Bay and is home to a mediaeval castle, beautiful subtropical gardens, and a complex tapestry of stories and tales. Whether reached on foot during low tide or by boat while the causeway is flooded, a trip to St. Michael's Mount seems like entering a realm of history, mystery, and natural beauty.

A Place of Myth and Legend

Saint Michael's Mount has long been steeped in legend. One of the most well-known stories is a giant named Cormoran, who is claimed to live on the island and terrorise the locals. According to tradition, a valiant boy named Jack deceived the giant and eventually beat him, resulting in the legend of Jack the Giant Killer.

The island is also rich in religious importance. It is thought that in the fifth century, a group of monks from Mont Saint-Michel in France founded a monastery here and dedicated it to the Archangel Michael. Some allege that St. Michael appeared to local fishermen on the island, strengthening its status as a holy location. This relationship to its French counterpart provides the island a distinct cultural and spiritual significance that has persisted for decades.

Mediaeval Castle and Family Legacy

St. Michael's Mount Castle, located in the middle of the island, is a beautiful building that has looked over the bay for nearly a thousand years. The property was first a Benedictine monastery, then a fortress, and finally a beautiful residence. Since the 17th century, the island has been owned and occupied by the St. Aubyn family, who now live there while overseeing its protection as a heritage monument.

Visitors can tour the castle's mediaeval halls, large dining rooms, and breathtaking terraces, all of which provide stunning views of the Cornish coastline. Inside, the castle is adorned with ancient artefacts such as armour, antique furniture, and paintings that tell the narrative of its long and adventurous history. One of the attractions is the Chevy Chase Room, which features a 17th-century frieze depicting a well-known mediaeval hunting scene.

The Chapel of St. Michael, which dates from the 12th century, is another must-see. This small yet evocative place of worship is famous for its stunning stained glass windows and the renowned "miracle chair," where individuals who sit on it are claimed to receive supernatural favours.

The Enchanted Gardens

The castle is surrounded by the island's famous subtropical gardens, which provide a lovely contrast to the wild Cornish seas. The island's unusual climate supports a diverse range of exotic flora, including aloes, succulents, agaves, and bright blooms cascading down the steep terraces.

Walking through the gardens is a sensory experience, with the scent of salt air blending with the fragrance of Mediterranean and subtropical plants. The meandering stone paths take tourists through a rainbow of colours and textures, with each turn presenting spectacular views of the castle above and the water below. Gardeners will appreciate the extraordinary efforts required to maintain this rich landscape, particularly given the island's vulnerability to the weather.

Tide timings and how to get there.

The fluctuating tides are one of the most fascinating features of visiting St. Michael's Mount, as they radically vary how tourists approach the island.

At low tide, an ancient cobbled bridge emerges from the sea, allowing visitors to walk between Marazion and the island. The experience of crossing the stone pathway with the sea gleaming on all sides is wonderful. The causeway is only accessible for a short time each day, so check tide times ahead of time to guarantee safe passage.

When the tide comes in, the causeway disappears beneath the waves, requiring tourists to take a short boat journey to access the island. The boat service runs often during high tide and provides a different, but equally spectacular, view of the island from the ocean. The voyage to St. Michael's Mount, whether on foot or by boat, is an adventure in and of itself.

The best time to visit.

St. Michael's Mount has its own distinct charm that changes with the seasons. The most popular periods to visit are spring and summer, when the gardens are in full flower and the weather is perfect for touring the island and castle grounds. However, these months tend to attract more crowds, so early morning or late afternoon trips are encouraged for a more relaxing experience.

Autumn is an excellent time to visit the island, since it is drenched in golden light and has less people and a more quiet environment. The changing greenery in the gardens enhances the beauty of the area.

Winter might be a beautiful season to visit if you appreciate dramatic scenery. The island frequently encounters rough waves and gloomy sky, creating a wild, magical atmosphere. While the gardens may be less vivid, the mediaeval castle, steeped in history, feels even more eerie during the winter months.

Explore Marazion and the Surrounding Area

A trip to St. Michael's Mount is incomplete without seeing the lovely town of Marazion, one of Cornwall's oldest settlements. Marazion's picturesque alleyways, unique shops, and cosy cafés make it the ideal location to relax before or after your island trip.

The shoreline at Mount's Bay is ideal for scenic walks, with stunning views of the island from a variety of vantage points. Marazion's sandy beach is ideal for swimming, sunbathing, and water sports, making it an all-around destination for history buffs and outdoor enthusiasts alike.

A Journey Through Time and Nature.

St. Michael's Mount is more than just a historical site; it's a place where myth, history, and natural beauty come together. From its legendary past to its majestic castle, lush gardens, and breathtaking coastal views, the island provides an unforgettable experience.

Whether you walk the historic causeway at low tide, take a boat across the glistening bay, or explore the island's mediaeval wonders, a visit to St. Michael's Mount is a voyage back in time that will stay with you long after you leave.

COASTAL HIKES WITH STUNNING VIEWS ON THE SOUTH WEST COAST PATH.

The South West Coast Path is one of the most stunning long-distance hiking pathways in the United Kingdom, spanning 630 miles along the mountainous coastlines of Cornwall, Devon, Dorset, and Somerset. This classic trail in Cornwall displays stunning cliffs, golden beaches, and secret coves, making it an ideal destination for hikers of all skill levels. Whether you're looking for a short scenic walk or a strenuous walk, the South West Coast Path provides an unforgettable opportunity to enjoy Cornwall's natural beauty.

Beauty of the South West Coast Path

Walking along the South West Coast Path is like stepping into a moving postcard. The walk follows the shore, providing stunning views of the Atlantic Ocean, wildflower-covered cliffs, and historic sites. With each step, the scenery varies, from windswept headlands to secluded beaches, and from tiny fishing communities to ancient ruins.

The trail is well-known for its abundant biodiversity. Seabirds including puffins, cormorants, and gannets can be seen swooping over the cliffs, while seals can be seen sunning on the rocks underneath. During the warmer months, lucky hikers may see dolphins or basking sharks gliding through the ocean.

Each season adds a unique charm to the trail. In the spring, the cliffs come alive with carpets of bluebells, sea pinks, and gorse. Summer brings long, bright days, making it excellent for enjoying sea breezes and panoramic vistas. Autumn changes the scenery into warm golden hues, and the less crowds provide for quiet hikes. Even in the winter, the road is breathtaking, with dramatic waves slamming against the cliffs and a refreshing sensation of solitude.

Best Routes for Hikers at All Levels

The South West Coast Path is divided into several portions that cater to both casual walkers and skilled hikers. For those going for a quiet, scenic stroll, there are numerous short, well-maintained trails that provide breathtaking vistas without needing extreme endurance. More daring hikers can tackle the steeper, more difficult sections, which offer a rewarding physical exercise as well as stunning views.

The stretch between St. Ives and Zennor is one of the path's most iconic parts. This 6-mile journey is one of Cornwall's most magnificent coastal walks, with craggy cliffs, ancient mining ruins, and views of the crystal-clear sea below. While the terrain can be difficult at times, the landscape makes it all worthwhile.

Padstow to Stepper Point is an excellent choice for a shorter but equally beautiful hike. This 5-mile round journey follows a moderate walk along the Camel Estuary, with stops in Padstow, a quaint seaside community noted for its seafood eateries and harbour views. The walk gives breathtaking views of Doom Bar, a well-known sandbank with shipwreck and mermaid legends.

For experienced hikers looking for a more strenuous trip, the Hartland Quay to Bude portion offers some of the most magnificent scenery along the coast route. This 15-mile trip is physically hard due to its high ascents and rough cliffs, but it rewards hikers with breathtaking vistas of secluded coves, jagged rock formations, and boundless ocean horizons.

Weather Considerations and Seasonal Differences

Cornwall's coastal weather may be unpredictable, so dressing for the occasion is key for a pleasant walk. During the spring and summer, the sun can be intense, and the exposed cliffs provide little shade, so sunscreen and plenty of water are essential. Autumn and winter bring strong winds and the possibility of rain, so waterproof clothing and sturdy footwear are advised.

Although the path is generally well-maintained, heavy rain can cause certain sections to become slippery or muddy. It is recommended that hikers check the weather forecast before heading out, and they should always be aware of high tides when walking near beaches or estuaries.

Wildlife & Nature on the Trail

The South West Coast Path is home to a diverse range of wildlife and plant life. Foxes, deer, and even otters are frequently seen in the early morning or evening near the more remote sections. Birdwatchers will see gulls, fulmars, and peregrine falcons swooping down to hunt.

The ocean is just as alive with marine life. During the late summer, dolphin pods can often be seen playing in the waves, while basking sharks glide beneath the surface in deeper waters. Grey seals are frequent visitors, typically seen relaxing on the peaceful beaches beneath the cliffs.

The plant life is equally as amazing. Springtime transforms the coastal route into a beautiful tapestry of wildflowers, such as purple heather, yellow gorse, and delicate sea campion. These vibrant colours contrast nicely with the deep blue of the ocean, producing an unforgettable visual experience.

Dog-Friendly Hiking on the South West Coast Path

For dog owners, the South West Coast Path is a fantastic place to explore with a four-legged companion. Many sections of the route are dog-friendly, with sufficient possibilities for canines to enjoy open areas, fresh air, and even a swim in the surf.

Some portions of the path can be hard for dogs, particularly those with steep inclines or tiny ledges. It's also necessary to be mindful of animal grazing areas, where dogs must be kept on leashes. Water bowls and additional supplies are advised, as certain areas of the trail have limited access to fresh water.

One of the most popular dog-friendly paths is the Lizard Peninsula walk, which offers a combination of coastal views, open fields, and ancient lighthouses. The Marazion to Perranuthnoe walk is another fantastic choice, with a flat, easy path that passes alongside dog-friendly beaches and cafés.

Local Pubs and Cafés for a Well-Deserved Rest

After a long hike, there's nothing better than stopping at a nice pub or seaside café to refuel and unwind. Fortunately, Cornwall is home to some of the best seaside cafés, many of which provide gorgeous sea views and delicious local cuisine.

In Padstow, The Golden Lion is a historic tavern with a pleasant ambiance and outstanding seafood meals. The Logan Rock Inn near Porthcurno is another wonderful stop, offering traditional Cornish pasties and ales in a picturesque village setting.

For those concluding their journey around St. Ives, Porthmeor Beach Café is a terrific site to enjoy freshly caught seafood, Cornish cream teas, and panoramic views of the ocean. The Tinners Arms in Zennor offers a traditional pub experience dating back to the 13th century, along with a menu including locally produced foods and hearty dishes.

The ultimate way to experience Cornwall's coastline

Hiking the South West Coast Path is one of the most enjoyable ways to explore Cornwall's natural landscapes, diverse wildlife, and breathtaking sea views. Whether you take a short and scenic route or embark on a multi-day expedition, each step along the coast reveals something new—hidden coves, old ruins, wildflower meadows, and the ever-changing beat of the ocean.

For nature lovers, photographers, and explorers alike, Cornwall's coastal treks provide a memorable tour through one of Britain's most magnificent settings.

SURFING IN NEWQUAY: RIDE THE WAVES ON FISTRAL BEACH

Newquay, known as the UK's surfing capital, is a dream destination for wave surfers of all skill levels. Among the various surf places along Cornwall's craggy coastline, Fistral Beach is the best destination for surfers. Fistral Beach, with its regular waves, gorgeous environment, and dynamic surf culture, attracts both novices and seasoned surfers from all over the world. Whether you want to take your first surf lesson, ride some of the most difficult waves in the UK, or simply soak up the lively environment, Newquay's surf scene will provide an amazing experience.

Why is Fistral Beach the Best Surfing Spot in the UK?

Fistral Beach's reputation as the UK's finest surfing destination stems from its powerful Atlantic swells and well-shaped waves. The beach faces westward, directly into the open ocean, so it gets some of the finest swells all year. It offers waves at all ability levels, from gentle rollers for beginners to strong barrels for advanced surfers.

The beach itself is over 750 meters long, giving surfers plenty of room to spread out and making the experience more enjoyable even during peak seasons. The golden beaches and steep cliffs surrounding the beach provide a breathtaking backdrop, adding to the attractiveness of the surfing experience.

Fistral Beach is also home to an active surfing culture. The existence of surf schools, board rental shops, and competitions ensures that the area retains its reputation as the heart of British surfing. The beach frequently organises international surf events, such as the Boardmasters Surf Festival, which attracts top surfers from across the world.

Best Months to Surf at Fistral Beach

While surfing is possible all year at Fistral Beach, different seasons provide unique conditions that suit a variety of skill levels.

Spring and summer waves are typically smaller and more forgiving, making them ideal for beginners wishing to practise on soft, rolling waves. The warmer weather also makes it a fun time for newcomers to the sport. This is the peak season for surf schools, and the beach is packed with both locals and visitors eager to get in the water.

Autumn brings ideal conditions for intermediate and advanced surfers. The water remains pretty warm from the summer, but the crowds start to dwindle out. The Atlantic swells grow stronger, producing more powerful waves that test those looking to improve their skills.

The most experienced surfers take to the water throughout the winter. During this season, the largest and most powerful swells arrive, creating waves up to 10 feet high. The lower temperatures and harsher conditions make it less appropriate for beginners, but for those looking for thrilling rides, winter offers some of the best surfing in the UK.

Surf Schools and Lessons for Beginners

For those new to surfing, Newquay is one of the best places in the world to start. Several top-rated surf schools operate near Fistral Beach, providing expert lessons for people of all ages and skill levels. These schools provide wetsuits, surfboards, and skilled instruction, assuring a safe and pleasurable learning environment.

Newquay Surf School, one of the most established surf schools in the area, provides both group and private lessons. The teachers concentrate on basic basics, ocean safety, and wave reading, ensuring that even complete beginners feel confident in the water.

Another popular option is Quiksilver Surf School, which is great for families and kids. With its welcoming atmosphere and high-quality equipment, it's an excellent choice for individuals wishing to take their initial steps into the world of surfing.

For surfers who already have some experience but want to enhance their skills, Cornish Wave Surf Coaching offers intermediate classes that focus on wave selection, paddling techniques, and turning on the face of the wave.

Equipment Rental and Pricing Details

If you don't have your own surfboard or wetsuit, Newquay offers plenty of rental shops offering a wide selection of equipment for all ability levels. Renting gear is quick and reasonable, making it feasible for tourists to enjoy a spontaneous surf session without needing to bring their own equipment.

Most rental companies, like Fistral Beach Surf Hire, provide beginner-friendly soft-top boards, regular shortboards and longboards, and high-performance boards for advanced surfers. Wetsuits are available in a variety of thicknesses depending on the season, with thicker 5mm suits recommended for winter and thinner 3mm suits suitable for summer.

A regular rental package, which includes a surfboard and wetsuit, usually costs between £15 and £25 for a half-day session or £30-£40 for a full-day rental. Some stores also provide multi-day discounts, making it easier for those planning a longer surfing trip.

Beginner-Friendly Surf Spots Around Newquay

While Fistral Beach is the major hub for surfers, Newquay boasts several additional outstanding surf areas that cater to all levels of ability.

Towan Beach is a good alternative for novices. Located in the town centre, it has mild waves and shallow waters, making it a great area for beginners to practice without the bigger swells found at Fistral.

Watergate Bay, just a short drive from Newquay, is another renowned surfing spot. With its large beach and steady waves, it offers plenty of room for surfers of all skill levels to enjoy the ocean without the crowds of more popular places.

Crantock Beach has lengthy, peeling waves that are ideal for intermediate surfers who want to practise their turns. This gorgeous beach is significantly less busy than Fistral, making it an excellent choice for those seeking a more relaxed surfing experience.

Safety Tips for Surfing in Newquay

Surfing, like any other water sport, requires a basic grasp of safety in order to provide an enjoyable and risk-free experience.

Beginners should always surf in approved lifeguarded zones, which are identified by red and yellow flags on the beach. Professional lifeguards patrol these locations and can aid in the event of an emergency.

Rip currents are widespread in the waters around Newquay, therefore understanding them is vital. If caught in a rip current, surfers should remain calm and avoid paddling directly against it, instead paddling parallel to the coast to escape the current's hold.

Wearing the appropriate wetsuit thickness for the season is critical to avoiding hypothermia, particularly during the winter months when water temperatures drop dramatically. In addition, wearing a surf leash keeps your board tethered and prevents it from drifting away after a wipeout.

For novices, having a session with a licensed surf instructor is the most effective way to acquire proper technique and water safety. Even individuals with some experience can benefit from a coaching session to fine-tune their techniques and improve their overall surfing abilities.

The Ultimate Surfing Experience in the United Kingdom

Surfing in Newquay, particularly on Fistral Beach, is more than a sport; it's a way of life. The combination of world-class waves, breathtaking coastline landscape, and a thriving surf culture make it an unrivalled wave riding destination.

Whether you're catching your first wave or slicing through huge winter swells, Newquay's surf scene has something for everyone. The town's warm attitude, high-quality surf schools, and beautiful beachfront views ensure that every visitor has unforgettable memories of riding the waves in one of Europe's best surfing destinations.

A MAGICAL DAY AT MINACK THEATRE, CORNWALL'S OPEN-AIR CLIFFSIDE THEATRE.

The Minack Theatre, perched spectacularly on the cliffs overlooking the Atlantic Ocean, is one of Cornwall's most outstanding cultural and historical sites. This breathtaking open-air theatre, carved into the granite rocks above Porthcurno Beach, offers guests a totally unique experience. Whether you're seeing a live performance under the stars, strolling the beautifully planted gardens, or appreciating the panoramic sea views, Minack Theatre provides a memorable experience.

With a history as dramatic as the plays presented on its stage, Minack Theatre is more than just a venue; it is a tribute to human ingenuity, resilience, and artistic passion. Minack Theatre, which began as a one-woman enterprise and is now one of Cornwall's most popular attractions, is a must-see for everyone visiting this region of England.

The Fascinating History of Minack Theatre

Rowena Cade, a visionary woman, created Minack Theatre, transforming a craggy cliffside into a world-class performing facility. In the early 1930s, Rowena Cade, who had built her home on Porthcurno's cliffs, volunteered her garden as a location for a staging of Shakespeare's The Tempest. Recognising the possibilities of the spectacular setting, she decided to build a permanent outdoor theatre.

She and her gardener began sculpting seating terraces, pathways, and the stage into the granite cliffs with only hand tools, cement, and a great deal of tenacity. Despite the severe seaside conditions, she worked on the theatre for decades, incorporating elaborate carvings and decorative embellishments that gave Minack its particular character.

Today, Minack Theatre honours Rowena Cade's steadfast passion and innovation. Her vision has left an indelible stamp on Cornwall's cultural environment, and millions of people travel each year to honour her memory and experience the wonder of this one-of-a-kind theatre.

Stunning location and breathtaking views.

One of the most appealing qualities about Minack Theatre is its location. Nestled on the craggy cliffs of Porthcurno, the theatre has unbroken views of the Atlantic Ocean, providing a beautiful natural background for performances.

During the day, tourists may see the turquoise waters and golden sands of Porthcurno Beach below, while the horizon spreads eternally into the open sea. On a clear day, you may even see dolphins or seals playing in the water.

As the sun sets, the ambiance at Minack Theatre becomes even more wonderful. Watching a play as the sky becomes golden, with the sound of crashing waves below and a nice coastal breeze caressing over your skin, is a unique experience. The combination of nature and theatre produces a compelling atmosphere that heightens the charm of each performance.

Performances & Events at Minack Theatre

Minack Theatre provides a broad range of performances throughout the year, including Shakespearean classics, modern tragedies, musicals, and even children's storytelling sessions.

The theatre season normally lasts from spring to early October, when the weather is pleasant and the outdoor setting is ideal. During this time, spectators can see anything from Shakespeare's tragedies and comedies to modern plays, opera performances, and live music concerts. Each show is carefully chosen to match the theatre's unique ambiance, providing visitors with an outstanding experience.

One of the most enjoyable aspects of seeing a show at Minack is how the natural environment is incorporated into the performance. Actors frequently have to project their voices over the sound of the waves, while birds occasionally provide an unexpected yet hilarious aspect to the act. Every Minack performance is unique due to the beautiful combination of nature and theatre.

When is the best time to visit and how can I get tickets?

The optimal time to visit Minack Theatre depends on the type of experience you want. If you wish to see a live performance, plan your visit between April and September, when the theatre's roster is jam-packed with intriguing shows. However, tickets frequently sell out quickly, so reserving in advance is strongly advised.

If you prefer a quieter atmosphere, visiting during the day allows you to explore the theatre at your leisure. You may wander down the terraces, enjoy the stunning coastline views, and learn more about Minack's history at the visitor centre and exhibition.

The price of performance tickets varies based on the production and the seating arrangement. Adult tickets often cost between £10 and £20, with discounts available for students, children, and seniors. Daytime entrance to sightseeing is typically around £10 for adults and £5 for children.

Minack Theatre also hosts unique events like workshops, presentations, and storytelling sessions, making it an ideal destination for both families and theatre fans.

Accessibility and Facilities

Because of the cliffside setting of Minack Theatre, some people may find it difficult to get there. However, attempts have been made to ensure that the site is as inclusive as possible.

Step-free access to certain portions of the theatre is available for people with restricted mobility, including a viewing platform that offers a wonderful view of the stage and the sea beyond. Wheelchair users and anyone who have difficulty walking are recommended to call the theatre in advance to provide the best possible access.

The Minack Theatre has a café with locally sourced food and drinks, a gift store selling souvenirs and theatre-related products, and well-maintained toilets. There are also picnic places where guests can eat a meal while admiring the breathtaking scenery.

Tips to Make the Most of Your Visit

To get the most out of your visit to Minack Theatre, come prepared. If you're attending an evening concert, bring warm clothing and blankets because the temperature can drop quickly once the sun goes down. A cushion or foldable seat is also recommended because the granite seats might be uncomfortable to sit on for extended periods of time.

Sunscreen and a hat are required for daytime visits because the theatre provides little shade. Comfortable footwear is also recommended, as some paths and steps are steep.

Photography is highly encouraged, so remember to bring your camera or smartphone to capture the amazing scenery. Whether you're watching a play or just touring the grounds, Minack Theatre provides numerous opportunity for excellent photographs.

A Timeless Theatre Experience on the Cliffs of Cornwall

Minack Theatre is more than just a venue; it is a space where history, nature, and art collide to produce something truly amazing. Whether you're witnessing a riveting Shakespearean drama, listening to live music against the backdrop of the sea, or simply admiring the wonderful craftsmanship that went into building this theatre, Minack is an experience you'll never forget.

Its distinctive cliffside location, intriguing history, and outstanding performances make it one of Cornwall's most valued attractions. Minack theatrical is a must-see for theatrical fans, history buffs, and nature lovers alike when visiting Cornwall.

The Iconic Cornish Pasty: History and Where to Get the Best

The Cornish pasty is more than just a savoury pastry; it is a cultural icon for Cornwall, firmly ingrained in the region's history and traditions. This delectable, hand-held supper, with its golden, crimped crust and rich, flavourful filling, has been a Cornish culinary mainstay for ages. The Cornish pasty is a beloved dish by both locals and visitors, and it tells a remarkable story of resilience, innovation, and culinary tradition.

A Brief History of Cornish Pasties

The Cornish pasty dates back to the 13th century, but it gained popularity in the 18th and 19th centuries, especially among Cornwall's tin miners. These hard-working guys required a convenient, healthy, and substantial lunch that could last long hours below, and the pasty provided the ideal solution.

Traditionally, the pasty was constructed with a thick, crimped crust that served as a handle, allowing miners to eat the filling while using unclean hands. This was especially crucial in the mines, where arsenic and other hazardous compounds were prevalent. The crust, which was frequently abandoned after eating, helped protect the dish from contamination.

Another intriguing historical element of the Cornish pasty is that it might have two sections—savory and sweet. This meant that miners could eat their main course and dessert in the same pasty, making it an extremely convenient meal.

The pasty has developed over the centuries, but its significance in Cornwall has not changed. Today, it holds Protected Geographical Indication (PGI) status, meaning that only pasties made in Cornwall using traditional methods and ingredients can legally be called "Cornish pasties."

What Makes a Cornish Pasty Authentic?

A true Cornish pasty adheres to strict requirements to maintain its originality and quality. A Cornish pasty, according to PGI criteria, must be filled with beef, potatoes, swede (rutabaga), onion, salt and pepper and wrapped in a shortcrust or rough puff pastry.

The filling must be uncooked when inserted inside the pastry, allowing it to cook while baking. This slow-cooking approach ensures that the flavours combine precisely, resulting in a soft, flavourful filling within a crispy, golden crust.

One of the most distinguishing characteristics of a Cornish pasty is its D-shaped shape with a crimped edge on one side. The crimping process is vital for sealing the pasty and keeping the filling intact.

Where to Find the Best Cornish Pasties?

Cornwall is home to some of the best pastry shops and bakeries, each with their own unique interpretation on the famous recipe. Whether you want a traditional pasty or a modern twist with unique fillings, there are lots of options to satiate your hunger.

- **Cornish Bakery (Various Locations)**

The Cornish Bakery is one of Cornwall's most popular pasty chains, serving award-winning pasties produced from high-quality ingredients. Their typical pasty is a must-try, but they also have a number of interesting flavours, such as cheese and onion and spicy chicken.

- **Phillips Bakery (Hayle, Marazion, Penzance)**

Philps Bakery has been manufacturing pasties for over 70 years and is renowned for its properly seasoned filling and flaky, buttery dough. Locals and visitors both enthuse about their amply stuffed classic pasties.

- **Ann's Pasties (Helston, Porthleven, and the Lizard)**

Ann's Pasties is the place to go if you want a pasty created by a family-run business that genuinely cares about Cornish tradition. Their hand-crimped pasties are produced fresh daily using locally sourced ingredients.

- **Warrens Bakery (several locations in Cornwall)**

Warrens Bakery, the world's oldest pasty producer, has a rich history dating back to 1860. They adhere to traditional ways while also providing exciting variants such as lamb and mint and vegan pasties.

- **Malcolm Barnecutt's Bakery (Bodmin, Wadebridge, Rock, St. Austell, and Beyond)**

This popular bakery offers some of Cornwall's best crust-to-filling ratio pasties. Their typical steak pasty is a client favourite, but they also serve gluten-free and vegetarian versions.

Modern twists on the traditional Cornish pasty

While the traditional Cornish pasty remains popular, modern bakeries and chefs are experimenting with new flavours. Some prominent versions are:

- **Vegetarian option**: Cheese & Onion Pasty, prepared with Cornish cheddar and caramelised onions.
- **Lamb & Mint Pasty** - A delectable combination of locally sourced lamb and fresh mint.
- **Popular Chicken & Chorizo** Pasty with spicy and smoky flavours.
- **Vegan Pasty:** Made with plant-based ingredients like mushrooms, sweet potatoes, and leeks.

Many bakeries now serve gluten-free pasties, making this Cornish staple more accessible to visitors with dietary restrictions.

Tips for Eating Cornish Pasty Like a Local

Eating a Cornish pasty is a cultural experience, and here are a few pointers to help you enjoy it the right way.

First, don't use a knife and fork; pasties are designed to be eaten by hand. Their sturdy, crimped edge makes them easy to hold, so follow tradition and eat straight from the bag.

Second, choose a scenic location to enjoy it. Cornwall's coastline makes an ideal setting for a pasty picnic. Whether you're sitting on the cliffs overlooking St. Ives Bay, relaxing on the sands of Porthcurno Beach, or stopping for a break after hiking the South West Coast Path, eating a pasty with a sea view is an unforgettable experience.

Finally, watch out for seagulls! These smart birds have a propensity of stealing pasties from people's hands, particularly in prominent tourist destinations such as St. Ives and Padstow. To avoid losing your lunch, keep it close and keep an eye on the sky.

The Cornish Pasty is a must-try culinary experience.

The Cornish pasty is not simply a meal—it's a piece of Cornwall's history and culture that continues to be cherished by locals and visitors alike. Whether you have a traditional steak pasty from a family-run bakery or experiment with a gourmet variety, this basic yet wonderful food is an essential element of any trip to Cornwall.

No visit to the region is complete without biting into a warm, freshly baked pasty, relishing its rich tastes, and appreciating the centuries of tradition behind this unique delicacy.

Cornwall, with its craggy coastline and profound marine past, has long been regarded as a seafood lovers' paradise. The region's proximity to the Atlantic Ocean assures a steady supply of fresh, high-quality seafood, making it a haven for people who enjoy the flavours of the ocean. From plump oysters harvested from Cornwall's pristine waters to delectable lobster rolls bursting with flavour, the county provides a diverse and mouthwatering seafood experience.

Whether you're dining at a Michelin-starred restaurant, picking up a seafood snack from a coastal food shack, or enjoying a simple plate of fish and chips by the harbour, the taste of Cornwall's seafood is one of the most memorable aspects of any visit.

The Rich Tradition of Seafood in Cornwall

For centuries, Cornwall's fishing industry has played a vital role in its economy and culture. Generations of fishermen have braved the Atlantic waves to bring in daily catches of mackerel, crab, lobster, and other prized seafood. Towns like Newlyn, Padstow, and St. Ives have thrived as fishing hubs, with local seafood markets supplying restaurants and homes across the region.

The Cornish fishing community is dedicated to sustainable techniques, ensuring that the region's seas remain teeming with marine life. Many local fisheries and restaurants emphasize ethically produced seafood, with an increasing number receiving MSC (Marine Stewardship Council) accreditation to promote responsible fishing.

The result is seafood that is not only extraordinarily fresh but also obtained in an environmentally responsible way, guaranteeing that future generations may continue to enjoy Cornwall's gastronomic riches.

Oysters - A Taste of the Cornish Coast

One of Cornwall's most sumptuous seafood products is the oyster, which has been produced in the province for centuries. The Fal River Estuary, in Falmouth, is home to one of the last remaining traditional oyster fisheries in Europe, where oysters are still picked using sail-powered boats and hand-hauled dredges.

The unusual blend of freshwater from the river and saltwater from the sea gives Fal oysters a peculiar flavor—mildly saline with a smooth, somewhat sweet finish. They are best consumed raw, served on a bed of crushed ice with a touch of lemon, or mixed with a shallot vinaigrette for an extra burst of flavor.

Visitors may get a truly immersive experience by taking oyster farm tours, where they can learn about traditional harvesting methods and even shuck and sample fresh oysters right from the water. The Falmouth Oyster Festival, held every October, is a must-see for seafood enthusiasts, with cooking demos, tastings, and exuberant celebrations honouring Cornwall's oyster legacy.

Cornish lobster is a delicious delicacy.

No vacation to Cornwall is complete without indulging in Cornish lobster, which is regarded as some of the best in the world. The calm, clean seas off the Cornish coast give perfect circumstances for lobsters to grow, producing firm, sweet, and juicy meat.

Many seafood restaurants and coastal eateries provide freshly caught lobster in a variety of preparations. Some like grilled lobster with garlic butter, which highlights the meat's natural sweetness. Others indulge in lobster thermidor, a rich, creamy dish with a decadent cheese and mustard sauce.

Lobster rolls are a popular option for visitors looking for a more casual experience. These delectable sandwiches include chunks of tender lobster meat tossed in a light, flavourful dressing and served on a buttery, toasted brioche roll. They're ideal for those exploring Cornwall's picturesque harbours and beaches as a quick meal.

Traditional Cornish Crab - Sweet and succulent

Cornwall is also renowned for its delicious crab, with brown crab and spider crab being the most commonly caught varieties. The mild, sweet flavor of Cornish crab makes it a favoured ingredient in many local cuisines, from simple crab sandwiches to more sophisticated crab bisques and seafood platters.

One of the best ways to enjoy Cornish crab is in a crab salad, where the fresh, flaky flesh is served with crisp greens, cherry tomatoes, and a light dressing. Another local favorite is crab linguine, a dish that mixes fresh pasta with white crab meat, garlic, chiles, and a dash of lemon juice for a dish overflowing with flavor.

Many restaurants serve whole crabs, freshly steamed or boiled, with crusty bread and homemade mayonnaise. This hands-on seafood experience allows diners to truly enjoy the delicate texture and flavour of Cornish crab.

Where to Find the Best Seafood in Cornwall

Cornwall has an incredible selection of seafood restaurants, fish markets, and coastal food stalls, each offering a distinct taste of the region's maritime bounty. Whether you prefer fine dining or a casual seafood shack by the water, there is something for every seafood lover.

Padstow, the Seafood Capital of Cornwall.

Padstow, a picturesque fishing hamlet on Cornwall's north coast, is widely regarded as the ultimate seafood resort. Celebrity chef Rick

Stein has helped to place Padstow on the culinary map with his well-known Seafood Restaurant, where customers can enjoy expertly prepared dishes crafted with the freshest local ingredients. Other great seafood restaurants in Padstow include Prawn on the Lawn, which is famed for its inventive small plates, and The Lobster Shed, which specialises in grilled lobster and crab.

St. Ives: Fresh Seafood with a View.

St. Ives is another popular seafood destination, with breathtaking ocean views and a wide range of excellent dining options. The Rum & Crab Shack is a local favourite, offering a wide variety of crab dishes and rum-infused cocktails. For a more upscale experience, The Porthminster Beach Café serves beautifully presented seafood dishes with breathtaking views of the beach.

Newlyn, the heart of Cornwall's fishing industry.

Newlyn, one of the busiest fishing ports in the UK, is the place to go for the freshest seafood direct off the boats. Mackerel Sky Seafood Bar is a must-visit spot, offering a relaxed atmosphere and a menu filled with seafood tapas-style dishes, including mussels, scallops, and mackerel pâté. The town's fish market also offers an excellent opportunity to get fresh seafood for cooking at home.

Cornwall's Seafood Scene—A Culinary Adventure

Cornwall's seafood scene is as diversified as its breathtaking shoreline. Whether you're indulging in a plate of fresh oysters in Falmouth, savoring a buttery lobster roll in Padstow, or cracking into a sweet Cornish crab in St. Ives, each dish offers a taste of the region's deep connection to the sea.

For those who love seafood, Cornwall is a dream trip, delivering not only some of the freshest and most flavorful seafood in the UK but also a memorable dining experience surrounded by magnificent coastal scenery.

Cornwall is famous for many things—its stunning coastline, rich history, and incredible seafood—but perhaps one of its most beloved traditions is cream tea. Cream tea, a Cornish cultural staple, consists of a freshly baked scone, a generous dollop of clotted cream, and a layer of sweet, fruity jam, all served with a steaming pot of tea.

This seemingly simple dish, however, has generated one of the UK's most heated culinary debates: should the jam or cream come first? For years, Cornwall and its neighbouring county, Devon, have fought bitterly over their respective traditions.

For tourists visiting Cornwall, trying a good Cornish cream tea is a must—not only for the excellent taste, but also for the opportunity to participate in this light-hearted yet deeply rooted cultural custom.

The History of Cream Tea

The origins of cream tea can be traced back millennia. Some historians claim that the custom began in the 11th century, when monks at Tavistock Abbey in Devon offered bread with clotted cream and jam to laborers repairing the abbey. However, the Cornish think that their own clotted cream history extends back much longer, with local farmers manufacturing the thick, golden cream as far back as the medieval period.

Regardless of its specific roots, cream tea became popular throughout the Victorian era, when afternoon tea rituals developed across Britain. As more people traveled to Cornwall and Devon, the tradition spread, and soon, tea rooms across both counties were serving scones with clotted cream and jam as a quintessential English indulgence.

Today, cream tea remains a beloved part of Cornwall's culinary identity, enjoyed in cozy cafés, grand hotels, and picturesque countryside tea gardens.

The Cornish Way: Jam First, Then Cream

In Cornwall, the correct method to eat a cream tea is to spread the jam first, followed by a thick coating of clotted cream. Locals feel that this method makes the most sense, as the jam functions as a basis, allowing the thick, velvety clotted cream to rest lightly on top without sliding off.

Cornish clotted cream, which bears a PDO (Protected Designation of Origin) designation, has a distinct thick texture and a rich, buttery flavour. It is traditionally made by gradually heating full-fat cow's milk and then cooling it until the cream rises to the surface and forms a thick, golden crust. Because of its luxurious consistency, Cornish clotted cream is best served in a generous layer rather than thinly spread.

Many Cornish residents passionately defend their "jam first" method, claiming that it improves the overall flavour balance. The experience is said to be more pleasant and flavourful when the jam's sweetness hits the taste receptors first, followed by the cream's decadent richness.

The Devonshire Approach: Cream first, then jam.

Just across the border in Devon, locals insist on putting the cream on first, followed by a dollop of jam. The Devonshire tradition treats the scone more like a buttered piece of bread, with clotted cream replacing butter and jam as a finishing touch.

While this method has its supporters, Cornish purists argue that it is not logical. They point out that Devon's approach forces the jam to slide off the cream, making for a messier and less balanced bite.

Although the two counties continue to disagree on the order of toppings, one thing remains constant: the quality of the scone, the richness of the cream, and the fruity sweetness of the jam all play an essential role in creating the perfect cream tea experience.

Where to Have the Best Cream Tea in Cornwall.

Cornwall is home to some of the best tea rooms and cafés in the country, with many serving award-winning cream teas in picturesque settings. Whether you want a cosy, traditional setting or an alfresco experience overlooking the sea, there are numerous places to enjoy a delicious Cornish cream tea.

The Duchess of Cornwall Inn at Poundbury

This elegant tea room provides a traditional cream tea experience in a charming, vintage-inspired setting. Their handcrafted scones, topped with Rodda's Cornish clotted cream and locally made jam, are a really authentic delicacy.

The Hidden Hut, Porthcurnick Beach

For a seaside cream tea experience, The Hidden Hut offers something truly special. This rustic outdoor café serves fresh, locally sourced treats, including warm scones served with Cornish clotted cream and jam, all enjoyed with breathtaking ocean views.

The Cream Tea Café, St. Ives

Nestled in the heart of St. Ives, this lovely café is well-known for its generously proportioned scones and extra-thick cream. It's a popular destination for people wishing to enjoy a traditional cream tea while visiting one of Cornwall's most lovely seaside villages.

Trevaskis Farm, Hayle

For those who love homemade, farm-fresh ingredients, Trevaskis Farm offers a delightful cream tea made with scones baked fresh daily, along with fruit preserves made from their own farm-grown produce.

The Ultimate Cream Tea Experience: Making Your Own

For visitors who want to fully immerse themselves in the Cornish culinary tradition, making homemade cream tea can be a rewarding experience.

Baking the Perfect Scones

The key to a great scone lies in its texture—it should be light, fluffy, and slightly crumbly, with a golden crust. Traditional Cornish scones are made with flour, butter, sugar, milk, and baking powder, and they are best enjoyed fresh out of the oven.

Choosing the Best Clotted Cream

While store-bought clotted cream might be excellent, nothing surpasses fresh, locally made Cornish clotted cream. If you visit Cornwall, consider purchasing a tub from a local dairy farm to take home with you.

Choosing the Right Jam

Strawberry jam is the most traditional topping for a Cornish cream tea, providing the ideal combination of sweetness and fruitiness. However, raspberry, blackberry, or even homemade plum jam can be delicious options.

A Delicious Tradition That Stands the Test of Time

The jam first vs. cream first debate may never be settled, but what truly matters is the shared love for this delightful Cornish tradition. Whether you're sitting in a cozy tearoom in St. Ives, enjoying a cream tea with ocean views in Padstow, or baking your own scones at home, the experience of indulging in warm scones, thick clotted cream, and fruity jam is a moment of pure bliss.

So, next time you find yourself in Cornwall, make sure to order a proper Cornish cream tea, spread your jam first, top it with a generous helping of clotted cream, and savor every bite of this delicious, time-honored treat.

CORNISH CIDER & LOCAL BREWS – BEST PUBS & TASTING SPOTS

Cornwall is not just recognised for its stunning coastline and rich history but also for its robust cider and brewing culture. The region has a long-standing tradition of cider-making, thanks to its warm temperature, which gives the right circumstances for producing apples. Along with its famed ciders, Cornwall has a thriving craft beer culture, with independent breweries creating some of the UK's best ales and lagers.

Exploring Cornwall's cider and brewing heritage is a must for any visitor wishing to enjoy true local flavors. Whether you like a refreshing, crisp cider made from heritage apple varieties or a smooth, full-bodied Cornish ale, there are plenty of great pubs, breweries, and cider farms to visit.

The History of Cornish Cider

Cider-making in Cornwall dates back centuries, with records suggesting that apples were being pressed for their juice as early as the medieval period. The region's fertile orchards provided an abundant supply of apples, and farmers quickly realized that fermenting the juice created a delicious, mildly alcoholic drink.

During the 18th and 19th centuries, cider became a staple beverage for farm laborers, typically provided as part of their daily salary. It was regarded as a safer alternative to drinking water, which was often contaminated. Over time, Cornish cider gained popularity beyond the farming community, and today, Cornwall is known for producing some of the finest traditional ciders in the UK.

Famous Cornish Cider Brands

Healeys Cornish Cyder Farm, one of Cornwall's most well-known cider producers, has been producing award-winning cider since 1986. Rattler, their signature cider, is popular with both residents and visitors, because to its robust, invigorating flavour and slightly harsh finish. Rattler comes in a variety of flavours, including traditional apple, pear, and even pineapple, to suit a wide range of tastes.

Cornish Orchards, located in the lovely town of Duloe, is another well-known cider producer. Their ciders are prepared from hand-selected apples that are naturally fermented to produce a smooth and well-balanced beverage. Cornish Orchards' Gold and Heritage Ciders are particularly popular, with nuanced flavours and crisp, clear finishes.

Smaller, independent cider farms can be found throughout the region, creating artisanal ciders with traditional methods. Many of these farms welcome guests for tours and tastings, providing a unique perspective on the cider-making process.

The Cornish Brewing Revolution

While Cornwall's cider legacy is well recognised, the region has also enjoyed a craft beer boom in recent years. Independent brewers have thrived, creating a broad range of lagers, pale ales, IPAs, and stouts that highlight the region's talented brewing community.

One of the most famous Cornish brewers is St Austell Brewery, which has been brewing beer since 1851. Their main beers, Tribute (a mellow, well-balanced pale ale) and Proper Job (a robust, hoppy IPA), are widely accessible in pubs around Cornwall and beyond. The brewery provides guided tours, which allow visitors to learn about the brewing process and drink their beers directly from the source.

Another noteworthy brewery is Harbour Brewing Co., noted for its unique, modern approach to beer-making. Harbour Brewing, based in Bodmin, specialises in small-batch, handcrafted beers with robust flavours and high-quality ingredients. Their selections range from crisp pilsners to rich, nuanced porters, making them a popular choice among craft beer fans.

Smaller microbreweries, such as Verdant Brewing Co. in Falmouth and Padstow Brewing Co., have also received attention for their innovative and experimental brews. Verdant is particularly well-known for its hazy, hop-forward IPAs, whilst Padstow Brewing is famed for its balanced, flavourful beers that represent Cornwall's seaside charm.

The Best Pubs and Tasting Spots in Cornwall

Cornwall has a superb collection of historic pubs, cider houses, and brewery taprooms where you can enjoy Cornish cider and beer in an authentic setting.

Pandora Inn (Restronguet Creek)

This lovely waterfront tavern is one of Cornwall's most popular drinking establishments. The Pandora Inn, which dates back to the 13th century, serves a superb selection of Cornish ciders and ales while providing spectacular views of the stream. The pub's thatched roof, wooden beams, and floating pontoon seating make it a memorable spot to have a drink.

Blue Anchor (Helston)

For those interested in Cornwall's brewing history, The Blue Anchor is a must-see. This historic alehouse is one of Cornwall's oldest pubs, having brewed its own beer on-site for almost 600 years. Their flagship ale, Spingo, comes in a variety of strengths, ranging from a light, malty brew to a rich, high-alcohol version.

The Sloop Inn, St. Ives

The Sloop Inn, located right on the harbour in St. Ives, is a charming, centuries-old pub with an excellent selection of local ciders and ales. Its cosy interior and outdoor seats with harbour views make it an ideal spot to relax with a drink while watching the boats come and go.

Healeys Cornish Cider Farm (Near Truro)

Healeys Cornish Cyder Farm is a must-see for cider enthusiasts. This family-run cider farm provides guided tours and tastings, allowing visitors to experience a variety of ciders, including their well-known Rattler series. Guests can also visit the historic cider press, distillery, and even a real farm, making it an enjoyable experience for the entire family.

Verdant Brewery Taproom, Falmouth

Craft beer enthusiasts should visit the Verdant Brewery Taproom, where they can sample some of Cornwall's best modern IPAs, pale ales, and stouts. With a relaxed ambiance and a rotating assortment of fresh, hop-forward beers, it's a must-see for beer enthusiasts.

Combining Cornish Cider and Beer with Local Food

Pairing Cornish cider and beer with traditional local meals is one of the greatest ways to fully enjoy them.

Cider pairs well with Cornwall's famous seafood, especially fresh oysters, mussels, and grilled mackerel. The crisp acidity and slight sweetness of cider complement the briny, delicate flavours of seafood, resulting in an ideal balance.

For those enjoying a Cornish pasty, a pint of amber ale or a traditional Cornish bitter is the ideal accompaniment. The malty, caramel tones of the beer accentuate the rich, flavourful filling of the pasty, providing for a very fulfilling supper.

Meanwhile, hops IPAs work well with spicy meals, cutting through the heat and intensifying the flavors, while dark stouts and porters are a perfect match for chocolate desserts and rich, creamy cheeses.

A taste of Cornwall in every sip.

Cornwall's cider and beer culture reflects the region's rich agricultural past, excellent workmanship, and long-standing traditions. Whether you're drinking a crisp, delicious cider made from Cornish apples or a pint of craft beer created by dedicated artisans, each taste represents a bit of Cornwall's culture.

Exploring Cornwall's cider farms, breweries, and historic pubs is an unforgettable experience for visitors who want to immerse themselves in the local flavours. So raise a glass to Cornwall's wonderful brewing and cider-making traditions, and enjoy the finest that this dynamic region has to offer.

VEGETARIAN AND VEGAN-FRIENDLY DINING OPTIONS IN CORNWALL

Cornwall is known for its rich culinary heritage, which includes fresh seafood, hearty pasties, and locally brewed beverages. However, in recent years, the region has embraced the rise of vegetarian and vegan restaurants, with a broad selection of plant-based dishes to suit all preferences. From quaint cafés serving hearty vegan breakfasts to sophisticated eateries generating creative plant-based cuisine, Cornwall has something for every vegetarian and vegan traveler.

The Increasing Popularity of Plant-Based Cuisine in Cornwall

Traditionally, Cornwall's cuisine scene was dominated by meat and seafood dishes, but a revolution in dietary choices has resulted in a thriving vegetarian and vegan community. With an increasing number of people adopting plant-based lifestyles for health, environmental, and ethical reasons, many Cornish restaurants, cafés, and bakeries have expanded their menus to include delicious vegetarian and vegan options.

One of the key reasons for this shift is Cornwall's strong focus on sustainability and locally sourced ingredients. The region's rich agricultural landscape produces an abundance of fresh vegetables, fruits, legumes, and grains, which form the foundation of many plant-based dishes. Additionally, Cornwall's seaside environment has encouraged the use of seaweed, samphire, and other foraged ingredients, bringing unique flavors to vegetarian and vegan cuisine.

Traditional Cornish Cuisine with a Plant-Based Twist

Cornwall's culinary legacy includes some renowned dishes that have been recreated for vegetarians and vegans. One of the most notable versions is the vegan Cornish pasty. Traditionally filled with beef, potatoes, swede, and onions, the vegan version replaces the meat with flavourful alternatives like lentils, mushrooms, or jackfruit, while retaining the rich, hearty flavour that makes pasties so popular. Many bakeries now serve vegan pasties, allowing plant-based diners to experience this Cornish delicacy.

Another popular dish that has been adapted is stargazy pie, originally made with whole fish poking out of the crust. Modern vegan variants of this meal replace the fish with smoked tofu, mushrooms, or jackfruit, seasoned with seaweed to replicate the taste of the ocean. Similarly, Cornwall's famous seafood chowder has been given a plant-based makeover, with creamy coconut or cashew milk bases replacing dairy, and potatoes, leeks, and nori seaweed providing depth of flavor.

For those with a sweet craving, Cornwall's famed cream tea is also available in a vegan variant. Many cafés now serve dairy-free scones made with plant-based butter, topped with coconut cream or oat-based alternatives and delicious homemade fruit preserves. The question over whether to spread jam or cream first remains just as significant for plant-based dining!

Top Vegetarian and Vegan Restaurants in Cornwall

Cornwall has a thriving plant-based food scene, with restaurants, cafés, and takeaways offering delicious meat-free meals.

The Bean Inn (Carbis Bay)

Located just outside St. Ives, The Bean Inn is one of Cornwall's best-known vegetarian and vegan restaurants. The menu features a creative selection of plant-based dishes, using fresh, organic, and locally sourced ingredients. Guests can enjoy flavorful curries, roasted vegetable platters, and indulgent desserts in a cozy, welcoming atmosphere.

The Cornish Vegan (truro)

For a completely vegan experience, The Cornish Vegan in Truro is a must-see. This restaurant serves vegan comfort food including jackfruit "fish" and chips, seitan burgers, and creamy dairy-free mac & cheese. Their handcrafted cakes and pastries, which include rich chocolate brownies and fruit crumbles, are equally popular.

Potager Garden Cafe (Constantinc)

Potager Garden Café, located in a lovely organic garden, provides a relaxing eating experience with a cuisine focussing on vegetarian and vegan whole foods. The café's menu changes with the seasons, with delicacies such as butternut squash risotto, roasted chickpea stews, and substantial bread sandwiches with plant-based spreads.

The Stable (Fistral Beach, Newquay)

For those who adore pizza with a sea view, The Stable in Newquay provides a superb assortment of vegetarian and vegan pizzas. Toppings include locally produced vegetables, plant-based cheeses, and handmade tomato sauces. The restaurant also serves vegan-friendly ciders, making it a great place to enjoy a relaxed meal by the coast.

Sam's Deli (Fowey)

For plant-based eaters on the go, Sam's Deli in Fowey offers a range of freshly made vegan sandwiches, wraps, and salads. Their falafel wraps and hummus-filled baguettes are popular with travellers searching for a quick and healthful supper.

Plant-Based Marketplaces and Food Festivals

In addition to restaurants and cafés, Cornwall has various food markets and festivals dedicated to plant-based cuisine.

The Penzance Farmers' Market is an excellent place to find fresh, organic produce directly from local farmers. Shoppers can pick up fresh veggies, handcrafted vegan cheeses, artisan bread, and plant-based condiments, making it an excellent visit for self-catering travelers.

Each year, Cornwall holds the Vegan and Ethical Market in Truro, which brings together vegan food vendors, eco-friendly items, and sustainable fashion manufacturers. This festival is perfect for those looking to explore new plant-based flavors, with vendors offering everything from vegan Cornish pasties to dairy-free ice cream and locally made kombucha.

Another excellent event is the Great Cornish Food Festival, which showcases local producers' latest innovations. Many vendors now provide vegan and vegetarian-friendly options, allowing visitors to enjoy some of Cornwall's best plant-based foods.

The Best Places for Vegan Afternoon Tea

Afternoon tea is a cherished tradition in Cornwall, and many tea establishments now provide plant-based versions of this iconic experience.

The Greenbank Hotel in Falmouth offers an elegant vegan afternoon tea that includes delicate finger sandwiches, dairy-free scones, and a variety of plant-based cakes. Their handcrafted almond milk lattes and herbal teas make the experience even better.

For a more rural environment, The Hidden Hut near Portscatho provides an outdoor afternoon tea experience, where guests can eat freshly baked vegan scones with locally made jams while admiring the magnificent Cornish coastline.

Sustainable & Ethical Dining in Cornwall.

One of the most appealing parts of Cornwall's vegetarian and vegan eating scene is the emphasis on sustainability and ethical food sourcing. Many of the region's plant-based restaurants and cafés collaborate with local organic farms, independent farmers, and ethical suppliers to guarantee that their supplies are of high quality.

Cornwall's commitment to eliminating food waste and supporting sustainable agriculture is shown in its numerous farm-to-table programs. Restaurants like The Rocket Store in Boscastle and Canteen in St. Agnes prioritise seasonal, locally farmed produce, ensuring that diners eat fresh, flavourful, and environmentally friendly meals.

A thriving plant-based food scene for all visitors.

Cornwall has fully embraced the vegetarian and vegan movement, making it an ideal location for plant-based travellers. There are numerous options to choose from, including a casual café serving substantial vegan breakfasts, a fine dining experience featuring innovative plant-based cuisine, and a traditional Cornish pasty with a meat-free twist.

Cornwall is a vegetarian and vegan foodie's dream, thanks to its devotion to ecology, fresh local products, and inventive culinary expertise. No matter where you go in this lovely region, you're likely to find tasty, plant-based recipes that reflect the finest of Cornwall's natural wealth.

How To Get To Cornwall: Flights, Trains, and Roads

Cornwall is one of the most gorgeous places in the United Kingdom, attracting visitors with its stunning coastline, historic villages, and rich cultural history. Cornwall is located in the far southwest of England, so getting there takes some planning, but there are several options to suit different travel tastes. Cornwall is well connected to the rest of the UK, whether you fly, take the train, drive, or utilise a coach service. Understanding your travel alternatives will help you have a seamless and pleasurable journey.

Flying to Cornwall is the fastest way to arrive.

Flying is the quickest method to get to Cornwall from other parts of the UK or internationally. Cornwall Airport Newquay (NQY) is the region's major airport, located just outside of Newquay and serves as a handy entrance point for passengers travelling to popular sites such as St Ives, Padstow, and Falmouth.

Cornwall Airport Newquay provides regular domestic flights from major UK cities like London, Manchester, Birmingham, Edinburgh, and Glasgow, as well as seasonal international flights to Spain, Portugal, and Germany. Airlines such as British Airways, Ryanair, and easyJet provide regular flights, making air travel an efficient option for people with little time.

Once you've landed, there are various options for continuing your voyage. The airport is connected to adjacent towns by bus and taxi, and vehicle rental options are available for people who want to explore Cornwall on their own. Travellers should be advised that flights to Newquay might be more expensive during the summer months, so booking early is recommended.

For those travelling from abroad, the best choice is to fly into London Heathrow (LHR), London Gatwick (LGW), or Bristol Airport (BRS) and then travel to Cornwall by train, coach, or car hire.

Travelling by train: A scenic and comfortable journey.

The train is a popular option for those seeking a relaxing and scenic journey to Cornwall. The principal railway line servicing Cornwall is the Great Western Railway (GWR), which runs direct from London Paddington to Penzance, passing through key Cornish cities such Truro, St Austell, and Bodmin Parkway. The train journey from London to Cornwall usually takes between 4.5 and 6 hours, depending on the destination.

Travellers can add to their comfort by booking seats on the Night Riviera Sleeper Train, which runs overnight from London Paddington to Penzance. This service offers private sleeping cabins, making it a handy and relaxing option to arrive in Cornwall without sacrificing crucial daylight hours.

Visitors from other parts of the UK can also reach the Cornish railway network by train connections from Birmingham, Bristol, Exeter, and Plymouth. Once in Cornwall, branch line services make it simple to explore the area, with scenic routes like the St Ives Bay Line, the Looe Valley Line and the Falmouth Maritime Line providing breathtaking coastal views.

Booking train tickets in advance can help you get reduced rates, as costs tend to climb closer to the departure date. Travellers could also look into railcards and discounts, which can drastically lower expenditures.

Drive to Cornwall: Flexibility and Adventure on the Road

For those who value independence and flexibility, driving to Cornwall is an excellent choice. The M5 motorway runs south from

Bristol to Exeter, where it connects to the A30 and A38, Cornwall's two main roads.

The drive from London to Cornwall takes about 5 to 6 hours, depending on traffic and the destination. From other big cities:

- Bristol to Cornwall: Around 2.5 to 3.5 hours
- Birmingham to Cornwall: Around 4.5 to 5.5 hours
- Manchester to Cornwall: Around 6 to 7 hours

The A30 is the fastest and most direct route, running all the way to Penzance, while the A38 gives access to towns in southeastern Cornwall such Liskeard and Saltash. The gorgeous drive through rolling countryside, craggy moors, and coastal highways makes road-tripping to Cornwall a great experience.

Visitors should be prepared for narrow country lanes when exploring rural Cornwall, particularly in coastal settlements where streets can be tight and winding. During peak summer months, traffic congestion can develop on key highways, so planning travel times outside of popular hours might assist minimise delays.

There are several service stations along the route, providing rest areas, food, and fuel stops. Travelers should also be mindful of parking limitations in several Cornish towns, as many sites have restricted parking or demand advance bookings.

Taking a Coach: An Affordable and Relaxing Alternative

For budget-conscious travelers, riding a coach to Cornwall is one of the most economical methods to reach the region. National Express and Megabus operate long-distance coach services from major UK cities, including London, Bristol, Birmingham, and Manchester, with stops in Cornwall's key towns such as Truro, Newquay, and Penzance.

The coach journey from London to Cornwall takes approximately 7 to 9 hours, depending on traffic and the number of stops. While slower than flying or taking a train, coaches provide a cost-effective option, especially for those traveling with large luggage or looking for a relaxing ride.

Many modern coaches are outfitted with WiFi, power outlets, and reclining seats to ensure a comfortable ride. Advance booking is encouraged because fares are typically lower when purchased in advance.

Arriving by ferry: A Unique Way to Enter Cornwall.

While Cornwall does not have direct ferry links from outside the UK, travellers from France or Spain can take a ship to Plymouth, which is just outside Cornwall. Ferry services from Roscoff (France) and Santander (Spain) arrive at Plymouth, from where travellers can go to Cornwall by car, train, or coach.

Once in Cornwall, ferries offer scenic local transportation between destinations. The King Harry Ferry, for example, connects Truro to the Roseland Peninsula, and the Padstow to Rock Ferry is a popular route for visitors exploring North Cornwall's coastline.

Choosing the Best Travel Option for Your Trip

The best way to get to Cornwall is based on your money, time limits, and preferences. Flying is the fastest alternative, although it is more expensive and needs additional travel from Newquay Airport. Trains offer a scenic and comfortable ride, particularly for those traveling from London, while driving provides the most flexibility and convenience. For individuals trying to save money, coaches are a trusted and budget-friendly choice.

Regardless of how you choose to travel, Cornwall's breathtaking scenery and lovely villages make the journey worthwhile. With careful planning, you can have a seamless and pleasurable journey that allows you to completely appreciate the beauty and culture of this popular coastal destination.

When planning a trip to Cornwall, one of the most important decisions travellers must make is how to move around the area. Cornwall has a multitude of sites to see, including magnificent coastline, attractive villages, and ancient landmarks. However, due to its rural nature, transport options vary greatly depending on where you want to go and how flexible you need to be.

Public transportation, such as trains, buses, and taxis, is an environmentally friendly and cost-effective way to travel, but it has limitations in terms of schedules and coverage. Renting a car, on the other hand, provides more freedom and access to off-the-beaten-path destinations, but it may present obstacles such as limited roads, parking limitations, and expensive rental costs. Understanding the benefits and drawbacks of each choice can help travellers make an informed selection based on their itinerary and preferences.

Exploring Cornwall via Public Transport

For those who prefer not to drive, Cornwall provides a dependable but limited public transit network that connects major cities and several tourist destinations. The region's public transport system includes primarily of trains and buses, with occasional ferry service in some places.

Train Travel in Cornwall.

Cornwall has a well-connected railway system, with the Great Western Railway (GWR) providing services to essential destinations. The main railway route connects Plymouth and Penzance, stopping in Liskeard, St Austell, Truro, Redruth and St

Erth. Branch lines connect these larger stations to smaller towns and villages, some of which provide outstanding scenic excursions.

One of the most popular train routes is the St Ives Bay Line, which runs from St Erth to St Ives and provides stunning coastline vistas. Similarly, the Looe Valley Line, which connects Liskeard and Looe, offers a scenic route through lush farmland and estuaries.

Trains in Cornwall are generally comfortable and convenient for reaching larger towns, but their main disadvantage is the restricted frequency. Unlike in large cities, train services in Cornwall are less regular, so travellers should plan their itineraries carefully to avoid excessive wait periods between connections.

Bus Service and Coverage

Buses are the principal means of public transit for accessing destinations not covered by the train network. First Kernow and Go Cornwall Bus operate the Cornwall Bus Network, which connects towns, villages, and tourist destinations throughout the county. Popular routes connect Land's End, The Lizard Peninsula, and coastal towns like Padstow, Newquay, and Falmouth.

Tourists who want to explore scenic areas without driving can take advantage of the Atlantic Coaster and Land's End Coaster buses, which provide convenient and picturesque transportation along Cornwall's rugged coastline. These seasonal services are designed exclusively for guests and offer hop-on/hop-off possibilities.

While buses do travel to many regions of Cornwall, they are sometimes rare and slow, particularly in rural areas. Travellers should prepare for lengthier journey durations owing to many stops and twisting roads. In smaller settlements, services may be restricted to a few buses each day, necessitating meticulous planning.

Taxis and Ride-Share Services

Taxis are available in Cornwall, albeit not in the same numbers as in big cities. It is recommended that you book a taxi in advance, especially in smaller towns and villages where taxis can be scarce. Ride-sharing services such as Uber are not generally available, thus travellers should rely on local taxis or pre-arranged transportation as necessary.

Taxis can be expensive for long travels, so they are best utilised for short trips, such as getting from a train station to a hotel or seeing a rural attraction that is not accessible by public transit. Some accommodations provide shuttle services or may organise local transportation for guests, so contacting hotels in advance might be beneficial.

Renting A Car: Freedom and Flexibility

For those who want complete flexibility to explore Cornwall at their own leisure, hiring a car is the best alternative. Cornwall's magnificent vistas, secret coves, and remote settlements are simpler to get by automobile, as public transport may not reach many of the most scenic sites.

Advantages of Renting a Car in Cornwall

One of the main perks of owning a rental automobile is the opportunity to go on your own timetable. Public transit in Cornwall, while functional, can be restrictive in terms of timetables and coverage. A car allows travellers to visit remote beaches, scenic viewpoints, and lesser-known villages without having to wait for a bus or train.

Driving also allows for impromptu detours, such as stopping at a quaint tea shop, exploring a lonely coastline trail, or enjoying an unexpected sunset vista. Furthermore, if you intend to visit multiple attractions in one day, a car is a far more efficient mode of transportation.

Renting a car is more comfortable and convenient for families, groups, and those travelling with a lot of luggage than taking buses or taxis. The ability to keep picnic supplies, beach gear, or shopping finds in the car makes day trips more convenient and enjoyable.

Driving Challenges in Cornwall

While renting a car offers more flexibility, there are some drawbacks to consider. Cornwall's road network is comprised of narrow, winding lanes, particularly in rural areas and small villages. Many roads are only wide enough to accommodate one vehicle at a time, forcing drivers to use passing lanes to allow oncoming traffic through.

Parking can also be an issue in popular tourist destinations like St Ives, Padstow, and Fowey, where parking lots fill up quickly during the peak season. Many historic towns have limited parking spaces, and some accommodations do not offer private parking, forcing visitors to use public parking lots that may be a short walk from their hotel.

Fuel prices and rental costs can add up quickly, especially during the summer months when rental cars are in high demand. It is advisable to book well in advance to secure the best rates and availability. Furthermore, some rental companies place restrictions on taking vehicles on narrow or unpaved roads, so double-check the rental terms before booking.

Which is the best option for you?

Finally, the traveler's preferences, budget, and itinerary determine whether to take public transportation or rent a car.

- Larger towns such as Truro, Newquay, and Penzance offer train and bus services that connect to popular attractions. If you prefer not to drive, you can still experience much of Cornwall by using a combination of trains, buses, and taxis.

- For visitors who want to explore remote areas, hidden beaches, or multiple locations in one day, renting a car is the best option. Having your own vehicle gives you the freedom to venture off the usual route and make the most of your time.
- For budget-conscious travelers, public transport is more economical, though it requires careful planning due to limited schedules.

Both options have their pros and cons, and in some cases, a combination of both may be ideal. For example, travelers could take a train to Cornwall and then rent a car for just part of their journey, using public transit when staying in major towns and switching to a rental car when driving to rural areas.

By considering factors such as accessibility, convenience, and travel goals, visitors can make the best choice for their trip and enjoy everything Cornwall has to offer.

CURRENCY, PAYMENT METHODS, & ATMS IN CORNWALL

When traveling to Cornwall, understanding the local currency and payment options is essential for a smooth and hassle-free experience. While the region is part of the United Kingdom and uses the British Pound (£), tourists will find that certain rural areas may have limited access to digital payment options. Being well-prepared with the right mix of cash and card payments will ensure that you can enjoy your trip without any financial inconveniences.

Understanding the British Pound (£) and Exchange Rates

Cornwall, like the rest of the United Kingdom, uses the British Pound Sterling (GBP), abbreviated as £. Each pound is divided into 100 pence. Coins are available in denominations of 1p, 2p, 5p, 10p, 20p, 50p, £1, and £2, while banknotes come in values of £5, £10, £20, and £50.

For overseas tourists, exchange rates will decide how much local money you get for your home currency. Exchange rates fluctuate frequently, so it is best to check them before your travel. Major airports, banks, and currency exchange offices offer foreign exchange services, but travelers often get better rates by withdrawing cash from ATMs or using credit/debit cards with favorable exchange terms.

Some businesses in Cornwall, particularly those in tourist-heavy areas, may accept Euros, but this is not widespread, and the exchange rate is usually not favorable. It is usually better to have British Pounds on hand to avoid any complications while making transactions.

Card Payments: Where and How They Work

In Cornwall, credit and debit cards are widely accepted, especially in towns, cities, and major tourist attractions. Most shops, restaurants, and hotels will accept major card providers, including Visa, Mastercard, and American Express. Contactless payments have become increasingly common, allowing for quick transactions using tap-to-pay technology.

While many companies support card payments, there are certain outliers, notably in tiny villages, independent markets, or isolated places where cash may still be the favoured means of payment. Travellers should always bring a small amount of cash, especially if they intend to visit local pubs, farm shops, or rural attractions.

Mobile payment methods such as Apple Pay and Google Pay are widely accepted. However, it is crucial to highlight that certain smaller businesses may have restricted access to card machines or internet connectivity, which can affect digital transactions.

Using ATMs in Cornwall

ATMs are widely available in Cornwall, particularly in bigger towns like Truro, Penzance, Newquay, and St Ives. Banks, supermarkets, petrol stations, and some tourist areas will have ATMs where visitors can withdraw cash.

When withdrawing money, international travelers should be aware of potential fees. Some ATMs, particularly those operated by independent providers in convenience stores or tourist hotspots, may charge withdrawal fees. To minimize costs, it is advisable to use ATMs attached to major banks such as Barclays, Lloyds, HSBC, and NatWest, as they typically offer better exchange rates and lower fees.

Before using an ATM, check to see if your home bank has any partnership agreements with UK banks, as this may allow you to withdraw money without incurring additional fees. If your bank charges foreign transaction fees, withdrawing bigger amounts at once can limit the number of transactions and lower the charges.

Always use caution when using ATMs, especially in popular tourist locations. Shield your PIN when entering it, and avoid withdrawing big sums of money in secluded settings.

Currency Exchange Options in Cornwall

For people who want to convert foreign cash rather than rely on ATMs, there are various options to obtain British Pounds in Cornwall. Currency exchange services are available at banks, post offices, and travel agencies, though they may not always offer the best rates.

Major airports, such as London Heathrow or Bristol Airport, have exchange counters where you can convert your money before traveling to Cornwall. However, exchange rates at airports tend to be less favorable due to high commission fees.

Some hotels and travel organisations may offer currency exchange services to tourists, however they sometimes come with additional fees. If you need to convert currency while in Cornwall, a bank or post office is usually the best option. Many tourists find that withdrawing money directly from an ATM is the most cost-effective option to receive British Pounds.

Tipping Culture In Cornwall

Unlike in other countries, tipping in Cornwall is not mandatory but is appreciated in some service industries. In restaurants, it is common to give a 10–15% tip if the service charge is not already included in the bill. Some high-end restaurants may automatically add a service charge, so verifying the bill before tipping is advisable.

In cafés and casual eateries, tipping is less frequent, although rounding up the bill or leaving modest change is a polite gesture if you had good service. Taxi drivers, particularly for long-distance journeys, appreciate a little gratuity (about 10%), though it is not demanded. Hotel employees, such as porters and housekeepers, may get minor tips for exemplary service.

Tipping is not common practice in pubs and bars, but buying the barman a drink (offering them 'one for yourself') is a traditional way to express gratitude.

STAYING CONNECTED: INTERNET, SIM CARDS, AND WIFI OPTIONS.

Staying connected while travelling in Cornwall is critical, whether for navigation, communicating with loved ones, sharing your experiences on social media, or working remotely. While Cornwall has excellent internet access in most areas, there are significant connectivity issues, especially in rural and coastal areas. Understanding the different WiFi, mobile data, and SIM card options can help you have a smooth and uninterrupted digital experience.

WiFi availability in Cornwall.

WiFi is commonly available throughout Cornwall, especially in large towns and tourist destinations. Most hotels, guesthouses, and holiday rentals offer free WiFi for visitors, though speeds and reliability can vary depending on location. Larger lodgings, particularly those in city centres or along the shore, typically provide good internet connectivity. However, due to infrastructural constraints, WiFi in distant villages or countryside getaways may be slower or less reliable.

Many cafés, restaurants, and taverns also offer free WiFi, though clients are typically required to make a purchase before receiving access. Popular chains like Costa Coffee, Starbucks, and some independent Cornish cafés provide free internet, making them ideal for travellers who need to check emails or browse the web.

Cornwall's public libraries and community centres frequently offer free WiFi, which can be useful for visitors looking for a quiet place to work or catch up on travel plans. Some tourist information centres have internet connection, albeit it is less prevalent than in larger cities.

While free WiFi is available in many locations, it is crucial to exercise caution when utilising public networks, as they are not necessarily safe. A VPN (Virtual Private Network) can provide an additional layer of security while viewing personal information online.

Mobile Networks and SIM Cards for Travellers

Purchasing a UK SIM card is an excellent alternative for travellers who want a more dependable and consistent internet connection. Several major mobile network providers operate in Cornwall, including EE, Vodafone, Three, and O2. These firms provide prepaid (pay-as-you-go) SIM cards that include mobile data, calls, and messages, allowing travellers to stay connected without using public WiFi.

Purchasing a SIM card is simple and can be done at large supermarkets, convenience stores, mobile phone shops, and even some airport kiosks before arriving in Cornwall. Here are some of the greatest prepaid SIM card options:

- EE is a top choice for reliable mobile data in Cornwall due to their robust coverage and fast 4G speeds.
- Vodafone provides good coverage and flexible prepaid data plans, but some areas may experience weaker signals.
- Three - Offers affordable data plans with generous allowances, though rural connectivity may be inconsistent.
- O2 is ideal for travellers seeking flexible pay-as-you-go plans with reasonable coverage.

For those travelling with an unlocked phone, installing a UK SIM card is a simple method to get mobile data. However, travelers with locked phones may need to check with their home operator regarding foreign roaming alternatives. Some UK companies also provide eSIM options, which allow consumers to activate a local cell plan without needing a physical SIM card.

Best mobile data plans for tourists

When selecting a prepaid SIM card, travellers should consider their data requirements based on how frequently they will be online. A low-data package (about 5GB) may be suitable for folks who only use the internet for navigation and messaging on occasion. However, if you are streaming videos, making video calls, or transferring huge files, an unlimited data or 20GB+ plan may be more appropriate.

Several UK cell operators provide tourist-friendly SIM plans, and some of the better alternatives include:

- Three's PAYG Data Pack is a cost-effective option for travellers with high data use needs.
- Why EE's Preloaded SIMs provide fast speeds, data, calls, and texts for short-term guests.
- Vodafone's Big Value Bundles offer affordable data, calls, and texts for holidaymakers.

Most prepaid SIM cards are valid for 30 days and can be filled up online or in convenience stores if more data is required.

Internet Access and Rural Connectivity

While Cornwall offers decent mobile coverage in large towns such as Truro, Newquay, Penzance, and St Ives, other regions, particularly coastal cliffs, lonely beaches, and rural countryside, may have a weak or no signal. This is due to the region's rocky environment, which might interfere with mobile towers.

For travellers wishing to explore off-the-beaten-path sites, it is advised to download offline maps on Google Maps or utilise apps like Maps.me, which allow navigation without an active internet connection. Additionally, some hiking trails and seaside pathways may have restricted network reception, making it vital to plan accordingly.

Travelers who require consistent high-speed internet for work or remote access may consider acquiring a mobile hotspot device. These portable WiFi routers employ a SIM card to provide a personal internet connection, allowing many devices to connect simultaneously. This is a good alternative for digital nomads, business travellers, and people who need a reliable connection when staying in remote places.

Roaming Charges for International Travelers

Visitors from outside the UK should check their mobile provider's international roaming policies before visiting Cornwall. Some providers include free UK roaming in their international plans, while others charge high rates for data usage abroad.

Some mobile plans still give free roaming in the UK for European Union travellers, however this varies by carrier and post-Brexit rules. Visitors from the United States, Canada, and Australia may incur significant roaming charges, making a UK SIM card the more cost-effective option.

Instead of acquiring a local SIM card, you can utilise travel SIM cards from international carriers such as Airalo or Holafly, which provide data plans across the UK and Europe without requiring a physical SIM switch.

PET-FRIENDLY CORNWALL: REGULATIONS, HOTELS, AND OUTDOOR SPACES

Cornwall is a haven for not only humans, but also pets, notably dogs. With its beautiful beaches, broad landscape, and inviting institutions, the region provides numerous chances for those who want to explore with their pets. However, understanding the local legislation, accommodation options, and finest outdoor locations is critical for a smooth and comfortable visit with pets.

Pet Travel Regulations and Entry Requirements

Visitors travelling to Cornwall from outside the UK should be aware of the UK government's pet entrance restrictions. Pets entering the country must comply with the Pet Travel Scheme (PETS), which requires microchipping, up-to-date vaccinations (including rabies), and in some cases, tapeworm treatment before arrival.

For domestic tourists travelling from within the UK, there are no specific entrance requirements. However, pet owners should check for train, airline, or ferry laws if utilising public transportation to reach Cornwall.

Once in Cornwall, pet owners must obey basic UK pet restrictions, such as keeping dogs on leashes in approved places, cleaning up after them, and according to local rules about where pets are permitted. Certain locations, such as nature reserves or protected wildlife regions, may have dog entry restrictions, so it is always a good idea to check ahead.

Pet-Friendly Accommodation in Cornwall

Cornwall provides a wide choice of pet-friendly accommodation options, from hotels and guesthouses to self-catering cottages, campsites, and lodges. Many places acknowledge the increasing number of vacationers carrying their pets and offer amenities customised to their needs.

In cities and towns such as Truro, St Ives, Newquay, and Penzance, pet-friendly hotels include specific facilities such as dog beds, food bowls, and welcome snacks. Some higher-end lodgings even provide pet-sitting services for owners who want to visit attractions that do not accept pets.

Self-catering cottages and holiday rentals are ideal for individuals looking for a more flexible and homelike environment. These choices provide pets greater space to explore and frequently include enclosed gardens. Many Airbnb houses and holiday parks in Cornwall advertise their rooms as pet-friendly, allowing owners to select a comfortable stay that meets their needs.

Campsites and lodges also appeal to pet owners, particularly those who want to spend time outdoors with their pets. Many campsites in Cornwall welcome dogs, as long as they are kept under control, and some even provide dog-washing stations to clean up after a muddy day of exploring.

When reserving accommodations, it is generally a good idea to confirm any additional pet costs or limitations. Some establishments may have breed or size restrictions, while others may charge a little cleaning fee for bringing a pet.

Best Pet-Friendly Outdoor Spaces.

One of the most appealing aspects for pet owners visiting Cornwall is the number of pet-friendly outdoor settings, such as beaches, parks, gardens, and walking paths.

Dog-friendly beaches

Cornwall has some of the best dog-friendly beaches in the UK, with long expanses of sand where dogs may run and play. Many beaches allow dogs year-round, while others have seasonal limitations during peak summer months (usually May to September).

Some of the most popular dog-friendly beaches include Watergate Bay, which is noted for its large, open space, Perranporth Beach, which even has a dog-friendly pub on-site, and Mawgan Porth, a calmer spot with magnificent coastline views. Before visiting any beach, make sure to check local signage or online resources for seasonal dog bans or leash regulations.

Scenic walking trails and country paths

Cornwall has numerous footpaths and countryside paths where dogs can roam freely. The South West Coast Path is a popular walking route that runs along Cornwall's coastline and offers beautiful vistas. While dogs are acceptable on the majority of the trail, owners should be cautious of steep cliffs and keep their pets under control in cattle areas.

Other excellent walking areas include Cardinham Woods, a beautiful forested area with designated dog-friendly trails, and

Tehidy Woods, which has shaded paths and a tranquil atmosphere for a peaceful walk with pets.

Dog-friendly gardens and parks.

Several of Cornwall's famous gardens permit dogs, allowing owners to appreciate the area's natural beauty while keeping their pets close by. The Lost Gardens of Heligan is one such location, with expansive grounds where dogs on leashes are permitted. Similarly, Trelissick Garden offers gorgeous parks and woodland trails for pets to enjoy.

For more leisurely walks, public parks in towns like Truro's Boscawen Park are ideal places for dogs to stretch their legs. These facilities frequently have dog waste bins and specific areas for pets to run freely.

Pet-Friendly Cafes, Pubs, and Restaurants

Cornwall is well-known for its dog-friendly dining scene, with numerous cafés, pubs, and restaurants accepting four-legged visitors. Some restaurants even go the extra mile by providing dog treats, water bowls, and pet-friendly menus.

Many pubs in coastal towns such as Padstow, St Ives, and Falmouth allow pets on their outdoor seating. Some even allow well-behaved dogs inside. The Watering Hole in Perranporth, a beachside pub, is popular with dog owners, as is The Bowgie Inn near Newquay, which offers breathtaking sea views.

For a more traditional experience, Cornwall's tea houses welcome dogs, allowing owners to enjoy a classic cream tea without leaving their pets outdoors. Many ice cream shops even serve dog-friendly ice cream, which is a refreshing treat for pets on hot days.

Before dining out, it is always a good idea to check with the restaurant first, since some may have limits on pet access indoors.

Top Tips for Travelling with Pets in Cornwall

There are a few things to consider when visiting Cornwall with pets to ensure a stress-free and enjoyable experience.

- To begin, always keep necessary supplies on hand, such as a leash, water bowl, food, and waste bags. Cornwall has many dog-friendly areas, but cleaning up after pets is strictly enforced, and failure to do so can result in fines.
- Second, be aware of hot weather conditions, particularly during the summer. Many beaches and trails have few shaded areas, so bring plenty of water and avoid walks during peak sun hours.
- Third, those visiting more rural areas should keep an eye on livestock and wildlife. Many country trails run past fields where sheep, cows, and other animals graze, thus keeping dogs on a leash is essential to avoid problems.
- Finally, always check for pet restrictions at hotels, beaches, and attractions. While Cornwall is incredibly pet-friendly, some locations still have seasonal bans or specific rules that must be followed.

Luxury Accommodation with Coastal Views in Cornwall.

Cornwall, with its stunning coastline and breathtaking scenery, is home to some of the best luxury hotels, providing both comfort and spectacular views of the sea. Whether you want a relaxing retreat, a romantic getaway, or a high-end base for your Cornish adventures, these luxury accommodations offer first-rate service, elegant interiors, and world-class amenities. Many of these hotels are situated in ideal coastal areas, providing breathtaking views of the ocean, direct access to sandy beaches, and exquisite dining experiences featuring fresh local seafood.

The Headland Hotel and Spa

Address: Fistral Beach, Newquay, Cornwall, TR7 1EW.

Nearby attractions include Fistral Beach, Newquay Harbour, and Blue Reef Aquarium.

Pet Policy: Dog-friendly accommodations and cottages are offered, with pet-friendly dining areas

The Headland Hotel & Spa is one of Cornwall's most recognizable luxury hotels, with an unrivaled blend of elegance and coastal beauty. This five-star hotel, perched on a dramatic clifftop overlooking the famous Fistral Beach, offers stylish rooms, luxury self-catering cottages, and an award-winning spa. Guests can enjoy panoramic sea views from their private balconies, dine at The Samphire Restaurant, and relax with world-class spa treatments.

For those traveling with pets, the hotel provides dog-friendly accommodations, including a dog-washing station for sandy paws after a day at the beach. With direct access to Fistral Beach and scenic coastal trails, The Headland is ideal for both relaxation and outdoor adventure.

The Scarlett Hotel

Address: Tredragon Road, Mawgan Porth, Cornwall TR8 4DQ

Nearby attractions include Mawgan Porth Beach, Bedruthan Steps, and Watergate Bay.

Pet Policy: Dogs are allowed in selected rooms with sufficient notification.

The Scarlet Hotel is an adults-only luxury resort located on Mawgan Porth's craggy cliffs, providing an eco-friendly and serene experience. The hotel is designed for ultimate relaxation, with floor-to-ceiling windows that capture sweeping views of the Atlantic Ocean, allowing guests to wake up to breathtaking sunrises and fall asleep to the sound of waves.

One of the major elements of The Scarlet is its emphasis on wellbeing. Guests can enjoy clifftop hot tubs, Ayurvedic spa treatments, and an eco-friendly indoor pool. The restaurant showcases locally sourced and sustainable cuisine, with fresh seafood being a highlight. While the hotel primarily caters to couples looking for a romantic getaway, some rooms allow pets, making it a perfect choice for tourists who wish to share their luxury experience with their four-legged pals.

Carbis Bay Hotel And Estate

Address: Carbis Bay, St Ives, Cornwall, TR26 2NP.

Nearby attractions include Carbis Bay Beach, St Ives Harbour, and Tate St Ives.

Pet Policy: Pet-friendly beach cabins are available on request.

Nestled along the picturesque sands of Carbis Bay, this premium hotel provides an exclusive beachfront experience along with world-class amenities. The Carbis Bay Hotel & Estate is well-known for its magnificent suites, self-catering beach huts, and access to a privately owned Blue Flag beach, which is among Cornwall's most beautiful.

Guests can unwind in the on-site spa, enjoy gourmet dining at The Sands Restaurant, and take part in water sports like as paddleboarding and kayaking. The hotel's position is just a short drive from St Ives, where tourists can explore local art galleries, small boutiques, and vibrant seafood restaurants.

For those traveling with pets, the hotel offers a range of pet-friendly beach cottages that provide direct access to the sand, allowing visitors to enjoy a gorgeous coastal hideaway without leaving their furry friends behind.

The Idle Rocks

Address: Harbourside, St Mawes, Cornwall, TR2 5AN

Nearby Attractions: St Mawes Castle, St Anthony Head, Roseland Peninsula

Pet Policy: Small dogs permitted in select rooms with prior arrangement

The Idle Rocks, a boutique luxury hotel in St Mawes, mixes modern elegance with timeless seaside charm. This tiny hotel is located directly on the port, offering breathtaking views of the water as well as a serene and relaxing atmosphere.

Each room is uniquely decorated with contemporary décor and luxurious furnishings, creating a pleasant yet classy ambiance. Guests can dine in the hotel's award-winning restaurant, which focuses on fresh, locally produced seafood and seasonal produce.

St Mawes provides a peaceful setting with stunning coastline walks and easy access to the Roseland Peninsula. While The Idle Rocks maintains an aura of luxury, it does allow small dogs in selected rooms, giving it a refined but pet-friendly option for guests.

Talland Bay Hotel

Talland Bay, Porthallow, Cornwall. PL13 2JB.

Nearby attractions include Looe, Polperro, and the South West Coast Path.

Pet Policy: We provide dog-friendly accommodations, snacks, and an enclosed exercise area.

Talland Bay Hotel is a great option for people looking for a luxurious resort that welcomes pets. Located between Looe and Polperro, this boutique hotel oozes coastal charm with its individually furnished rooms, manicured gardens, and spectacular sea views.

Talland Bay Hotel is one of Cornwall's most dog-friendly luxury lodgings, providing a warm welcome for canines. Dogs are welcome not only in guest rooms, but also in common spaces such as the bar and lounge. Special pet amenities like as dog treats, pet-friendly dining, and a fenced exercise space make it ideal for guests who want their pets to feel as pampered as they do.

The hotel's proximity to the South West Coast Path makes it ideal for lengthy coastal walks, while the neighboring beaches offer ample area for dogs to run free. Talland Bay Hotel's warm welcome and breathtaking views create a magnificent and relaxing environment for both pets and their owners.

Cornwall has a large selection of mid-range and boutique hotels that offer outstanding hospitality, stylish lodgings, and unique appeal to guests looking for a blend of comfort and cost. These hotels frequently combine modern convenience with local culture, ensuring that guests have a pleasant and comfortable stay without the excesses of high-end luxury resorts. Many of these businesses are independently owned, with personalized service and unique decor that reflects Cornwall's coastal beauty and rich history.

The Gannet Inn: A Chic Retreat Near St Ives.

Address: St Ives Road, Carbis Bay, St Ives, Cornwall, TR26 2SB

Nearby attractions include Carbis Bay Beach, Tate St Ives, and Porthminster Beach.

Pet Policy: Limited pet-friendly rooms are available on request.

The Gannet Inn is an excellent alternative for those looking to experience the charm of St Ives while relaxing in the calm surroundings of a boutique hotel. This beautiful hotel, located within a short walk from Carbis Bay Beach, offers distinctively designed rooms with vintage decor and modern elements. The atmosphere is cozy yet beautiful, making it an ideal hideaway for couples and lone travelers.

The hotel's on-site restaurant serves regionally influenced cuisine, including fresh seafood and seasonal ingredients. The hotel's proximity to St Ives gives for easy access to art galleries, independent shops, and stunning coastal walks, while also providing a calm retreat from the bustling town centre.

The Greenbank Hotel: Riverside Comfort in Falmouth

Harborside, Falmouth, Cornwall, TR11 2SR.

Nearby attractions include Pendennis Castle, the National Maritime Museum, and Gyllyngvase Beach.

Pet Policy: Dog-friendly rooms are available upon prior booking.

The Greenbank Hotel, located on the edge of Falmouth Harbour, is a mid-range boutique hotel with spectacular waterfront views and a strong nautical heritage. With origins reaching back to the 17th century, this hotel flawlessly integrates traditional elegance with modern comforts, providing spacious accommodations with views of the harbor and surrounding coastline.

Guests can begin the day with a traditional Cornish breakfast while watching boats meander over the lake. The hotel also houses the famed Water's Edge Restaurant, which serves fresh, locally sourced seafood. A stay at The Greenbank Hotel provides a unique opportunity to discover Falmouth's thriving cultural scene, seaside walking routes, and historic landmarks in a tranquil and scenic location.

The Alverton - A Historic Retreat in Truro

Address: Tregolls Road, Truro, Cornwall, TR1 1ZQ

Nearby Attractions: Truro Cathedral, Royal Cornwall Museum, Boscawen Park

Pet Policy: Pet-friendly rooms available on request

For visitors who want to stay in Cornwall's only city, The Alverton in Truro is an excellent mid-range boutique hotel with a distinct blend of history and elegance. This former convent, housed in a stunning Grade II-listed building, has been transformed into a stylish and inviting hotel. The interiors have high vaulted ceilings, arched windows, and period details, resulting in a peaceful and sophisticated atmosphere.

The hotel's extensive grounds offer a calm respite, but its central position allows guests to easily explore Truro's shops, galleries, and cultural attractions. The Alverton's award-winning Afternoon Tea experience is a must-have for guests looking to partake in a traditional Cornish tradition. Visitors can expect top-notch service and a memorable stay, whether they're relaxing in the cozy bar or dining in the elegant restaurant.

St Enodoc Hotel: A Boutique Escape in Rock.

Address: Rock, Wadebridge, Cornwall, PL27 6LA

Nearby Attractions: Padstow, Daymer Bay, Polzeath Beach

Pet Policy: Selected pet-friendly rooms available

St Enodoc Hotel, located in the picturesque coastal village of Rock, provides a stylish yet relaxed retreat for those seeking boutique accommodations with a touch of luxury. Overlooking the Camel Estuary, the hotel is recognized for its light and airy rooms, many of which offer stunning views of the water.

A highlight of this boutique hotel is its exceptional restaurant, which is profoundly entrenched in Cornwall's culinary traditions. The menu emphasizes on locally produced seafood, farm fresh produce, and contemporary British cuisine, making eating at St Enodoc a true experience.

Outdoor enthusiasts will adore the neighboring sandy beaches, scenic coastal walks, and chances for watersports. Guests can also take a short ferry ride to Padstow, a thriving fishing village known for its culinary scene. With its charming environment and great service, St Enodoc Hotel is an excellent choice for guests seeking a comfortable yet elegant stay.

Fowey Harbour Hotel: Coastal Elegance in a Historic Setting.

Address: Esplanade, Fowey, Cornwall, PL 23 1HX

Nearby Attractions: Fowey Estuary, Readymoney Cove, Polruan

Pet Policy: Dog-friendly accommodations available

Nestled in the gorgeous Fowey Estuary, the Fowey Harbour Hotel is a charming mid-range option that offers coastal elegance with a boutique flair. This wonderfully renovated Victorian structure is noted for its sophisticated décor, pleasant ambiance, and unparalleled sea views.

Guests can relax on the hotel's outdoor terrace, which overlooks the harbor, or take a short walk to the picturesque town center, where independent shops, tea cafes, and waterfront pubs await. The hotel's restaurant delivers outstanding seasonal Cornish cuisine, with a focus on locally caught fish and fresh ingredients.

Readymoney Cove Beach and the South West Coast Path are both nearby for individuals who enjoy spending time outside. The hotel's pet-friendly policy makes it an excellent choice for tourists who want to bring their four-legged pets along for the journey.

BUDGET-FRIENDLY B&BS AND GUESTHOUSES IN CORNWALL

Cornwall is a dream location for many tourists, but it doesn't mean you have to spend a fortune on lodging. Budget-friendly Bed & Breakfasts (B&Bs) and guesthouses offer pleasant and charming locations to stay while keeping travel costs under control. These lodgings provide comfortable surroundings, friendly hosts, and personalized service, making them ideal for single travelers, couples, and families seeking a more authentic Cornish experience.

Affordable guesthouses can be found all around Cornwall, in coastal villages, countryside getaways, and bustling harbor towns. Many of these facilities are family-run and focus on local charm, offering cooked breakfasts, pleasant rooms, and insider information from the hosts on the finest locations to explore.

Chy a Gwedhen: A Cozy B&B with Stunning Views.

Location: St. Ives.

Chy a Gwedhen, a wonderful budget-friendly B&B near St Ives, offers comfortable accommodation as well as spectacular seaside views. Every morning, guests are treated to a delicious Cornish breakfast with locally sourced food and freshly baked delicacies.

The warm and inviting hosts create a calm and friendly atmosphere, making it ideal for guests seeking individualized suggestions on the best local attractions. The nearby beaches, art galleries, and charming streets of St Ives make this an excellent base for exploring Cornwall's artistic and coastal heritage.

The Smuggler's Rest: A Traditional Cornish Guesthouse

Location: Newquay.

For those looking for a low-cost stay near Cornwall's surf capital, the Smugglers Rest in Newquay is an excellent choice. This family-run guesthouse blends traditional Cornish hospitality with a relaxed beach atmosphere, making it ideal for surfers, backpackers, and budget-conscious travelers.

Guests can start their day with a great full English breakfast before heading to the famed Fistral Beach or Watergate Bay for some surfing, sunbathing, or coastal hikes. The guesthouse provides a comfortable stay at an affordable price, allowing visitors to experience the best of Cornwall's coastline without breaking the bank.

Treverbyn House – A Homely Escape in Padstow

Location: Padstow

Treverbyn House provides a charming and affordable stay for travelers looking to experience Padstow's famous seafood scene and picturesque harbor without paying premium hotel prices. This tiny bed and breakfast offers light and airy rooms with great rural views, making it a pleasant refuge from the bustling harbor town.

A stay at Treverbyn House includes a freshly prepared breakfast made from local products, preparing you for a day of exploration. Just a short walk from Padstow's bay, tourists may enjoy Rick Stein's seafood restaurants, independent shops, and gorgeous coastal walks before returning to their warm accommodations.

If you're searching for an economical yet comfortable stay in Penzance, The Firs Guesthouse is a hidden gem offering a quiet and homey environment. Conveniently positioned near the Penzance coastline, this guesthouse provides easy access to St Michael's Mount, the Minack Theatre, and the Isles of Scilly ferry terminal.

The Firs offers clean and comfortable rooms, with many featuring sea views. The guesthouse prides itself on warm hospitality and a hearty breakfast, making it an excellent choice for travelers who want to explore West Cornwall's rugged coastline and charming villages.

The Countryman – A Countryside Retreat Near St Agnes

Location: St Agnes

One of the greatest advantages of staying in a B&B or guesthouse is the personal touch. Unlike larger hotels, these accommodations are often family-run, meaning you receive local insights, homemade food, and a welcoming atmosphere.

Major airlines fly to Cornwall and nearby airports.

Cornwall, located in the southwest region of England, is well-connected by air, making it accessible to both domestic and foreign visitors. While it lacks a large international airport, it is served by Cornwall Airport Newquay (NQY), the area's primary airport. Travelers can also fly into nearby airports including Exeter Airport (EXT), Bristol Airport (BRS), and London Heathrow (LHR) before continuing on to Cornwall by train, coach, or automobile.

Whether flying directly into Newquay or utilizing a neighboring hub, researching the available airlines and routes is critical for arranging a smooth and efficient journey.

Cornwall Airport Newquay (NQY)—The Gateway to Cornwall

Overview

Cornwall Airport Newquay (NQY) is the region's primary airport, providing direct domestic and seasonal international flights. The airport is only five miles northeast of Newquay, making it an easy choice for tourists visiting Cornwall's beautiful beaches, coastal villages, and countryside attractions.

Domestic Airlines and Routes

For those flying within the UK, several airlines offer direct services to Cornwall Airport Newquay from major cities, making the region easily accessible.

- British Airways' seasonal flights from London Heathrow (LHR) provide a convenient connection for both local and international travelers passing through one of the world's busiest airports.

- Loganair provides regular flights from Manchester (MAN), Edinburgh (EDI), and Glasgow (GLA), making it easier for passengers from Scotland and Northern England to reach Cornwall.
- Eastern Airways offers flights between London Gatwick (LGW) and Humberside (HUY), serving travelers from the southeast and northeast of the UK.
- \tRyanair, a cheap airline, offers affordable flights from Dublin (DUB) to chosen European destinations during peak seasons, catering to Irish and European tourists.
- Emerald Airlines' Aer Lingus Regional service connects Dublin (DUB) to Newquay, making it a handy choice for Irish travelers.
- These domestic links allow you to fly into Cornwall from major UK cities in about two hours, avoiding the need for lengthy car or rail journeys.
- International Airlines and Routes
- While Cornwall Airport Newquay predominantly serves domestic passengers, it also operates seasonal international flights.
- Ryanair and Aer Lingus offer flights from Dublin (DUB) to North America and Europe, making it convenient for Irish travelers.

During the summer, select carriers may operate seasonal flights from Düsseldorf (DUS) in Germany, providing a direct connection between Cornwall and mainland Europe.

For international visitors arriving from other locations, the best choice is to fly into London Heathrow (LHR), London Gatwick (LGW), Bristol (BRS), or Exeter (EXT) and then take a connecting flight, train, or rental car to Cornwall.

Alternative Airports near Cornwall

While Newquay is the most convenient airport, passengers might also consider flying into surrounding smaller airports, which provide a greater range of airlines and routes.

Exeter Airport(EXT)

Exeter Airport, located around 90 miles northeast of Cornwall, is an excellent choice for visitors who want more airline alternatives while staying close to their destination.

- Flybe, Ryanair, and TUI offer flights from Manchester, Belfast, Dublin, and select European cities.
- Exeter Airport offers direct train and coach connections to Cornwall, making onward travel easier.

Bristol airport (BRS)

Bristol Airport, located approximately 150 miles from Cornwall, is a major hub with more international connections.

- Offers flights from major airlines such as easyJet, Ryanair, TUI, and KLM, with a diverse range of European and international itineraries.
- To get to Cornwall from Bristol, passengers can take a train, rent a car, or employ a coach service, which takes about 3-4 hours.

London Airports: Heathrow and Gatwick

For long-haul tourists flying from North America, Asia, or other overseas destinations, London's Heathrow (LHR) and Gatwick (LGW) airports offer the most airline options and onward travel connections.

- The UK's largest international airport, London Heathrow (LHR), serves destinations globally. British Airways offers flights to Newquay, and a rail from Paddington Station to Cornwall is also available.

- London Gatwick (LGW) is another key hub for international flights. It provides a seasonal direct route to Newquay with Eastern Airways, or travelers can use a rail or domestic flight to continue their journey.

While traveling into London requires more travel time to reach Cornwall, it remains a popular choice for visitors from the United States, Canada, Australia, and Asia.

Choosing the Best Airport and Airline for Your Trip.

Your choice of airport and airline is determined by your departure location, affordability, and convenience.

- Cornwall Airport Newquay (NQY) is the finest alternative for direct access to Cornwall, especially for flights from UK locations such as London, Manchester, Edinburgh, and Dublin.
- Exeter Airport (EXT) and Bristol Airport (BRS) provide additional airline options and international connections within a few hours of Cornwall.
- Long-haul travelers can reach Cornwall by train, domestic aircraft, or rental vehicle from London Heathrow (LHR) and London Gatwick (LGW) airports, which offer global connections.

Understanding the available airlines, flight routes, and nearby airport options allows travelers to plan a smooth and efficient journey to Cornwall, ensuring a hassle-free arrival to explore the region's breathtaking coastline, historic landmarks, and charming villages.

BAGGAGE POLICIES AND FEES: WHAT YOU SHOULD KNOW.

Traveling to Cornwall by air necessitates a grasp of airline baggage restrictions, particularly when traveling into Cornwall Airport

Newquay or connecting through another UK airport. Each airline's baggage allowance, prices, and restrictions differ, which might have a big impact on your trip plans. Knowing what to expect in terms of checked luggage, cabin baggage, and special allowances will help you have a smooth travel.

Carry-on Baggage Allowances

Most airlines that fly into Cornwall allow customers to bring one piece of carry-on luggage and one personal item, such as a handbag, laptop bag, or small backpack. However, particular size and weight restrictions differ by airline.

For example, British Airways permits one cabin bag of up to 56cm x 45cm x 25cm and one personal item, with a total weight limit of 23kg. Budget airlines, such as Ryanair and EasyJet, have tougher baggage policies, often allowing only one small bag that fits beneath the seat unless an upgraded ticket is purchased.

It is critical to confirm your airline's specific policy before flying, as breaching size or weight restrictions may result in additional costs at the airport. If you are taking vital items such as medications, travel documents, or electronics, make sure they are packed in your carry-on bag to avoid any trouble caused by lost or delayed luggage.

Checked Baggage Fees and Policies

The restrictions regarding checked luggage vary greatly depending on the airline and ticket class. Some airlines include a checked bag with the ticket price, while others charge an extra fee.

Standard economy rates on full-service carriers such as British Airways and Aer Lingus often include one free checked bag weighing up to 23 kilograms. However, travelers flying with cheap airlines such as Ryanair or EasyJet must pay for checked luggage individually, with rates ranging depending on the route, season, and weight of the bag.

Checked baggage fees typically vary between £20 and £50 per bag, however charges can jump dramatically if the allowance is purchased at the airport rather than in advance. If you anticipate having a checked bag, it is best to reserve it online before leaving to save money and avoid last-minute stress.

When flying into Cornwall, it is also important to examine luggage transfer procedures if connecting with various airlines. Some low-cost carriers do not automatically transfer checked luggage between flights, so travelers may have to collect and recheck their bags during a layover.

Excess baggage charges

If your luggage exceeds the weight limit, airlines will usually charge you an extra baggage fee, which can be rather expensive. Depending on the airline, fees for excess kilograms can range between £10 and £20.

To avoid surprise charges, weigh your bags before heading to the airport. Many travelers use a small luggage scale to ensure they stay inside the permissible weight limit. If you anticipate needing more luggage space, purchasing an extra baggage allowance online in advance is frequently less expensive than paying for excess weight at the check-in counter.

Some airlines also allow you to pool luggage allowances when flying in a group. This means that if one traveler's bag is slightly overweight but another's is under the limit, the total weight can be merged to avoid further penalties. Checking your airline's policy on pooled baggage can aid in optimising luggage distribution.

Special baggage and sporting equipment

Travelers visiting Cornwall for outdoor activities such as surfing, hiking, or cycling may need to bring appropriate equipment. Most airlines allow passengers to check recreational equipment like surfboards, golf clubs, and bicycles, although these items frequently require special handling and involve extra expenses.

For example, British Airways and Aer Lingus enable travelers to check sporting equipment as part of their usual baggage allowance, as long as it meets size and weight restrictions. However, Ryanair and EasyJet charge separate costs that can range from £30 to £60 per item.

Surfboards, in particular, have tight size limits and may necessitate advance reservations with the airline. Many travelers choose to rent equipment upon arrival rather than deal with the inconvenience and expense of bringing large equipment. If you opt to bring your own, make sure it's carefully packed in a suitable travel case to avoid damage during transit.

liquids, prohibited items, and security regulations

Those flying to Cornwall, like all other flights in the UK, must follow tight security restrictions for liquids, gels, and forbidden items. The standard regulation for liquids in carry-on luggage applies, which states that all liquids must be in containers no larger than 100ml and fit into a single, transparent, resealable bag.

Sharp things, volatile materials, and huge lithium-ion batteries are sometimes banned or require particular handling. It is critical to review the most recent airport security standards to ensure compliance and avoid unnecessary waits at security checkpoints.

If you are taking duty-free liquids purchased at another airport, they must be sealed in a tamper-proof bag with the receipt visible to pass through security.

Tips for Managing Baggage Effectively

When packing for your trip to Cornwall, keep these practical tips in mind to reduce baggage-related stress.

First, pack light whenever possible to save money on baggage fees and make traveling easier, especially if you intend to visit Cornwall by train, bus, or rental car. Using packing cubes might help you organize your stuff more efficiently and maximize travel space.

Second, be aware of your airline's luggage rules in advance to prevent unexpected fines at the airport. Check the weight and size limits for both carry-on and checked baggage, and consider paying for any excess baggage online before your departure.

Finally, if you're taking precious items like cameras, laptops, or essential documents, keep them in your carry-on luggage rather than checking them in. This protects against potential harm or loss.

Understanding airline luggage restrictions and planning accordingly can help tourists secure a pleasant flight to Cornwall without needless delays or charges. Whether you're flying with a big airline or a budget carrier, understanding baggage prices, restrictions, and best practices will help you have a stress-free journey.

PET TRAVEL REGULATIONS FOR AIRLINES AND ENTRY INTO THE UNITED KINGDOM

Traveling with pets to Cornwall necessitates careful planning and adherence to airline laws and UK immigration requirements. Understanding the proper papers, airline pet rules, and quarantine regulations is critical for a pleasant journey, whether you're traveling with a dog, cat, or other small pet.

Cornwall is a pet-friendly location, with many lodgings, beaches, and outdoor spaces that welcome canine companions. However, pet owners must adhere to severe UK government regulations regulating animal transportation, vaccinations, and health inspections.

Airline Policy for Pet Travel

Pet travel restrictions differ per airline and whether your pet will be traveling in the cabin, as checked baggage, or in the cargo hold.

Pets are allowed on major airlines such as British Airways, KLM, and Lufthansa, but size, weight, and breed limitations apply. Small dogs may be allowed in the cabin provided they fit into an airline-approved carrier under the seat. However, many airlines require dogs to be transported in the cargo hold, particularly on foreign flights.

Budget airlines, such as Ryanair and EasyJet, often prohibit pets in the cabin or as checked luggage, with the exception of guide dogs. If you're flying with a pet to Cornwall, make sure to choose an airline that allows pets.

Many airlines have a limited number of spots available per flight, thus it is recommended that you plan pet travel well in advance. Additionally, passengers should confirm the particular size and weight limits for pet carriers, as these regulations vary by airline.

Health and Vaccination Requirements for Pet Entry into the United Kingdom

Before traveling with a pet to Cornwall, owners must check that their animals fit the UK's stringent entrance regulations. The UK follows the Pet Travel Scheme (PETS), which allows pets from recognized countries to enter without quarantine if they meet vaccination and microchipping requirements.

The main prerequisites for bringing a pet into the UK are:

1.All pets must be microchipped before obtaining a rabies vaccination. The microchip must conform to ISO 11784 or ISO 11785 requirements and be scannable upon delivery.

2.Rabies Vaccination - Pets must have an up-to-date rabies vaccine delivered at least 21 days before to travel. The vaccination date must be included on the pet's official health certificate.

3.Animal Health Certificate (AHC) or Pet Passport - Travelers from the European Union or Northern Ireland may utilize an EU Pet Passport. Travelers from outside the EU (including the United States) must present an Animal Health Certificate issued by a licensed veterinarian. This document must be completed within 10 days of travel and include immunization records and microchip information.

4.Tapeworm Treatment for Dogs - Dogs traveling from specific countries must undergo an approved tapeworm treatment between 24 and 120 hours before arriving in the United Kingdom: A veterinarian must record the treatment on the health certificate.

Failure to follow these regulations may result in quarantine or rejection of entry for the pet.

Flying to Cornwall with a Pet

Because Cornwall Airport Newquay is a small airport with few international flights, most pet-friendly visitors arrive in the UK via large international airports such as London Heathrow, London Gatwick, or Manchester Airport before traveling to Cornwall.

Pets coming in the UK by air must pass through an approved pet entry point. Heathrow Airport has a specialized Animal Reception Centre (ARC) for processing pets upon arrival. Pets are scanned for microchips, health certificates, and immunization records before being returned to their owners.

Pet rules vary on domestic flights within the United Kingdom. British Airways permits pets to travel in the cargo hold, whereas smaller regional carriers like Loganair may have different rules. Before booking, make sure to check with the airline.

Pet-Friendly Transportation Options From Airports to Cornwall

Once in the UK, pet owners have several alternatives for getting to Cornwall with their animals.

By train:

The UK train network welcomes pets, enabling small pets to ride free of charge. Larger dogs may require a ticket, but are normally accepted on board as long as they are kept on a leash. The GWR Night Riviera Sleeper Train from London to Cornwall permits pets in select cabins, making it an ideal overnight travel choice.

By car:

Driving is frequently the most comfortable method to get to Cornwall with a pet because it provides flexibility and reduces stress for the animal. Rental car companies may allow pets, but it is best to examine their policy ahead of time.

By Ferry:

When coming from Europe, catching a pet-friendly ship to the UK and then driving to Cornwall is a popular option. Many ferry operators provide onboard pet accommodations, such as kennels and pet-friendly rooms.

Pet Travel Costs and Airline Fees

Airline rates for pet travel vary greatly depending on the carrier and whether the pet flies in the cabin, as checked luggage, or as cargo.

For example, British Airways charges between £800 and £3,500 for pets traveling in the cargo hold, depending on the route and pet size. Airlines like Lufthansa and KLM have similar pricing schemes.

If a pet is permitted to fly in the cabin, the prices are often lower, ranging between £50 and £200 each flight. However, this option is typically only offered to tiny pets.

In addition to flight fees, pet owners should plan for charges such as microchipping, vaccines, health certifications, and overnight stays at pet reception facilities.

Pet-Friendly Accommodation and Outdoor Spaces in Cornwall.

Cornwall is one of the most pet-friendly places in the UK, with many hotels, cottages, and bed and breakfasts welcome pets. Many motels provide pet-friendly features including dog beds, water bowls, and designated walking spaces.

Cornwall's outdoor spaces, which include beaches, coastal walks, and national parks, are great for pet-friendly outings. However, some beaches impose seasonal dog restrictions, notably during the summer months. Here are some popular pet-friendly beaches:

- Watergate Bay is open to dogs year-round and offers great opportunities for long walks and wave play.
- Perranporth Beach is another pet-friendly destination that allows dogs off-leash.
- Gwithian Towans Beach provides plenty open room for dogs to run freely.

To preserve Cornwall's natural ecology, dog owners should follow local restrictions and tidy up after their pets.

BEST TIPS FOR A SMOOTH JOURNEY TO CORNWALL.

Traveling to Cornwall involves careful planning, whether by air, train, or road. Every step of the process, from ordering your tickets to negotiating airport procedures and ensuring a comfortable travel, can be streamlined for efficiency and convenience. Preparing ahead of time can help you avoid delays, reduce stress, and enjoy your trip more fully.

Planning and booking your trip

The first step to a hassle-free journey is picking the right form of transport. Cornwall is accessible by air, train, car, and bus, so travelers should choose their decision based on price, accessibility, and personal preferences.

Booking flights early is critical, especially during peak tourist seasons. Major airports such as London Heathrow, Gatwick, and Manchester offer flights to Cornwall Airport Newquay, but they can fill up rapidly during the summer months. If you are flying internationally, you may find it more practical to arrive in London or Bristol and then take a connecting domestic flight or alternate transportation to Cornwall.

Reserving seats in advance ensures a more comfortable journey, especially when using services such as the Great Western Railway (GWR) Night Riviera Sleeper Train from London Paddington to Cornwall. This overnight train is a practical choice for tourists looking to make the most of their time in Cornwall without the strain of long daytime travel.

Driving to Cornwall provides flexibility, allowing visitors to explore smaller villages and gorgeous coastal routes at their leisure. When renting a car, confirm booking details in advance and check for any restrictions, such as mileage limits or drop-off fees, to avoid last-minute surprises.

Packing Smart for the Journey

Efficient packing is essential for a stress-free trip. Checking airline luggage allowances and regulations ahead of time helps passengers avoid surprise fines or delays at the airport. Cornwall's weather is unpredictable, so bring layers, a waterproof jacket, and suitable walking shoes.

For train and vehicle passengers, having refreshments, water, and entertainment options on hand makes the journey more enjoyable. Cornwall's rural terrain means that there are few dining alternatives along the road, so taking light refreshments can be beneficial, especially for families with young children.

Travelers bringing pets should take food, water, waste bags, and any necessary documentation for pet-friendly lodgings or transportation.

Navigating Airports and Train Stations Effectively

Arriving at the airport early is one of the most effective methods for a stress-free flight. Domestic flights normally require passengers to check in at least 90 minutes before departure, whilst international travelers should arrive at least three hours before their trip.

Security checks can travel time-consuming, but making sure liquids are within the airline's limits, electronic gadgets are conveniently accessible, and forbidden items are removed from carry-on luggage will help speed things up. Many airports provide fast-track security lanes, which are useful during peak travel times.

Checking departure boards and platform numbers ahead of time at train stations reduces last-minute rush. Cornwall-bound trains from London and other large UK towns can be crowded, especially during the summer, so arrive at the station early to obtain a good seat. Bringing a small travel pillow and eye mask on the sleeper train can help passengers stay comfortable during the evening journey.

Managing layovers and transfers.

If your route to Cornwall includes a layover or transfer, careful planning might make the procedure go more smoothly. Air travelers with layovers at major airports such as Heathrow or Gatwick should research the airport layout and know how long it will take to get to the connecting gates. Heathrow, for example, has several terminals, and the journey between them might take up to an hour.

Understanding transfer times and station distances is critical for train passengers who are transferring trains. The London Paddington to Penzance route is one of the most popular rail journeys to Cornwall, but some passengers may need to change trains at Exeter or Plymouth. Checking plans ahead of time and allowing for unanticipated delays will help ensure a seamless transfer.

If you're hiring a car upon arrival, confirm pick-up locations, fuel policies, and insurance coverage ahead of time to minimize unnecessary waits at the rental counter.

Once in Cornwall, traveling about is made easier by renting a car, using a bus, a rail, or a ferry. While driving is the most flexible alternative, people who use public transportation should be familiar with Cornwall's bus and train networks.

The First Kernow bus service connects important towns and tourist spots, but the schedule varies depending on the season. Travelers should verify timetables ahead of time, particularly in outlying places where services may be less frequent.

Cornish branch line trains, such as the St Ives Bay Line and the Looe Valley Line, provide spectacular views while avoiding traffic congestion. These train routes are especially handy during the high summer months, when road travel can be slow.

Avoiding Common Travel Challenges.

A few easy strategies can help you avoid common travel concerns. Booking lodgings in advance guarantees availability, especially during high season when hotels and guesthouses fill up rapidly. Travelers traveling by automobile should inquire about parking availability at their lodging, as some smaller hotels and inns may have limited space.

Visitors to Cornwall during festival or public holiday times, such as the Boardmasters Festival in Newquay, should plan ahead of time because roads, public transportation, and hotels will be busier than usual.

Staying informed about weather conditions is also important, as Cornwall's coastal climate might alter travel plans. Ferry services, in particular, may be delayed or canceled due to heavy seas, so checking for real-time updates before leaving might help you avoid delays.

International visitors should have a backup plan for internet access, such as a portable Wi-Fi gadget or a local SIM card, to ensure connectivity when traveling in unfamiliar places.

HOW TO BOOK FLIGHTS AND FIND THE BEST DEALS IN CORNWALL.

Planning a vacation to Cornwall necessitates careful planning to acquire the greatest airline fares, especially if you're flying from overseas or rural places. With fluctuating airfares, seasonal demand, and numerous travel routes, learning the best methods for booking flights can save you time and money. This guide will bring you through the necessary procedures for locating cheap flights, booking effectively, and maximizing comfort on your trip to Cornwall.

Choosing the Best Time to Book Flights.

Booking flights at the proper moment can result in big cost savings. Airfares fluctuate depending on demand, season, and how far in advance tickets are booked. Domestic flights to Cornwall are best scheduled one to three months in advance, while international flights should be booked three to six months ahead of travel.

Peak travel seasons, such as summer (June to August) and school holidays, experience an increase in demand, causing costs to climb. If you intend to visit Cornwall during these dates, book as soon as possible. Traveling during the off-season (October through March) can result in reduced rates and fewer crowds.

Airlines occasionally issue discounted fares for last-minute travelers as departure dates approach, but this is not guaranteed. Monitoring airline costs and activating ticket alerts can help you get a great deal when prices fall.

Choosing the Right Airports and Routes

Cornwall has a single principal airport, Cornwall Airport Newquay (NQY), which is the most convenient entrance point for air travelers. It offers direct domestic flights from places like London, Manchester, and Edinburgh, as well as some seasonal international trips. However, flight availability may be limited, forcing passengers to investigate other neighboring airports.

If direct flights to Cornwall Airport Newquay are not available from your location, the best options are Exeter Airport (EXT), Bristol Airport (BRS), and London Heathrow (LHR). Travelers can continue their journey from these airports by taking domestic planes, trains, or rental vehicles.

For international passengers, flying into London Heathrow, Gatwick, or Manchester Airport offers the most airline options, followed by a connecting domestic flight or train ride to Cornwall.

How to find the cheapest flights.

There are various approaches to finding the most affordable flights to Cornwall.

First, airfare comparison websites like Google Flights, Skyscanner, Kayak, and Momondo allow you to compare prices from numerous airlines and booking platforms. These apps frequently offer adjustable date options, allowing passengers to choose the cheapest days to fly.

Being flexible with travel dates is another great approach to save money. Midweek flights, especially on Tuesdays and Wednesdays, are typically less expensive than weekend departures. Furthermore, early morning or late-night flights are frequently less expensive than peak-time flights.

Booking directly through an airline's website can occasionally result in lower pricing, as third-party booking systems may charge service fees. Airlines periodically provide exclusive discounts and promotions on their official websites.

For individuals prepared to go further, flights with layovers rather than direct routes can result in significant savings.

Utilizing Fare Alerts and Discount Programs

Travellers looking for the greatest deals could use fare alert services provided by websites such as Google Flights, Hopper, and Skyscanner. These systems alert users when costs for their selected routes drop, allowing them to book at the lowest possible fare.

Joining airline loyalty programs or frequent flyer programs can also result in discounts, free upgrades, and bonus miles that can be used on future journeys. Furthermore, subscribing to airline newsletters frequently grants access to unique promotions and early booking discounts.

Credit cards with airline miles or travel benefits can be useful for frequent travelers. Some credit card companies additionally provide travel discounts or free checked baggage, resulting in further savings.

Comparing Budget Airlines to Full-Service Airlines

When purchasing tickets to Cornwall, passengers have the option of flying with a budget airline or a full-service carrier, each with their own set of benefits.

Budget airlines like Ryanair and easyJet offer low-cost flights on domestic and European routes. However, these airlines frequently charge additional fees for checked baggage, seat selection, and onboard beverages, so it is critical to check the total price before booking.

Full-service carriers, such as British Airways and Loganair, offer more amenities in their fares, such as baggage allowance, in-flight beverages, and more flexible cancellation policies. While the initial ticket price may be greater, some tourists may find that the enhanced convenience is worthwhile.

Full-service airlines often have superior pet travel rules, such as allowing small pets in the cabin or offering designated pet transport services. Budget airlines, on the other hand, may have stricter pet regulations.

Book Multi-City and One-Way Tickets.

Travelers planning a longer journey in the United Kingdom or Europe may profit by reserving multi-city or one-way tickets rather than round-trip pricing. For example, you may travel into London Heathrow and spend a few days exploring the city before taking a domestic flight or train to Cornwall. This strategy can occasionally be less expensive than reserving a direct round-trip ticket.

Using multiple airlines for departure and return flights might also help you save money. Some flight comparison tools let travelers mix and match airlines to discover the most cost-effective or convenient alternative.

Depending on promotions and availability, one-way tickets from low-cost carriers to Cornwall can occasionally be less expensive than return flights.

Timing your arrival and departure

The timing of arrival in Cornwall can affect overall travel convenience. whether you arrive late at night, check to see whether local transportation options like as taxis, buses, or car rentals are available to get to your accommodation. Some sections of Cornwall have limited late-night transportation options, so transfers may need to be scheduled ahead of time.

Arriving at the airport early is critical for departing flights, especially when traveling during peak holiday seasons. Check-in for domestic flights is required at least 90 minutes before departure, while international flights require at least three hours.

When traveling out of Cornwall, keep in mind that Cornwall Airport Newquay is a small airport with limited amenities for dining and shopping. If departing from a larger airport, such as Heathrow or Gatwick, allow extra time for security checks, baggage drop, and navigating terminal transfers.

Lesser-Known Villages to Explore

Cornwall is famous for its gorgeous coasts, quaint harbor towns, and historical sites. While many people travel to major places like as St. Ives, Padstow, and Falmouth, the true magic of Cornwall is frequently found in its lesser-known communities. These hidden jewels provide a real Cornish experience, allowing visitors to escape the throng, admire breathtaking scenery, and interact with the region's rich cultural heritage.

Zennor, a village steeped in myth and folklore.

Zennor, located on the craggy Penwith Peninsula, is one of Cornwall's most magical communities. It is well-known for the mythology of the Mermaid of Zennor, which speaks of a mermaid seducing a young man to sea. Visitors can explore St. Senara's Church, which is home to the mythical Mermaid's Chair, a wooden bench carved with a mysterious mermaid figure.

Beyond its folklore, Zennor has breathtaking coastline beauty. The South West Coast Path goes through the hamlet, providing stunning climbs along the cliffs with panoramic views of the Atlantic Ocean. The area is also noted for its prehistoric sites, including Zennor Quoit, a Neolithic burial chamber that reflects the region's historical history.

The Tinners Arms, a historic bar dating back to 1271, offers a warm and inviting atmosphere for visitors. With its ancient stone walls and substantial Cornish meals, it's the ideal location to unwind after a day exploring the countryside.

Portloe: A Hidden Fishing Village on the Roseland Peninsula.

Portloe is the ideal spot for anyone looking for an unspoiled slice of Cornwall. Nestled within the Roseland Peninsula, this charming fishing community is largely unknown to popular tourists. Unlike more commercialized harbors, Portloe maintains its traditional beauty, with tiny alleyways, whitewashed houses, and a working fishing boat that brings in fresh seafood every day.

Portloe's calm atmosphere is one of its most notable features. The lack of huge hotels and tourist attractions makes it a perfect destination for those seeking peace and serenity. The neighboring Carne Beach provides a secluded length of beach ideal for relaxing, while coastal treks lead to stunning views of the English Channel.

The Lugger Hotel, a tiny boutique hotel with an award-winning restaurant, offers visitors a completely unique dining experience with fresh seafood. Watching the sunset over the water while eating locally caught lobster and crab is an unforgettable experience.

Polperro: A Step Back in Time

Polperro is one of Cornwall's most well-preserved fishing communities, providing tourists with an insight into the region's marine past. With its small winding alleyways, slate-roofed cottages, and thriving harbor, Polperro feels like a step back in time.

The community has a fascinating smuggling history, which is documented at the Polperro Heritage Museum of Smuggling and Fishing. Visitors can learn about the daring exploits of Cornish smugglers, who used the village's hidden coves to convey illegal goods.

Walking through Polperro, visitors will come across art galleries, independent stores, and quaint cafés serving traditional Cornish cream teas. The Blue Peter Inn, a centuries-old tavern, is a must-see destination for a pint by the waterfront.

The adjacent coastline is also magnificent, with scenic walking trails going to Talland Bay and Lansallos Beach, both of which provide calm beach retreats from the throng.

Mousehole: A Quaint Harbor with Timeless Charm.

Mousehole (pronounced "Mowzel"), a small yet stunning seaside treasure, is frequently referred to be one of Cornwall's most attractive villages. Mousehole, just a few miles from Penzance, is well-known for its Christmas light show, which transforms the harbor into a dazzling spectacle throughout the holiday season.

The village's cobblestone streets and stone homes create a postcard-perfect scene. Mousehole is also noted for its rich creative legacy, which includes several small galleries displaying the work of local artists and crafters.

One of Mousehole's beauties is its harbor beach, a modest but picturesque strip of sand suited for a relaxing day by the sea. The Ship Inn, a historic bar with wonderful seafood and magnificent harbor views, can also be found in the village.

Visitors can have a one-of-a-kind cultural experience by learning about Dolly Pentreath, who is thought to be the last native Cornish speaker. Her legacy lives on in the village, helping to preserve Cornwall's linguistic history.

St. Keverne is a village with a rich maritime history.

St. Keverne, located on the Lizard Peninsula, has a long history of maritime activity in Cornwall. It was originally the epicenter of Cornwall's wrecking trade, with residents salvaging items from shipwrecks off the hazardous coast.

The St. Keverne Churchyard is a must-see for history buffs, since it is the final resting place for many sailors who died in shipwrecks. The village's Marconi Monument commemorates Guglielmo

Marconi's pioneering radio experiments, which were essential in the development of wireless communication.

Today, St. Keverne is a tranquil village with a friendly community. The village square holds local markets and food festivals that highlight Cornish vegetables and artisanal goods. Nearby attractions include the Manacles Reef, a popular diving destination noted for its historic shipwrecks and diverse marine life.

Gorran Haven: A Seaside Retreat for Nature Lovers.

Gorran Haven is ideal for those who want to reconnect with nature. This small seaside community near Mevagissey features golden sand beaches, stunning cliffs, and crystal-clear waters. The sheltered harbor makes it ideal for swimming, kayaking, and paddleboarding.

The neighboring Vault Beach is one of Cornwall's best-kept secrets, offering a calm respite from the busier beaches. Walkers will also enjoy the picturesque pathways that lead to Dodman Point, Cornwall's tallest point, which provides stunning panoramic views.

Gorran Haven has a strong community spirit, and its small harbor is still bustling with local fisherman. The village bakery and seafood shops serve fresh local produce, making it an ideal visit for foodies.

Why visit Cornwall's lesser-known villages?

While Cornwall's main sites provide enough to see and do, its lesser-known settlements offer a more in-depth, personal experience. These hidden jewels allow visitors to avoid the tourist crowds, immerse themselves in Cornwall's original culture, and experience the region's natural beauty without interruption.

From folklore-filled Zennor to the peaceful shores of Gorran Haven, each settlement has its own distinct charm and history. Whether you're looking for coastal activities, cultural heritage, or a calm getaway, these off-the-beaten-path destinations are well worth visiting on your trip through Cornwall.

Cornwall is a haven for local market and artisanal craft shop enthusiasts, allowing tourists to immerse themselves in the region's creative traditions and culinary delights. Whether you're looking for handmade souvenirs, fresh local vegetables, or one-of-a-kind works of art, Cornwall's lively markets and charming artisan stores provide a real flavor of the region's culture and customs.

From weekly farmers' markets showcasing the best Cornish vegetables to independent craft stores stocked with handmade pottery, linens, and jewelry, these sites offer the ideal opportunity to support local artisans while also taking home a piece of Cornwall.

Exploring Cornwall's vibrant markets.

Markets have always been an important part of Cornish culture, with vendors selling anything from locally grown vegetables to freshly caught seafood. Many markets are held weekly or seasonally, bringing visitors and locals together to sample the finest of Cornwall's food, drink, and crafts.

Truro Farmers' Market - The Heart of Cornwall's Local Produce

Truro Farmers' Market is one of Cornwall's most popular and well-established markets, held every Wednesday and Saturday on Lemon Quay. It is a foodie's haven, with a diverse selection of locally sourced and organic produce. Visitors can peruse stalls selling fresh vegetables, artisanal cheeses, artisan breads, and Cornish pasties, as well as handcrafted preserves and honey prepared by local beekeepers.

Aside from the culinary delights, the market also sells handcrafted candles, pottery, and textiles, making it an ideal spot to find one-of-a-kind souvenirs. The welcoming ambiance, along with live music and street food sellers, produces a lively shopping experience that showcases Cornwall's creative and agricultural scene.

St. Ives Farmers' Market: A Coastal Delight.

This weekly market, hosted at The Guildhall in the lovely village of St. Ives, takes place every Thursday. Given St. Ives' position as an artistic powerhouse, the market combines cuisine and handcraft. Along with fresh food and organic meats, guests can find gorgeous handmade jewelry, sea glass art, and locally woven fabrics.

The market is also a great opportunity to try some of Cornwall's best delights, including handcrafted fudge, Cornish cream teas, and traditional saffron buns. The proximity to St. Ives' gorgeous beaches and art galleries makes it an excellent stop on a day trip around the area.

Penzance Country Market: A Hidden Gem.

Penzance Country Market is a must-see for anyone looking to experience the best of Cornwall's indigenous talent. Every Friday at St. John's Hall, this market provides an intimate environment for people to sell their handcrafted items, homemade chutneys, and freshly baked cakes. Many of the items sold here are created in traditional ways, offering an authentic and high-quality variety.

This market is well-known for its homemade Cornish saffron cakes and locally grown flowers, making it an ideal place to get a unique and considerate present.

Exploring Cornwall's Artisanal Craft Shops

Cornwall has long been an inspiration to artists and craftspeople, and its independent craft businesses highlight the region's tremendous talent. These businesses provide one-of-a-kind items manufactured by local artisans, such as hand-thrown pottery and delicate silver jewelry.

The Leach Pottery: A Legacy of Cornish Craftsmanship

The Leach Pottery, located in St. Ives, is a well-known pottery workshop in the United Kingdom. Bernard Leach founded it in 1920, and it has become a staple of Cornish ceramics, combining traditional Japanese and English techniques. Visitors can explore the operating studio, observe potters at work, and purchase gorgeous handmade items that will serve as everlasting souvenirs.

Each piece bears the hallmarks of skillful craftsmanship, with earthy glazes and distinct textures that reflect Cornwall's harsh landscape. The Leach Pottery is more than simply a shop; it's a living museum where visitors can learn about the region's rich pottery history.

Jubilee Wharf, a creative hub in Penryn.

Jubilee Wharf, located in the bustling town of Penryn, is a creative hub that houses independent workshops, galleries, and artist studios. Visitors can browse handcrafted wooden furniture, sustainable fashion, and eco-friendly home décor, all created by local artisans.

The Wharf also has art workshops where guests can try their hand at pottery, painting, and jewelry making. This makes it an ideal location for people who want to experience Cornwall's artistic flair firsthand.

The Cowhouse Gallery is a collective of Cornish artists.

The Cowhouse Gallery, located in the village of Perranuthnoe, is an artist-run facility that features works by painters, sculptors, and textile artists. The gallery's exhibits vary on a regular basis, resulting in a fresh and diverse collection of art inspired by Cornwall's coastline and countryside.

Many of the items reflect the region's natural beauty, including magnificent seascapes, handwoven scarves dyed with plant-based dyes, and driftwood sculptures that capture the character of the Cornish coast.

Why Go to Local Markets and Craft Shops in Cornwall?

Exploring Cornwall's local markets and artisanal craft shops provides more than simply a shopping experience; it is also an opportunity to engage with the region's culture, customs, and creative community. Unlike mass-produced souvenirs, the goods seen in these marketplaces and shops are deeply personal, with each telling a story about the maker's passion and expertise.

Supporting these local companies not only helps to preserve Cornwall's artistic heritage, but also guarantees that visitors take home authentic and meaningful souvenirs. Whether it's a hand-thrown porcelain mug from St. Ives, a handcrafted silver necklace from a jeweler in Penzance, or a jar of homemade Cornish honey from a Truro market stall, these treasures serve as enduring mementos of a really unique tour across Cornwall.

SECRET BEACHES AND SECLUDED COVES

Cornwall's coastline is known for its stunning cliffs, golden dunes, and pure waters. While major beaches such as Fistral, Perranporth, and St. Ives Bay draw tourists, there are other hidden treasures around the Cornish coast where visitors can enjoy tranquil privacy. These private beaches and isolated coves provide an opportunity to escape the crowded tourist areas and discover Cornwall's raw, unadulterated beauty.

Cornwall's lesser-known beaches, which range from tucked-away inlets only accessible by foot to calm sandy stretches hidden behind craggy cliffs, offer the ideal refuge for those seeking tranquility, visual beauty, and adventure.

Why should you visit Cornwall's hidden beaches?

Exploring Cornwall's secret beaches offers a completely different experience than the well-known tourist destinations. Many of these hidden coastal beauties need some effort to reach, whether by a stroll along a seaside trail or a scramble down a precipitous fall. However, the payoff is well worth it: peaceful surroundings, smooth sands, and the opportunity to appreciate the gorgeous Cornish coastline away from the masses.

These beaches are also known for their wilder, more untamed ambiance, which allows tourists to enjoy nature's raw splendor. Many are surrounded by high cliffs, caverns, or stunning rock formations, resulting in a magnificent and private hideaway.

Prussia Cove: A Timeless and Secluded Retreat.

Prussia Cove is one of Cornwall's most enchanting secluded beaches, situated between Penzance and Helston. This cove, named for the 18th-century smuggler John Carter, who referred to himself as the "King of Prussia," evokes mystery and history.

The cove itself is made up of a collection of small, sheltered beaches with craggy cliffs and rock pools ideal for exploration. The trek to Prussia Cove is part of its allure—visitors must take a lengthy coastal trail, which keeps the location blissfully peaceful and free of tourists. It's an ideal location for individuals seeking privacy, with clear waters for swimming and stunning coastal views.

Lansallos Cove: A Hidden Gem on the South Coast.

Lansallos Cove is the ideal destination for those looking for a secluded beach that seems like a true vacation. This gorgeous bay, located on the south coast near Polperro, is accessible via a scenic half-mile walk through lush trees and fields.

The trek culminates in a quiet, serene bay with golden dunes and blue waves. Lansallos Cove's sheltered location makes it a great site for a peaceful swim or picnic while listening to the waves gently lap against the shore. The cove's natural beauty and lack of commercial development make it an ideal spot to relax and enjoy Cornwall's untouched surroundings.

Nanjizal Beach—The Most Magical Hidden Beach

Nanjizal Beach is one of Cornwall's most breathtakingly gorgeous and secluded beaches, located near Land's End. Nanjizal, unlike many of Cornwall's more accessible beaches, has remained relatively undiscovered due to its distant location and lack of parking nearby. The only way to get there is by walking along the South West Coast Path, which keeps it a calm and unspoiled refuge.

Nanjizal is distinguished by its spectacular rock formations, which include the well-known "Song of the Sea" arch—a natural rock arch that frames the blue waters beyond. The coastline is filled with caverns, rock pools, and even a freshwater waterfall, adding to its unearthly appeal.

During low tide, the golden sand is uncovered, providing an ideal backdrop for sunbathing or beachcombing. The crystal-clear waters make it an ideal location for snorkeling, with tourists able to find marine life in the small pools.

Porthcurno's Secret Neighbor: Pedn Vounder Beach

While Porthcurno Beach is well-known in Cornwall, few people visit its more secret cousin, Pedn Vounder Beach. This gorgeous cove is frequently referred to be one of the most beautiful beaches in the UK, thanks to its white sand and sparkling blue waters that resemble a tropical paradise.

Pedn Vounder is not easily accessible, requiring a steep and difficult descent down stony cliffs. Those who make the journey are rewarded with one of Cornwall's most stunning and quiet sites. The sheer cliffs that surround the beach provide a sense of privacy, and at low tide, a sandbar forms, providing shallow, warm lagoons ideal for wading and swimming.

This beach is also noted for being clothing-optional, making it popular with naturists. However, its secluded location ensures that even on the busiest summer days, it remains a peaceful getaway from the masses.

Lantic Bay: A Secret Paradise on the Fowey Coast

For those who enjoy a nice hike, Lantic Bay is a must-see. This gorgeous beach, located on Cornwall's south coast at Polruan, is only accessible via a steep and hard trek down from the South West Coast Path.

The bay is made up of two sandy coves surrounded by steep cliffs, giving the region a dramatic and wild character. The golden sand and crystal blue waters make it a perfect location for sunbathing and swimming, while strong currents need caution when entering the sea.

Because of the effort required to get there, Lantic Bay is relatively untouched and rarely crowded, making it an ideal destination for anyone looking for a truly hidden treasure along Cornwall's coastline.

Tips for Visiting Secret Beaches in Cornwall.

Finding and visiting Cornwall's secret beaches can be a wonderful journey, but preparation is essential. Many of these secret coves involve some hiking, so bring suitable shoes. It's also a good idea to verify the tide times before coming, as some beaches may become inaccessible during high tide.

Most secluded beaches lack facilities such as cafés, restrooms, and lifeguards, so visitors should carry their own water, snacks, and sunscreen. Furthermore, responsible tourism is essential—removing any trash and respecting the natural environment helps to maintain these beautiful places pristine for future visitors.

SUSTAINABLE TOURISM: TRAVELING RESPONSIBLY IN CORNWALL

Cornwall is one of the most attractive places in the United Kingdom, attracting visitors with its stunning coastline, quaint settlements, and rich cultural heritage. However, the growing number of tourists each year presents new issues in terms of environmental effect, conservation, and local community well-being. Sustainable tourism is critical to maintaining Cornwall's natural beauty and cultural identity for future generations. Visitors who make good decisions can help conserve the environment, support local businesses, and provide a positive experience for both travelers and inhabitants.

Why Sustainable Tourism Matters in Cornwall.

Cornwall's magnificent landscapes, from golden beaches to craggy moorlands, are fragile ecosystems that can be quickly harmed by excessive human activity. Tourism growth has resulted in overpopulation, increased carbon emissions, littering, and a strain on local resources. Many Cornish communities rely heavily on tourism, but they also confront issues such as seasonal overpopulation and increased living costs, making it difficult for residents to maintain their way of life.

Sustainable travel guarantees that tourism benefits the community rather than harms it. Every visitor can help make tourism a positive force in Cornwall by reducing trash, saving water, respecting animals, and supporting ethical companies.

Choosing eco-friendly accommodations.

Choosing environmentally friendly accommodations is one of the most effective strategies to pursue sustainable tourism. Many Cornwall hotels, guesthouses, and vacation cottages are reducing their carbon footprint through green initiatives such as solar electricity, water conservation, and eco-friendly toiletries.

Eco-lodges and sustainable getaways, such as those in St. Agnes and the Roseland Peninsula, provide an opportunity to reconnect with nature while reducing environmental impact. Some facilities prioritize decreasing single-use plastics, providing plant-based meal options, and encouraging visitors to participate in conservation activities such as beach clean-ups.

Visitors who choose sustainable accommodations help to safeguard Cornwall's natural environment.

Reducing waste and plastic pollution.

Cornwall's coastline is one of its most valuable assets, yet it is also prone to contamination, notably from plastic garbage. Disposable objects such as plastic bottles, food packaging, and beach litter can end up in the water, endangering marine life and destroying the landscape's natural beauty.

Visitors can help reduce plastic waste by carrying reusable water bottles, coffee cups, and shopping bags. Many cafés and restaurants in Cornwall support plastic-free campaigns, urging customers to bring their own containers or engage in refill programs.

Another approach to help is to take part in or organize a beach cleanup. Several local organizations, notably Surfers Against Sewage, organize community clean-ups to keep Cornwall's beaches clean. Even picking up a few pieces of garbage while touring the coast has a big impact.

Respecting the local wildlife and natural habitats.

Cornwall has a rich assortment of fauna, including seals, dolphins, seagulls, and unique plant species. While seeing these species in their natural environment can be a thrilling experience, it is critical to approach wildlife properly.

Disturbing wildlife can have major repercussions, such as interrupting breeding patterns or putting animals through undue stress. When admiring the coastline, visitors should keep a respectful distance from seals and seabirds, avoiding loud noises and unexpected movements. Boat cruises and kayak excursions should adhere to ethical rules that prioritize marine conservation and do not pursue or disturb dolphins.

Hikers and outdoor enthusiasts should stick to marked pathways to avoid causing erosion and trampling delicate plant life. Many coastal trails in Cornwall run through protected areas, thus adhering to the "Leave No Trace" philosophy is critical—this includes taking all litter home, preventing vegetation damage, and abstaining from collecting pebbles or shells that benefit the ecosystem.

Supporting Local Businesses and Ethical Tourism

Sustainable tourism is about more than just protecting the environment; it is also about helping the local economy in ways that benefit the community. Cornwall is famed for its small enterprises, ranging from family-run eateries to artisanal craft shops, and shopping locally helps to preserve the region's cultural identity.

Dining at locally owned cafés, farm-to-table eateries, and seafood shacks keeps earnings in the community while lowering the carbon footprint of imported products. Many of Cornwall's greatest culinary attractions prioritize sustainability by obtaining food from local farmers, fishermen, and organic suppliers.

Shopping at local markets and buying handmade items from Cornish craftsmen also helps to preserve traditional skills and crafts. Rather than purchasing mass-produced souvenirs, visitors can purchase unique, locally crafted objects that represent the tale of Cornwall's heritage, such as handwoven fabrics, pottery, and sea glass jewelry.

Choosing ethical tourist experiences, such as guided walks led by locals, trips to sustainable wineries, or seminars on traditional Cornish crafts, allows for a more authentic and enriching experience while directly helping inhabitants.

Using Sustainable Transportation Options.

Transportation is a major element to a traveler's carbon footprint. While driving is often required to explore Cornwall's most rural places, there are alternatives to reduce the environmental impact.

Visitors can take advantage of Cornwall's public transportation system, which includes trains and buses, for picturesque and environmentally friendly travel throughout the county. The beautiful St. Ives Bay Line, for example, provides stunning vistas of the coast while decreasing traffic congestion.

Cycling is an excellent way to explore Cornwall responsibly. The Camel Trail, which runs from Padstow to Bodmin, provides a lovely and environmentally responsible opportunity to explore the countryside without contributing to emissions. Many cities and villages also provide bike rental services, making it easier for visitors to choose two wheels over four.

For those who must drive, adopting electric or hybrid vehicles is a more environmentally friendly option. Cornwall has an increasing number of electric vehicle charging stations, notably in environmentally minded locations such as Newquay, Falmouth, and Penzance.

Conserving Water and Energy

Cornwall experiences large tourist numbers throughout the summer months, putting severe strain on local resources such as water and energy. Visitors can help lessen their effect by conserving water, taking shorter showers, and reusing towels instead of asking new ones every day at hotels.

Turning off lights, heating, and air conditioning when leaving a room also saves electricity. Many sustainable accommodations already include energy-saving features, such as motion-sensor lights, but individual efforts can help reduce wasteful consumption.

Engaging in Sustainable Activities

Choosing low-impact activities is another method to promote responsible tourism. Instead of powered water sports, guests can choose eco-friendly activities such as kayaking, paddleboarding, or sailing to enjoy Cornwall's beautiful coastline without destroying the environment.

For hikers, the South West Coast Path is an ideal way to explore Cornwall's stunning cliffs and scenic landscapes while reducing the carbon imprint of car travel. Many conservation organizations also provide volunteer opportunities for tourists who want to give back by helping with nature restoration projects or educational programs.

FINAL TRAVEL CHECKLIST: DON'T FORGET THESE ESSENTIALS!

Planning a vacation to Cornwall involves careful consideration to ensure a seamless and pleasurable experience. While Cornwall has gorgeous coasts, picturesque villages, and a rich cultural past, tourists need be aware of necessary things, practical arrangements, and local customs to make the most of their trip. A well-prepared tourist can thoroughly enjoy Cornwall's splendor without undue stress.

Essential Travel Documents and Booking Confirmations

Before embarking on your vacation, ensure that all relevant travel paperwork are in order. If going from another country, ensure that you have a valid passport and all necessary visas. A government-issued ID may be useful for domestic travelers in the UK, especially when checking into hotels or hiring a car.

It is also important to have paper or digital copies of your hotel reservations, vehicle rental agreements, and any pre-booked activity confirmations. Although many companies in Cornwall accept digital proof of booking, carrying a printed backup can be useful in the event of a low phone battery or a poor connection in isolated places.

When utilizing public transportation, pre-booking train or bus tickets might help you avoid last-minute price increases and ensure seat availability, especially during peak seasons. Cornwall's picturesque train routes and bus services can get crowded, so plan beforehand.

Weather-appropriate clothing and footwear

Cornwall's weather can be unpredictable, especially during the summer. Packing appropriate apparel will assure your comfort throughout the trip. A lightweight waterproof jacket is required because unexpected showers are common. Layering is essential because temperatures might vary between warm afternoons and cool evenings.

Proper footwear is required when exploring Cornwall's magnificent coastline walks. Sturdy walking shoes or hiking boots offer the required grip and support on difficult terrain. Sandals or water shoes are also handy for beach vacations, especially in rocky places where the bottom may be uneven.

If visiting Cornwall in the winter, bring a heavy coat, gloves, and a hat, as coastal gusts can make temperatures feel colder than expected.

Tech & Gadgets for a Trouble-Free Trip

A well-packed travel backpack should include important electronic tools to improve the journey and enable clear communication. A fully charged smartphone with navigation programs like Google Maps or Ordnance Survey maps will be quite useful for locating trails, picturesque areas, and hidden gems.

Cornwall's rural areas may have limited phone reception, so downloading offline maps before leaving can be a lifesaver. A portable power bank keeps gadgets charged while touring, which is especially useful for those who frequently use their phones for photography or navigation.

To capture Cornwall's magnificent environment, photography aficionados should use a high-quality camera or a waterproof action camera. Drones are very popular for aerial photography, but tourists should be careful of local drone rules, especially in protected regions and near wildlife habitats.

Those who intend to work remotely or stay connected throughout their trip may also want to bring a UK travel adaptor (for international visitors) and a portable laptop or tablet. Some Cornwall motels and cafés provide free Wi-Fi, but service is restricted in rural regions.

Beach and Outdoor Essentials.

A trip to Cornwall is incomplete without visiting its beautiful beaches and coastal sceneries. Packing the necessary beach supplies will make these outings more enjoyable. UV rays can be powerful even on cloudy days near the seaside, so use a high-SPF sunscreen.

A nice pair of sunglasses and a wide-brimmed hat will provide additional sun protection.

If you plan on swimming, surfing, or paddleboarding, bring a quick-dry towel, rash guard, and a wetsuit (if you travel during the cooler months). Many surf businesses in Cornwall rent wetsuits and boards, although having your own gear is more convenient.

A reusable water bottle is essential for staying hydrated when touring, and many towns in Cornwall have refill stations to help decrease plastic waste. Cornwall promotes plastic-free activities, so eco-conscious guests should bring a reusable shopping bag to carry their local market purchases.

A lightweight backpack is useful for day journeys, as it may hold refreshments, a first-aid kit, and a windproof travel umbrella. Cornwall's seaside hikes can be long, but packing an easy-to-carry rucksack with basics guarantees a comfortable journey.

Health and Safety Precautions

Traveling with a basic first-aid kit is usually a smart idea, especially if you plan to walk or participate in outdoor sports. A pack should include bandages, antiseptic wipes, pain painkillers, motion sickness medicines (for boat voyages), and any personal prescription medications.

When touring coastal locations in Cornwall, keep in mind the tide times. The region has some of the greatest tidal ranges in the UK, and specific beaches or coves may become inaccessible during high tide. Checking tide schedules before going to the beach helps prevent becoming stranded.

It is recommended that persons with allergies, particularly seafood or pollen allergies, carry the essential medication, such as antihistamines or an EpiPen. Cornwall's rural environments might result in high pollen counts during particular seasons.

Travel insurance is generally advised, especially for foreign travelers. Having coverage for medical emergencies, trip cancellations, and missing luggage gives you piece of mind.

Money and Payment Methods

Although most places in Cornwall take credit and debit cards, it is still a good idea to bring some cash, especially for modest purchases at local markets, independent cafés, and distant attractions. ATMs are present in major towns, while some rural communities may have limited banking options.

Many shops in Cornwall accept contactless payments, making it easy for travelers to tap and pay for services. However, having a backup payment option, such as a supplementary credit card or prepaid travel card, is always a good idea in the event of technological difficulties.

Sustainable Travel Considerations.

Cornwall supports eco-friendly tourism, therefore visitors should be careful of their environmental impact. Packing a reusable cutlery set and a food container for takeaway meals will help you avoid single-use plastics. Many Cornish eateries and food booths offer discounts to guests who bring their own containers.

Visitors that are environmentally conscious might also pick sustainable amenities, such as biodegradable shampoo bars and reef-safe sunscreen. Chemical pollution can harm Cornwall's marine life and coastal ecosystems, therefore choosing ecologically friendly goods helps to protect the area's natural beauty.

When visiting rural areas, bring a small trash bag to guarantee that no litter is left behind, especially on beaches or picnic areas where waste disposal bins may not be easily available.

Cultural Etiquette and Local Customs

Understanding Cornwall's unique culture and traditions improves the whole trip experience. Cornish people have a strong sense of identity, complete with their own language, rituals, and festivities. Respecting local traditions, such as attending events like Padstow May Day or the St. Piran's Day parade, allows tourists to fully immerse themselves in the local culture.

When visiting tiny communities, travelers should be aware of noise levels, especially in residential areas. Many Cornish settlements have tiny roads, thus giving way to pedestrians and local traffic is considered courteous.

Supporting independent companies like family-run bakeries, seafood vendors, and artisan enterprises is greatly appreciated. Ordering a classic Cornish pasty from a local shop or tasting locally brewed ciders supports the local economy while also providing an authentic experience.

CONCLUSION
Your ultimate Cornwall adventure awaits.

Cornwall captivates the senses with its craggy coasts, quaint settlements, rich cultural past, and variety of outdoor activities. Whether you're traveling for the stunning beaches, historic landmarks, or vibrant food scene, this guide will provide you with the necessary information to make your trip smooth, pleasurable, and memorable.

From the best travel routes and lodging alternatives to insider recommendations on hidden jewels, this book has provided a complete look at what makes Cornwall unique. By planning ahead of time, respecting local customs, and adopting sustainable travel practices, you may ensure a meaningful and fulfilling vacation while reducing your environmental impact.

As you embark on your adventure, remember to immerse yourself in Cornwall's natural beauty, sample its traditional delicacies, and interact with its welcoming residents. Whether you're trekking along the South West Coast Path, discovering hidden coves, or enjoying a delicious Cornish pasty by the water, your time in Cornwall will be filled with amazing experiences.

Above all, go with a curious and open heart. Allow the spirit of Cornwall to inspire you, and may your journey be filled with exciting discoveries, relaxation, and a deep respect for this magnificent region. Safe travels, and enjoy every bit of your Cornwall adventur

Printed in Dunstable, United Kingdom